ENDOR&

When you put a priest and a psychologist together, what do you get? Healthy minds and healthy souls. Nicholas and Roxanne Louh have blended not only their lives in marriage, but what they have learned in their vocations, to provide insights and practical suggestions for becoming the person you were designed to be. I highly recommend this book for all who aspire to reach their potential for God and good in the world.

—GARY CHAPMAN, PHD, *New York Times* bestselling author and author of *The Five Love Languages*

We all want to live healthier, more productive lives. Yet so often we get sidetracked by unhealthy habits and addictions. That leads to discouragement about our lack of spiritual progress. Father Nicholas and Dr. Roxanne Louh can help. *Renewing You* is a practical primer on how to become your best self. Here are the tools you need to build better habits and stronger relationships, starting today!

—MICHAEL HYATT, *New York Times* bestselling author, podcaster, blogger, speaker, and founder and CEO of Michael Hyatt & Company

Drawing deeply from Scripture and the wisdom of the ancient Church, Father (Dr.) Nicholas and Presvytera (Dr.) Roxanne Louh inspire you to grow in relationship with the Lover of your soul, expel guilt, receive peace, nurture life and health in personal relationships, and aspire to spiritual and emotional maturity for the greater benefit of the Kingdom of God. I highly recommend this book!

—HANK HANEGRAAFF, president of the Christian Research Institute, host of the *Bible Answer Man* broadcast and the *Hank Unplugged* podcast, and author of numerous books, including *Truth Matters, Life Matters More: The Unexpected Beauty of an Authentic Christian Life*

Father Nicholas and Dr. Roxanne have summarized the key principles for living a healthier life spiritually, emotionally, physically, and mentally in this insightful book. These are life lessons grounded in both wisdom and experience.

—TIM TASSOPOULOS, president and COO, Chick-fil-A

I absolutely LOVE, LOVE, LOVE this book! It is spiritually uplifting, very funny, informative, poignant, touching, candid, thought-provoking, and challenging. When you read it, you can just feel the time, energy, and thought that they put into writing this book. And, boy, did they succeed. This book has an anointing on it. So many GREAT passages in it. For those of you who are looking to be spiritually renewed (and who isn't?), don't look any further. This book does exactly what it says: It will renew your spirit and bring you closer to God. Amen.

—ROBERT KRANTZ, actor and producer

Spiritual "power couple" Fr. Nick and Dr. Roxanne Louh, a parish priest and psychologist, have combined their considerable personal and professional experience to create a book which naturally and seamlessly integrates psychology, physiology, and faith. The Louhs address the challenge of how to envision and create a life of purpose and satisfaction which soars above and beyond what we might imagine possible. Practical guidelines, proven methods, and various techniques provide a plan to conquer our ruts, inaction, excuses, and bad habits. Employing solid scientific information, relatable examples from daily life, biblical insights, and spiritual inspiration, the Louhs encourage us to discover the God-given potentiality within each of us.

—DR. JEANNIE CONSTANTINOU, host of the podcast *Search the Scriptures Live!* on Ancient Faith Radio and professor of biblical studies and early Christianity at the University of San Diego

Renewing You is a call for self-improvement. But unlike self-help books that focus on self-improvement alone, *Renewing You* views self-improvement as a non-selfish exercise, as a road map to a Christ-centered life. For the authors, self-improvement calls us to become the hands, the feet, the comfort, the wisdom, and the love of God for others. By acquiring such gifts of the Spirit, one becomes the vehicle for God's healing and God's comforting Spirit for the sake of the world.

Perhaps the single most important message pouring forth from each of the chapters of this book is the emphasis on intentionality. The authors, both trained and experienced in helping others improve their lives spiritually and emotionally, share their many years of experience in private practice, leading retreats, and ministering to large and diverse communities of faith. Both their professional training and deep-rooted Orthodox faith advocate for the foundational role that intention plays in spiritual and emotional growth. At the center of this is love; and love, as our authors insist, is always intentional.

—JAMES C. SKEDROS, Michael G. and Anastasia Cantonis Professor of Byzantine Studies at Hellenic College Holy Cross and lecturer on Greek at Harvard Divinity School

Renewing You

*A Priest, a Psychologist,
and a Plan*

Rev. Dr. Nicholas G. Louh
AND
Dr. Roxanne K. Louh

ANCIENT FAITH
PUBLISHING

CHESTERTON, INDIANA

Renewing You
A Priest, a Psychologist, and a Plan
© 2020 The Rev. Nicholas and Dr. Roxanne Louh

PUBLISHED BY:
Ancient Faith Publishing
A division of Ancient Faith Ministries
PO Box 748
Chesterton, IN 46304

ISBN: 978-1-944967-84-0

Library of Congress Control Number: 2020942022

store.ancientfaith.com

Published in the United States of America.

IN MEMORY OF
OUR BELOVED FATHERS
George and André

TABLE OF CONTENTS

Meet Father Nick and
Dr. Roxanne Louh

W E ARE A PRIEST AND A PSYCHOLOGIST, and together, we represent a marriage of two different worlds and two different fields of study. Our seemingly opposite fields of faith and psychology join forces to provide you with the type of inward reflection that leads to lasting outward transformation. We cast practical life strategies through the lens of biblical aspiration and self-reflection, with the intent to give you the foundation to approach a life that more closely resembles the potential God sets forth for all of us.

For almost twenty years, we've worked together to merge our professions to help people seek the changes they want most for their lives. We have thirty years of combined experience working with individuals and families. Our education and training inform the suggestions, insights, and advice we share with you.

We enjoy the many opportunities we have to share our work in person: through speaking engagements and retreats, on our weekly show *Live with the Louhs* on 77 WABC Radio in New York City, via television and radio in Jacksonville, Florida, and on *Healthy Minds Healthy Souls*, our live call-in program on Ancient Faith Radio. We invite you to stay in touch with us at TheLouhs.com.

INTRODUCTION

And do not be conformed to this world, but be transformed by the renewing of your mind, that you may prove what is that good and acceptable and perfect will of God. —ROMANS 12:2

Do YOU FEEL like your walk with Christ has become stagnant and stale? That you're no longer able to enjoy the continual transformation of your life and faith that used to energize you? Perhaps you used to wake each morning with a sense of purpose and excitement for the coming day, but now you get out of bed and face your daily to-do list with heaviness of heart—and no amount of coffee can help you rekindle the energy you need so desperately for the day ahead.

All of us experience this struggle from time to time, and we all have areas in our lives that can lock us out of God's purpose for us. Whether we struggle with unhealthy thoughts, baggage from the past, loving our spouses, or just managing the everyday chaos of modern life, our personal and spiritual challenges can start to feel like locked prison doors that keep us inside and prevent us from living the full life our faith promises us.

But today is a new day! It's never too late to return, reset, and refocus our lives—to rediscover God's dream for us. As Romans 12:2 says above, transformation comes through the renewing of our minds. And by picking up this book, you've already made the first step to starting your renewal, because in this book we give you eight keys to help you unlock the areas of your life that keep you from fully experiencing God's purpose for you.

The word *renew* is a word of power: it means to "restore to freshness." Vigor. To make "extensive changes"[1]—not just minor changes but all-encompassing, profound changes that will, as 2 Corinthians 5:17 says, help you become a new creation in Christ. The "old things have passed away," this verse says, and "all things have become new."

God's Purpose for Us

As Christians, we believe God has a special plan for our lives, a will He has created us for, and that He has made us *on purpose for His purpose.* Yet all too often, we struggle to fulfill this greater purpose, don't we? Whether it's our inability to forgive, our difficulty coping with loss and setbacks, or our frustration when we attempt to create peace and harmony within our marriages and our relationships with our children—we wrestle with challenges that sidetrack and waylay us as we attempt to live up to our calling as followers of Christ and find our purpose in Him.

But what is God's purpose for us? Certainly, thousands of books, sermons, podcasts, Twitter threads, worried parents, and people at church potlucks have a lot to say on this subject, but it all boils down to this: Our purpose as Christians is to become increasingly like Christ in order to fulfill our calling as people created in God's image (Gen. 1:27). Simple, right? As the multitude of discussions on this subject proves—not so much! But maybe we can understand it a little better if we think first about what it means to be made in the image of God. We can think of this in terms of what distinguishes us from the animals: things such as our ability to reason, think abstractly, participate creatively in the world, make choices, and have free will. So as we look to find our purpose in life, our task as Christians is to strive to bring our choices and behavior more and more in line with those of God. It's also important to note that this is a *process*. We aren't born perfect, with complete knowledge and awareness of God's plan for our lives; rather, we're born with the potential to grow more and more into ourselves as people made in His image.

Luckily, God doesn't expect us to do it correctly from the outset. He knows our journey toward finding our purpose will be full of trials and failures, stops and starts, a few steps forward followed by many steps back. And He never promised the path would be easy—as Matthew 7:14 says, "Narrow is the gate and difficult is the way which leads to life." But we believe the rewards are worth the struggle, as discovering your purpose will not only bring you closer to God, it will also allow you to renew yourself daily and live your best life in Him!

The goal of this book, then, is to give you the keys to unlock your ability to renew yourself and live increasingly closer to the image of God. We'll look at the obstacles that can sabotage us and keep us locked inside the prisons we have (often unknowingly) created for ourselves, and each chapter will provide a principle that will help us live our lives with purpose. Chapter 1 talks about how we must first invite God into our lives and make faith our foundation, before we do anything else. Then, Chapter 2 discusses common thinking errors and how we can learn to become healthier thinkers, and Chapter 3 helps us find victory over our vices. Chapter 4 addresses the trials we encounter and how to triumph over them. Chapter 5 discusses the importance of self-care, and Chapters 6 and 7 help us strengthen our relationships with our spouses and children. Finally, Chapter 8 shows how to take your renewed self out into the world and shine your light in the darkness for Christ. Additionally, each chapter is followed by discussion questions to help you put these principles into practice or enable you to use the book in a group setting.

With our blended perspectives as priest (Father Nick) and psychologist (Dr. Roxanne), we draw principles from both our Christian faith and the science of human behavior to inform our discussion. So, the principles we've developed generally fall into these two categories: *self-awareness,* which entails understanding ourselves better and strengthening our relationship with ourselves; and *spiritual discipline,* which focuses on the battle we must engage in between the spirit and the flesh. Through this two-pronged approach, we'll look at the tools that help us conquer and better manage our strong emotions, struggling relationships, and difficult circumstances so that *we can lead lives of purposeful action rather than reaction.*

Self-Awareness: "How can we connect to Him if we don't connect within?"

Despite our best intentions, we often react to situations in the moment without thinking, rather than respond with purposeful action, or *intentionality*. This happens when we become emotionally and spiritually locked into our harmful habits and attitudes, and we lack the necessary keys to break out of them. From the time we leave our childhoods behind, our lives are like books where each chapter presents a new challenge, and in some chapters, we resort to unhealthy coping mechanisms in order to manage life's tough moments. Even though the difficulties we face offer us opportunities to renew our faith, draw nearer to Christ, and live more closely in His image, we often find ourselves lacking the emotional and spiritual resources to do so. But if we want our relationship with Christ to truly direct our steps, we must learn to strengthen our relationship with ourselves.

We can't conquer the problems within ourselves that we're not willing to confront, nor can we address what we don't have the tools to understand or change, but we truly believe *it is possible* to understand just *why* we struggle and have difficulty putting into practice our deepest beliefs. Gaining insight into our habits, misconceptions, and weaknesses is a powerful first step; from there, we can begin to make changes and develop tools for growth. Ultimately, we'll experience the joy that comes from putting into practice the habits and attitudes we aspire toward and pray for—even in the midst of difficult moments.

Without self-awareness and inward reflection, we often risk reducing our faith to mere statements of belief rather than a path of life we follow. As Christians, our challenge isn't to simply proclaim that we are followers of Christ but to *live out this reality* through the way we think and the way we act in our everyday lives.

It's important to note that self-awareness doesn't equal self-absorption; rather, we truly believe inward reflection is part of the foundation necessary for outward transformation. While we may resist working on ourselves because it initially feels selfish and we want to put others first, St. Paul reminds us that not only should we bear one another's burdens, but God also calls us to "bear [our] own load" (Gal. 6:5 [New International Version]). And Mark 12:31 instructs us to love our neighbor *as ourselves,* implying that we can't truly love and care for another person if we don't do the same for ourselves.

Spiritual Discipline: The Battle between Flesh and Spirit

Self-awareness isn't the only tool we have for getting more closely aligned with God's purpose for our lives and renewing ourselves in His image. We must also consider spiritual discipline, which poses a great challenge, because what our spirit desires and where our flesh leads us are rarely one and the same! Saint Paul helps us understand this battle between flesh and spirit in Romans 7:15-20 (English Standard Version), where he describes his own struggle with it:

> For I do not understand my own actions. For I do not do what I want, but I do the very thing I hate. Now if I do what I do not want, I agree with the law, that it is good. So now it is no longer I who do it, but sin that dwells within me. For I know that nothing good dwells in me, that is, in my flesh. For I have the

desire to do what is right, but not the ability to carry it out. For I do not do the good I want, but the evil I do not want is what I keep on doing. Now if I do what I do not want, it is no longer I who do it, but sin that dwells within me.

Simply put, we don't find it easy to honor God through our actions and reactions. If you don't think your flesh is at work within you, threatening to take charge, try praying for ten minutes straight, and notice how quickly your mind begins to wander. Try committing to daily Bible reading, and watch how quickly other tasks threaten to replace it. Try to be patient when you're tired, or loving when you're angry, or to honor Christ in your reaction after someone cuts you off in traffic! The truth is, we have a hard time choosing well, and we're all still learning how to conquer the temptations of the flesh.

To envision how this battle plays out, imagine that in one corner we have our spiritual person. This person wants to continually live for God, maintains godly thoughts, produces fruits of the Spirit, and views each situation through the lens of the spiritual walk. This person desires to act as a witness to others and seeks what is upright, good, and virtuous. He or she faces life's difficult moments relying on God's strength and trusting in His power, knowing that all things work together for the creation of an ultimate good.

Our fleshly nature stands in the other corner, the weaknesses of body and mind we can always count on to fuel the habits and attitudes that oppose the spiritual life. Our flesh embraces our free will with the temptations of the world and stirs up strong feelings and impulses we don't always know how to control. It encourages the disobedient and rebellious side of us and leads us away from God. We know this side of our nature is in control when we find ourselves giving in to pride, selfish ambition, jealousy, impatience, and fear. Our fleshly nature lives only for the moment and whatever that moment invokes.

The sobering truth is, we can't bear fruit unless we regularly confront *with discernment* the areas of our lives where our flesh is winning the battle over our spirit. We must remain watchful and awake so that we notice when we're about to follow anything not fueled by the spirit. Why does it matter if we engage in this battle? Because we can't *conquer* our fleshly natures if we don't *confront* them, and we can't confront what we don't *catch*. So this book also gives you some principles to help you unlock the door to the spirit while keeping the doors to those pesky messages of the flesh shut tight.

Say Nay to Your Inner Naysayer

Many of you may now be shaking your heads and thinking, "This sounds like a lot of work" and "I don't have the necessary strength to grow and change," or maybe even just, "I'm already overwhelmed with everything I have to do and am too busy to attempt to change anything." But we encourage you to approach this work with a positive attitude and a heart full of prayer, rather than becoming your own naysayer. Naysayers always attempt to discourage people of vision. Before Pedro Menéndez or Christopher Columbus ever traveled to the New World, people in Spain believed nothing existed beyond their own territory and that venturing off into the ocean would lead to danger and death. A favorite phrase of theirs was *ne plus ultra*, the Latin phrase for "nothing more beyond."[2] In other words, according to them, nothing existed beyond Spain and the known world!

Does this sound familiar? We often adopt a *ne plus ultra* attitude. "This is it," we tell ourselves with resignation. "There's nothing more to experience, nothing more to feel, nothing more to become." As you read this, we ask you to remember that there *is* something more, something beyond what you have known in life so far—new seasons, improved relationships, new opportunities, and new stories that God wants to write in the book of your life. Can you see yourself as calmer or more patient? Can you see yourself connecting more deeply with your spouse? Can you see yourself as more merciful and compassionate? More tolerant and less critical? Can you see yourself possessing the energy to impact your world the way you've always wanted? Or on the other side of a tragedy, truly living again rather than nursing old wounds? The spiritual goals we set will determine the kind of life we live and the kind of choices we make.

We encourage you to set aside all naysaying, then, and let this be your first prayer at the start of this journey: "Lord, I desire to grow; help me to be patient and willing! Give me the eyes to see what I need to change and the tools and the will to make it happen." As famed psychologist Victor Frankl once said, "When we are no longer able to change a situation, we are challenged to change ourselves."[3] This is our challenge to you, dear reader, as you begin this book. Don't wait another day—it's time to start!

CHAPTER ONE

Make Faith Your Foundation

Seek the Kingdom of God above all else, and live righteously,
and He will give you everything you need. —MATTHEW 6:33
(NEW LIVING TRANSLATION)

WHEN YOU FIRST wake up in the morning, what thoughts swim through your mind as you lift your head groggily from your pillow? What do you think about first, before you have even swung your legs over the side of the bed to stand up? Does your to-do list dominate your thoughts? Do you feel immediately stressed by all the tasks you have to balance, the people you need to care for, the long day stretching out ahead of you? Do you feel heavy-laden with worries? What if, instead, you could wake up each morning with God's peace ruling over your heart, His Word dwelling in your mind, and a renewed sense of purpose for your day because you have sought to "put on your new nature, and be renewed as you learn to know your Creator and become like Him" (Col. 3:10 [NLT])?

This is what it means to put God first in our lives: just as we get ourselves ready for the day, so also must we get ourselves spiritually prepared for our day. We hear from the

Apostle Paul in the Book of Ephesians about how to clothe ourselves spiritually for our day: "For shoes, put on the peace that comes from the Good News so that you will be fully prepared. In addition to all of these, hold up the shield of faith to stop the fiery arrows of the devil. Put on salvation as your helmet, and take the sword of the Spirit, which is the word of God" (6:15-17 [NLT]). As we put on these things of the Spirit, we must choose *consciously* to allow God's Spirit to guide us. And if we want our faith to direct our steps, then we must begin this path with a level of self-awareness that allows us to be intentional with seeking and choosing to practice our faith, even at moments when life tries to keep us away from it, even when it doesn't come naturally, and even when anger hits or dark moments seize us.

As you journey with us through this book, you'll start to notice that *we can't put any of the principles for renewal in this book into practice without relying first on God to guide us.* Whether we want to conquer our vices, build a stronger marriage, renew our relationships with our children, or learn to care for ourselves better, God remains at the center, loving us, guiding us, renewing us, strengthening us, and helping us to see all His signposts along the way. He helps us build that strong foundation upon which all other things rest: the foundation of our faith in Him. Just like the wise man in Matthew 7 who "built his house on the rock," when we have Christ as our foundation, our house will stand, even when "the rain descend[s], the floods [come], and the winds [blow] and [beat] on that house" (7:24-25).

So if we want to experience God's renewing power and find His purpose for us, we must make Him our foundation and center our lives on Him. But how do we do this? We do it by learning to listen to His voice and by prioritizing this listening above all else. We know this is a huge challenge, since the pressures of modern life overwhelm all of us with busyness, and we often feel exhausted just trying to keep up with our daily tasks. Who has the time to squeeze yet another item onto the calendar? Even Father Nick finds this challenging—and his work as a priest focuses on God and the church!

It helps if we can view listening to God as the thing from which all the rest of our work springs. Even those items on our to-do lists that seem to lack spiritual significance can benefit from God's influence, as you'll find as you make your way through this book. It may not seem so at first glance, but everyday tasks like going to the grocery store, returning emails, attending our children's sports events, walking the dog, and commuting to work can all provide opportunities to listen to and serve God.

On the other hand, if we don't make listening to God our number-one priority throughout the day, we find ourselves locked into the busyness and distractions of the world, rather than pursuing what's *actually* important! Listening to God helps us live every moment of our lives with wisdom, knowledge, and discernment—how can we possibly live well without these things, no matter what we're doing at any given moment? Proverbs 2:1-5 puts this so beautifully:

If you receive My words,
And treasure My commands within you,
So that you incline your ear to wisdom,
And apply your heart to understanding;
Yes, if you cry out for discernment,
And lift up your voice for understanding,
If you seek her as silver,
And search for her as *for* hidden treasures;
Then you will understand the fear of the LORD,
And find the knowledge of God.

Attending our kids' soccer games has really brought home to us this concept of listening to God and how hard it can be for all of us. Our children, George and Gabriella, both play competitive soccer. They love playing, and we love going to the games. We wish we could tell you we're the kind of parents who just kept quiet and casually observed. Unfortunately, we're not those parents. We're the parents at the game who are "loud and proud" on the sidelines, rooting the entire team on—and once one of our kids gets the ball, we scream out to them, "Go! You've got this! Watch out for that defender!" Of course, in our minds, we're certain they can hear every word, and more importantly, that they will follow our guidance. Funny thing is, that's not what usually happens. So one day after a game, we asked, "George, did you hear us when you were out there playing? We tried to tell you that you had someone behind you. We were cheering you on." George looked up and said, "No, I didn't hear your voices at all. There was just so much noise coming from the sidelines that I really couldn't hear you."

How similar this must feel for God as He tries to coach us. As we journey through life, so many voices come at us from the sidelines that we can't hear what our heavenly Father is saying. Could He be trying to encourage and renew our spirits in certain ways or give us a warning? To guide us or direct us in our renewal, but too many other competing voices drown out His? Every day the world bombards us with so much noise! Sounds come from every direction, and we hear a multitude of voices from other people who try to define us. We also hear the voices in our own minds that downplay our gifts and make us doubt our worth. We hear the voices of our responsibilities and mundane tasks that compete with our time for God. And we hear the disruptive voices of phones, televisions, emails, and social media—all vying for our attention with messages that seek to entice our flesh with values that aren't our own: deception, vulgar language, verbal attacks, egoism, vainglory, violence, infidelity, and degradation, to name a few. These messages compete with God's voice every day to counsel us on morals, faithfulness, our self-worth, and how we make decisions. "Dig in," they say. "Why would you offer forgiveness?" "Go for it; don't worry about who you could hurt in the process." "It's all about you: your glory, your money, your recognition. Don't worry about being a witness for something greater, like Christ." "You will never be good enough." And yes, "You really *are* the sum total of your insecurities."

Do you hear any of these messages in your head as you go about your day? We sure do! What, then, is the solution? The Bible answers this question very clearly, "Be still, and know that I am God!" it says in Psalm 46:10. This implies we'll never know God *until* we quiet ourselves enough to experience Him. When we do finally stop and listen, we allow Him to know us as well, as John 10:27 tells us: "My sheep hear My voice, and I know them, and they follow Me." We serve a God who yearns to know us and for us to know Him—who wants to have a relationship with us. And the Book of James reminds us that we play a role in creating that relationship: "Come near to God and he will come near to you" (James 4:8 [NIV]).

So how do we create this stillness—this quiet—so we can learn to listen better to God's voice? The rest of this chapter goes through several practices that have helped us invite God into our lives and the lives of people we've worked with, both as priest (Father Nick) and psychologist (Dr. Roxanne). Please consider taking this journey alongside us as we strive to unlock the doors of our hearts and allow God's voice to come through more clearly.

Seek Silence

Many Christians throughout the past two thousand years have sought to draw closer to God and experience His renewal by seeking solitude away from the world. We experienced this so vividly when God blessed us recently with a Holy Land pilgrimage to Jerusalem, where we walked in the footsteps of our Lord. On that trip, one thing we noticed over and over again, in every place we visited, was just how often Jesus withdrew from the noise of the world to seek solitude, stillness, and silence. He sought solitude in order to encounter God when He went into the Judean desert and spent forty days and nights preparing to launch His public ministry (Matt. 4:1-11). He sought it before choosing His disciples, when He spent the whole night on a mountain in silence, solitude, and prayer, seeking the will of His Father in one of the most important decisions of His ministry (Mark 3:13-19). Jesus also sought solitude and silence in order to simply pray, like in Mark 1:35 (NIV): "Very early in the morning, while it was still dark, Jesus got up, left the house and went off to a solitary place, where he prayed." He could often be found alone on a mountain or walking along the Sea of Galilee.

Jesus also withdrew into solitude when He felt agony: "When Jesus heard [about John the Baptist's beheading], He withdrew by boat privately to a solitary place" (Matt. 14:13 [NIV]). When tormented by His own emotions about the Cross and facing the agony of His impending death, Jesus sought God in the Garden of Gethsemane on the Mount of Olives. In essence, He sought solitude whenever He wanted to draw near to God. Seeking stillness is also a common theme in the Old Testament. In fact, God would often reveal Himself to others when they took time for silence, like to the Prophet Elijah in a cave when he fled to the wilderness (1 Kin. 19:11-12) and to Moses in the desert with the burning bush (Exodus 3).

If Jesus needed solitude in order for God to renew Him, how much more do *we* need it?! Most of us can't take forty days and nights to flee to a quiet place of solitude or find a nearby mountain to spend the night on, but we can find other ways of creating that type of space. For one, we can make a quiet place in our homes where we can practice silence a bit every day. Maybe you have a home office where you can go in and shut the door for few minutes before making dinner, or you can sit in your bedroom in silence as your spouse heads off to get ready for work. We also find that walking or running can provide the kind of quiet we need. So just as Jesus once walked about ninety miles from Galilee to Jerusalem (which gave Him about five days of solitude, John 7:10), we, too, can go for a walk or run early in the morning or after the sun has gone down in the quiet of day. Though Jesus would often sit on a mountain, we can simply sit outside on the front porch or in a nearby park, in the quiet of nature and away from competing distractions. Jesus often went outside the walls of the city to seek solace, and we too can step outside the walls of our busy lives to place boundaries around our solace. And as Jesus would walk along the Sea of Galilee, we can walk in nature to open up our minds and connect back to God in prayer.

When we step into stillness, we notice what's on our hearts. And in that silence, God speaks to our hearts, informing our spirits with His direction, encouragement, renewal, and wisdom. When we listen closely, we can begin to make sense of the patterns we see in our lives, the doors He keeps closing, and the convictions He places on our hearts, encouraging other directions. This will help us better see and know His purpose for us.

What happens when we don't renew ourselves in Christ by practicing the discipline of stillness? A disconnect can form in our relationship with God because we can't hear His guidance, and the world presses in, eroding our ideas, feelings, minds, and hearts with its own values, motivations, and principles. Our faith gets reduced to a mere statement of belief rather than a source of direction and guidance for living out our daily lives. The more we quiet our souls before Him, the more we'll hear His voice. God isn't in our noise; rather, *He enters into the stillness* as we create space for Him.

Avoid Chronic Busyness

The world also crowds out God's voice by demanding busyness from us. In many ways, we can think of our connection with God as a relationship, and good relationships require our time and attention, away from the everyday tasks that tend to consume us. From cover to cover, the Bible portrays our relationship with God as analogous to a marriage. At Easter, the church even refers to Christ as a Bridegroom, marrying His church through the wedding band of His Holy Cross. And just as a marriage depends on regular communication, so does our relationship with God. Although we can let someone know they're important to us in many ways, giving our time is probably one of the most difficult things to do because it's not quick. It requires a real, in-the-moment sacrifice of something most of us feel today is a rare and precious commodity: uninterrupted, undistracted, committed, and invested time. It's not as easy as quickly sending a gift at the click of a button, or dropping an occasional "I love you," or giving a hug to someone on their way out the door. No, giving of our time requires sacrificing something else in our day that we've prioritized. And it's up to us to choose this, because we don't worship a God who *forces* us into a relationship with Him; we worship a God who knocks on the doors to our hearts and has given us the free will to *choose* whether or not we spend time with Him. Christ puts it this way, in the Book of Revelation: "Here I am! I stand at the door and knock. If anyone hears My voice and opens the door, I will come in and eat with that person, and they with Me" (3:20 [NIV]). Notice, here, that God can only come into our hearts when there's synergy between His knock and our opening.

God knocks on our hearts in so many ways: He disrupts our plans, places people in our paths, sends unexpected blessings, and allows disappointments that provide a small tug for us to move in a different direction. He convicts us. He allows for challenging situations and opens up our hearts to notice uncomfortable feelings or restlessness or a lack of peace about something. We most often experience His knock on our hearts when we read His Word, and the Book of Hebrews tells us that "the word of God is living and active, sharper than any two-edged sword, piercing to the division of soul and of spirit, of joints and of marrow, and discerning the thoughts and intentions of the heart" (4:12 [ESV]). We have to make sure that when God knocks at the doors of our hearts, our chronic busyness doesn't keep us from letting His renewing presence into our lives and providing direction to our souls. The biblical story of Mary and Martha really drives this home:

> Now it happened as they went that He entered a certain village; and a certain woman named Martha welcomed Him into her house. And she had a sister called Mary, who also sat at Jesus' feet and heard His word. But Martha was distracted with much serving, and she approached Him and said, "Lord, do You not care that my sister has left me to serve alone? Therefore tell her to help me."
>
> And Jesus answered and said to her, "Martha, Martha, you are worried and troubled about many things. But one thing is needed, and Mary has chosen that good part, which will not be taken away from her." (Luke 10:38-42)

Father Nick has struggled with this sort of chronic busyness himself:

> As a priest, I could visit the sick and spend time with people twenty-four hours a day and still not finish all the work in front of me. As I moved through my years in ministry, I saw the collateral damage of doing too much. It affected my health, my family, and most of all, my own time to connect with God. It became

very clear to me that I would have to set intentional time aside for God—even to the point of putting it on my calendar just like any other appointment. My assistant will tell you that now, on Fridays, no matter what else I have on my schedule, I have time reserved for prayer and quiet reflection. This way, I can offer a message to our community on Sunday born out of this time of stillness with God. If I don't make the time, it won't happen.

So, what can we do to invite God in amidst our busyness? We make sure to set aside dedicated time each week for our own stillness. During that time, we turn off our phones, computers, televisions, and our mental to-do lists, and we sit down with God. We delight in the gift of just being present. If we truly invest our focused attention on simply *being in that moment*, having no other agenda in mind, we'll find we can experience God's renewal in a very real way. Try setting aside a few moments today to try it out! And *as you allow this interruption in your day, listen to the tugs on your heart.* Allow yourself to notice all the ways God has blessed you, savoring them with gratitude and thanking Him for all He's doing in your life.

Try Using the "First Fifteen" Method

We've found that unless we provide some structure for our quiet times with God, our minds tend to wander in unproductive ways. So we suggest using the very simple "First Fifteen" method to provide a framework for your solitude.

Each day, devote five minutes to reading the Bible, five minutes to prayer, and five minutes to reading books that help you grow in your faith. We use this method ourselves, and we find this daily practice of faith helps to renew and nourish our spirits and keep our inner voices and energies centered on matters that honor God, our family, and ourselves. Here are some more details about how to do it:

The First Five: Read the Bible. What better way to hear God's voice and experience His renewal than to read His Word? As Joshua 1:8 (NIV) says, "Keep this Book of the Law always on your lips; meditate on it day and night, so that you may be careful to do everything written in it. Then you will be prosperous and successful." The Bible helps us avoid faulty logic as we navigate messages from the world that seek to derail us. The more we read, the more we know God's voice and can hear Him convict us of certain truths and call us in a certain direction. When we know God's voice, we can better discern the voices in our own minds that may not be from Him yet may still attempt to lead us. And the more we read the Bible, the more our own lives will mirror it.

Many people have a hard time reading the Bible because it feels overwhelming. "I just don't know where to begin," we hear. But there are many strategies that can help us make reading Scripture a habit. It may help to purchase a study Bible, because these offer guidance on where to turn for help with specific areas of your life, and as you read, they provide a guide and a context to help you understand what you're reading. You can also try using an app, or sign up for a daily delivery of Scripture right to your in-box. Just take five minutes, and start with what you need to hear: perhaps a psalm of encouragement or a chapter from the Book of Proverbs, which offers practical wisdom, as contemporary today as it was thousands of years ago when it was first written.

Keep in mind that it's better to read one sentence of Scripture a day than to ignore it altogether. And one sentence adds up over time! Try to read it at the same time every day, which will encourage the habit to form. For us, it works best to read Scripture when we first wake up in the morning, before the day gets busy. We find that a morning dose of God's media does far more good than a morning dose of social media, *so instead of looking at Facebook, we put our faces in the Holy Book.* We also have an encouragement from Scripture that comes to our phones at a specific time each day, and it always seems perfectly chosen for what we need to hear that day. The wisdom of Scripture provides encouragement, guidance, and an opportunity for self-reflection. The more we read, the more we begin to see the truth of the scriptural metaphor that God's Word is a lamp to our feet and a light along our path (Ps. 119:105).

If uncertainty about the accuracy or efficacy of Scripture has kept you from reading it in the past, consider this. Dr. Peter Stoner, former professor of math and science at Westmont College in Santa Barbara, California, researched all 456 prophecies in the Bible related to the coming of the promised Messiah. Dr. Stoner discovered that Jesus Christ fulfilled *every single one.* As a mathematician, he then asked, "What are the chances that one person could fulfill even eight of these prophecies?" He gathered a symposium of mathematicians who researched his question, and their conclusions astonished them. The researchers determined that the odds were one in one hundred thousand trillion that Christ could have even fulfilled *eight* of those prophecies— and yet we know He fulfilled all of them!

Dr. Stoner illustrated the findings this way: If just eight of the 456 prophecies were correct, it would be as if you covered the state of Texas with silver coins two feet deep, painting just one of those silver coins black. Then you would blindfold someone and ask him or her to travel the entire state of Texas, pulling over just once to pick up one coin. How likely would it be that this blindfolded traveler would pick up *the one painted coin* amongst the millions of coins blanketing the entire state of Texas? This is how likely it is that the prophets could have written these eight prophecies in advance and had them all come true in the same person.[1]

What's the point of this? The Bible contains God's life-giving words. As 2 Timothy 3:16-17 (NIV) confirms, "All Scripture is God-breathed and is useful for teaching, rebuking, correcting and training in righteousness, so that the servant of God may be thoroughly equipped for every good work." It will transform your life if you let it! So if you want to invite God in to renew your life, make a habit of reading and applying His words every day. It's been said that dusty Bibles lead to dark lives. The more you read and learn, the more you'll come to know and develop your relationship with the Author Himself.

The Second Five: Prayer. Worship isn't just for Sunday mornings! When the world competes for our time and life gets busy, our prayer life is often the first thing to go. And when this happens, we may find ourselves *only* turning to prayer when we need something or when things get difficult, rather than making prayer part of our daily practice of renewal. We all experience times when *prayer functions as a last resort instead of a first response,* so to gauge the robustness of your current prayer life, see if any of these four types of prayers resemble yours:

- The *emergency prayer.* This happens when we move along through life without much awareness of or connection to God—until something unexpected happens that overwhelms us. And then we pray!
- With the *rehearsed prayer,* we simply recite the same words in the same order every day without thought or feeling. We probably know these prayers by heart, but we may not truly connect to them emotionally, or maybe we just feel too tired to do so.
- Then, there's the *contingent prayer,* where we say to God, "Okay, if You'll do this for me, I promise I'll do that for You."
- Lastly, we have the *firehouse prayer.* We pray this when we've tried to handle everything on our own, but nothing's working, and life feels like it's falling apart. *Only then do we pray! But God doesn't want to be our afterthought; He wants to be our first thought.* In the Old Testament, God talks about offering our firstfruits to

Him (Prov. 3:9-10), and we should think of prayer as one of those fruits.

So now the question is, *when should we pray?* Here's an illustration from Dr. Roxanne that helped her find the answer to this question:

> I'll never forget one particular client (whom I only saw once) who, through God's voice, taught me more in one sentence than I could have ever taught him. Just like any other initial appointment, I first tried to learn about my client, and part of that includes asking about his relationship with his faith. "Tell me about your faith," I said. "Do you feel your faith is an important source of strength and support in your life?" He said, "Absolutely. Of course. I wouldn't be here without it."
>
> Then I asked him about his prayer life: "So tell me, then, how do you connect to your faith? Do you pray often?" And what he said at that moment, I will never forget. "Do I pray often?" he chuckled. "Ma'am, *I never stop praying. I'm in a constant conversation with God. My mother taught me from a young age that you should never stop talking to God. In everything I do, I'm talking to Him too.*"

Pray always! How can we expect to renew our spirits daily in God if we don't? And in the Book of John, Jesus confirms this when He says,

Remain in me, and I will remain in you. For a branch cannot produce fruit if it is severed from the vine, and you cannot be fruitful unless you remain in me. Yes, I am the vine; you are the branches. Those who *remain in me, and I in them,* will produce much fruit. For apart from me you can do nothing. (15:4-5 [NLT])

The word *remain* means to stay or continue in the same state without ceasing. So, when should we pray? The answer is, "without ceasing." We should probably *never stop* having a conversation with God!

Saint Paul also affirms this idea of praying without ceasing when he says in I Thessalonians 5:16-18 (Good News Translation): "Be joyful always, pray at all times, be thankful in all circumstances. This is what God wants from you in your life in union with Christ Jesus." But how do we do this? One simple way is to remember that *how we begin anything affects the turnout of everything.* So we can pray first before anything we do, remembering what King David says in the Book of Psalms, "I rise before dawn and cry for help; / I have put my hope in your word" (119:147 [NIV]). So before you get out of bed in the morning, pray first. Before you eat breakfast, pray first. Before your children get out of the car to go into school, pray first. Before you begin a conversation or walk into an important meeting or start that difficult phone call, pray first. When we communicate with God regularly, He keeps our spirit full, arming us in every battle with our flesh.

So what is prayer, and why do we pray? Prayer is a willing connection to God we make through a deliberate or intentional practice—and we can't really have a relationship with God without it! Prayer gives us the opportunity to connect our lives back to God. It reminds us of our gratitude, helps us unpack our thoughts and release our worries, and gives us an opportunity to seek God's guidance and renewal. Prayer also reminds us we're never alone and that God's presence surrounding us is far more powerful than any difficulty we face. We remember feeling this presence so vividly during certain times of our own lives. One prayer I (Dr. Roxanne) find myself saying over and over again throughout my life is, simply, "God, please be with me." And in that same moment, I immediately experience, and say with awareness and feeling, "I know that You are." Simply reaching out in prayer is all I truly need to remind me of something I already know but can't necessarily feel until I tune into it.

So, what do we pray for? There's nothing we can't pray about! We pray for God to give us His words when we struggle to find our own words in a difficult conversation. We pray for His patience and strength in long and enduringly stressful situations. Or for enlightenment so we can see our faults and manage them better. We pray for Him to renew us when we feel our spirits sagging. We pray for His wisdom and guidance when we struggle to make a difficult decision.

We remember, especially, how much we've relied on prayers for guidance, praying together many, many times for God to enlighten us and help us decide on the right path—like when

Father Nick had to decide whether to take over the parish after the church asked him to. Father Nick also remembers how much he relied on prayer when it came to the decision to get married:

> I graduated from seminary at the age of twenty-five. Upon graduation, I didn't know whether God had called me to be a celibate or married priest. (The Orthodox Church doesn't pressure up-and-coming priests to make a decision about marriage, but you do have to make that decision *prior* to your ordination.) But I knew I wanted to move back to my hometown of Jacksonville, Florida.
>
> One day, while visiting my home church, I went into the main sanctuary. From time to time, during a break or holiday, I would come by just to say a prayer. That day as I stood in the altar, I felt drawn to ask God for guidance. I stood before the icon of Christ and looked into His eyes and said, "Lord, I'm ready. I want to serve You. If it's Your will that I be married, put someone in my life who can help me serve You." It wasn't a long prayer, just a simple one, but one thing I was always taught is that the greatest distance you will ever travel is the twenty-two inches from standing up to when your knees hit the ground in prayer.
>
> Later, a friend's father, also a priest, spoke to me about my plans for the future. I told him I still

had some uncertainty but that I felt drawn to serve the church. He told me about some good friends of his who both worked as professors and lived in Gainesville, Florida (approximately a one-hour and fifteen-minute drive from Jacksonville), and were very active in their church. "Because you're already doing campus ministry," he said, "perhaps you could go down and meet them." At the time, I didn't think anything of it. I just figured the next time I went to Gainesville I'd call them and get to know them.

Several days later, I planned to meet with some students at the University of Florida, so I called this family up to introduce myself. They very kindly invited me to their home after my meeting. Then, right as they warmly welcomed me in, their daughter showed up for a surprise visit. She was living in Orlando at the time, working on her master's degree. When I saw their daughter, I have to admit I could no longer focus on what they were saying.

I would love to say it was love at first sight for her, but it definitely felt like love at first sight for me! I knew at that moment that God had answered my prayers. Long story short, their daughter is now my wife, Roxanne. Now when we talk about that moment, she too says that she somehow "just knew" that night that I was the person she was supposed to marry. We both felt something divinely planned and orchestrated.

What's my point? Prayer guides our lives! Today, our ministry at church, our radio show, this book, and our beautiful family all came out of that one prayer. And, you know, looking even further back, Roxanne's fate to marry a priest might even have been evident by her last name, *Khuri*, which in Arabic actually means "priest."

So is it okay to pray for certain requests? Yes! When we pray for ourselves and others like this, God promises that our prayers are not in vain but are "powerful and effective" (James 5:16 [NIV]) and that when we "ask anything according to his will, he hears us" (I John 5:14 [NIV]). And God has said that we often go without because we don't ask Him for something (James 4:2). For example, if the blind man outside of Jericho had not called out to Christ, he would have remained blind instead of experiencing healing (Luke 18:35-43).

In one sense, prayer has similarities to sharing the gospel with people. We don't know who will respond, or how they will respond, until we share it. In the same way, we'll never see the results of answered prayer unless we actually pray. Remember, just because God already knows our needs doesn't mean we shouldn't state them. And if we struggle to find the right words when we pray, we can trust that the Holy Spirit will empower us. The truth is, we don't always know what we need, but St. Paul reminds us that "the Holy Spirit helps us in our weakness." If we don't know what to pray for, "the Holy Spirit prays for us with groanings that cannot be expressed in words. And the Father who knows all hearts knows what the

Spirit is saying, for the Spirit pleads for us believers in harmony with God's own will" (Rom. 8:26-27 [NLT]).

We can also remember the importance of prayer as an expression of gratitude. As in any relationship, our communication with God shouldn't be purely need-based. Think of how you would feel about a relationship if all the person did was ask for things, yet she never thanked you!

So, how do we pray? We pray with an open heart. The greatest obstacles to a good prayer life are those things we don't want to share—the things we feel ashamed of. But God desires our honesty so He can provide the healing and guidance we most need. As the Book of James states, above all, we should pray with sincerity, honor, and humbleness before God, for "the earnest prayer of a righteous person has great power and produces wonderful results" (5:16 [NLT]).

Jesus also told us we can use the Lord's Prayer as a model, which has a helpful structure to follow. It begins with gratitude and praise ("Our Father, who art in heaven, hallowed [holy] be Thy name"), then moves on to God's will ("Thy Kingdom come, Thy will be done on earth as it is in heaven"), then to our requests ("Give us this day our daily bread"), and then forgiveness and repentance ("Forgive us our trespasses as we forgive those who trespass against us"). When we use the Lord's Prayer as a template, we make sure to include all the necessary components of prayer.

The Third Five: Other resources that help you grow. Do you believe you should only read the Bible, when it comes to growing your faith? Certainly the Bible is so important, but other materials can also help us unlock our renewed selves. Daily devotionals, readings on the lives of the saints, books just like this one—and even music—can also enhance our walk of faith. For this reason, the third five includes any of these types of sources. In every way, we should look for opportunities to grow in our faith, to ensure that *growth isn't just a season in our life but a way of life.* God doesn't expect us to stay where we are today, so if we want to experience renewal, *we shouldn't just go through life; we should grow through life.* As the Bible tells us, we must grow in every way in Christ, "As a result, we aren't supposed to be infants any longer who can be tossed and blown around by every wind that comes from teaching with deceitful scheming and the tricks people play to deliberately mislead others" (Eph. 4:14 [Common English Bible]).

Another powerful verse instructs us to not only seek growth but to crave it constantly: "Like newborn babies, you must crave pure spiritual milk so that you will grow into a full experience of salvation. Cry out for this nourishment, now that you have had a taste of the Lord's kindness" (1 Pet. 2:2-3 [NLT]). This passage mirrors our own biology: Once a baby is born, feeding is no longer automatic. Now, it must *cry out* to let its mother know when it needs nourishment. In much the same way, we don't receive spiritual food automatically by simply living our lives. We, too, have to reach out and look for ways to receive the spiritual nourishment our soul cries out for!

Put God at the Center

Prayer helps us renew ourselves because it weakens the voice of the world and strengthens our ability to hear God's voice instead. But how else does the world threaten to drown out God's voice? Through all the forces that compete to rule over our hearts! What forces do you struggle with? Maybe it's the pull of money, material possessions, popularity, image, or notoriety. Or perhaps you feel attracted to greed, envy, pride, or resentment. Or maybe your worldly vices threaten to replace your deeper-seated values with powerful urges you can't seem to control.

Ultimately, any of these forces, if we let them rule over our hearts, can stop us from doing all God desires us to do. No matter how good of a person we aim to be, the world exposes us to many temptations that seek to take our hearts away from goodness. *And whatever we allow as master over our lives will have control of our lives.* For this reason, Scripture warns us not to worship two masters because:

> where your treasure is, there your heart will be also. The eye is the lamp of the body. If your eyes are healthy, your whole body will be full of light. But if your eyes are unhealthy, your whole body will be full of darkness. If then the light within you is darkness, how great is that darkness! *No one can serve two masters.* Either you will hate the one and love the other, or you will be devoted to the one and despise the other. You cannot serve both God and money. (Matthew 6:21-25 [NIV])

So it's important to ask ourselves regularly, "Who do I allow to have ultimate authority over my life?" "What am I a slave to?" "What force leads me most?" "What am I worshipping today that I probably shouldn't worship?" "Which values guide my decisions and actions?" To wrap up this chapter, let's hear from Father Nick about how this has played out in his life.

Back when I was still considering becoming a priest, I can remember finding every excuse in the book not to get ordained. I didn't feel ready! I didn't know if I could handle the stress and the responsibility! Or if I could balance the demands of ministry with also having a family. I didn't know if I would even be good at it—if I would have what it takes to bring people to Christ. In those moments, fear, worry, and distress ruled over my heart, but I started to notice that I only felt truly myself—truly at peace—when I let Christ rule as King over my heart. When we let Him rule over our hearts in all things and in all ways, only then will the "Lord of peace Himself give you peace at all times and in every way" (2 Thess. 3:16 [NIV]). This really drives home the fact that God doesn't give us peace just on Sundays at church but at all times. And how does He do that? He does it when we take Him home, bring Him with us, and let Him show up in every part of our lives.

We can easily see the benefits of believing in a Savior who died for us: a Savior who can get us into heaven.

But we may struggle with allowing a Lord—a King—to guide us in *all* our decisions and choices. In fact, we all tend to compartmentalize God. We'll let God guide certain parts of our lives but then tell Him, "No, I don't want You to tell me how I should live my life when it comes to tough things like controlling my temper, my vices, or my selfish desires." Or maybe we invite God in when we want Him to punish someone for hurting us, but then we disinvite Him when it's our turn to forgive. Or we'll ask God to help us through a struggle, but when everything returns to normal, we forget Him and never come back in gratitude to thank Him for how it turned out.

It helps me to remember that Christ paid His life to sit on the throne of my heart, and you can always tell the value of something by the amount someone was willing to pay for it. What else—or who else—deserves more to reign as King over my life? That means that wherever I go, Christ goes: speaking to me, guiding me, renewing me. When I'm out with my friends, He sits right next to me. Whenever I'm at my home, He's there leading me. When I'm about to send that email or make that hard phone call, I'm making sure He guides me. In short, I do what He would do.

PRAYER

✠ ✠ ✠

OH HEAVENLY FATHER, as I accept this challenge of renewal, remind me that apart from You, I can do nothing. That before I begin a journey, I need to have You as my guidepost. You tell me to seek You first, and today I recommit to putting You first in my life. I realize that if I don't put You at the center of my life, You can't guide me. I recognize that if I don't take the time to be still with You, the voices of the world may begin to define my life. I ask You to strengthen me during this journey of renewal, when I find myself tired or wanting to give up. Please place in me the hope for tomorrow.

✠ ✠ ✠

FOR DISCUSSION:
THE THREE Rs—REST, REFLECT, AND RESPOND

1. How can you make the Holy Spirit more present in your everyday life?

2. Name one way you tune in so that you can hear God speak to you. How do you seek stillness? How can you incorporate more stillness into your life?

3. What are the top three things that keep you chronically busy? What mundane tasks seem to swallow up much of your time? Which of them could you let go of, ask for help with, or simply re-prioritize to make more time for God?

4. Name one practice that might help you be still before the Lord.

5. During which time of day could you stop and read a Scripture passage? Can you come up with a daily plan that will work for your schedule?

6. Worship isn't just for Sunday mornings. Identify one thing you can do during the week to make more time for active conversation with God. Which important parts of prayer might be missing from your typical

prayer routine? What do you need to pray about, but haven't?

7. Name three additional sources of spiritual nourishment you can fold into your life.

8. Is there an area of your life you're holding on to, that you need to give over to Christ? Which goals have you put in place to address it?

CHAPTER TWO

Remodel Your Mind

Our life depends on the kind of thoughts we nurture. If our thoughts are peaceful, calm, meek, and kind, then that is what our life is like. If our attention is turned to the circumstances in which we live, we are drawn into a whirlpool of thoughts and can have neither peace nor tranquility.[1] —ELDER THADDEUS

And do not be conformed to this world, but be transformed by the renewing of your mind, that you may prove what is that good and acceptable and perfect will of God. —ROMANS 12:2

As WE CONTINUE to focus on renewing our lives in Christ, we quickly realize we need to renew and strengthen our minds. Our minds are powerful allies in helping us to break out of the prisons unhealthy thinking can create. They can also allow us to better ourselves through our various decisions, thoughts, perceptions, and behaviors because they direct everything we do and feel. But often, we don't really pay attention to what our minds tell us. How often do we walk into a room and then can't remember why we are there? Have you ever gotten in the car and followed your same route to work, even though you were supposed to go to a doctor's appointment in the other direction? Our distracted minds often lead us astray, so we may look up one day and find ourselves wondering, "How have I gotten so far off track?"

Incredibly, scientists tell us we entertain between eighty thousand and one hundred twenty thousand thoughts on any given day. To put that into perspective, there are only 86,400 seconds in a day—so this means our thoughts vie for our attention nearly every waking moment. Plus, we spend around 50 percent of the day thinking about things unrelated to our present experiences![2] Put simply, we can't possibly notice all our thoughts, yet they still create a storyline for our lives—informing our moods, choices, and interactions; shaping our decisions; urging us to action; and impacting our feelings at every turn. You see, your thoughts create the script for the movie that becomes your life. Don't you want to have a say?

Think about it. For each decision you consciously make, you've likely spent some time thinking it through first. For example, before you bought this book, you might have considered whether you'd find it relevant to your life—whether it would speak to you. And before we decided to write this book, we thought it through first. We asked ourselves questions like: Would readers find it relevant? Would it make a difference in people's lives? Do we have the time? We also thought about the "why." Why should we take this on? Why is it important? Why has God brought us together, and what has He called us for? It was, in fact, these thoughts that later inspired us to take the first steps.

Think of it like this: Our thoughts shape our actions, our actions shape our character, and our character ultimately shapes our lives. Even when we do something that seems impulsive, chances are, our reactions are driven by related thoughts we've had at some point in the past.

Take a look at some of the ways our often-unnoticed thoughts can profoundly affect our lives:

- If our thoughts focus on blame and judgment, we will likely feel defeated and insecure about our self-worth.
- If our thoughts instead concentrate on understanding, grace, and self-compassion, we will more likely feel loved and worthy.
- If empathy informs our thoughts about others, we're more inclined to show mercy, love, and compassion.
- If our thoughts fill us with fear, worry, and stress, we set ourselves up to succumb to the "fight-or-flight" response more readily (which is an instinctive and immediate reaction to either fight or run away without thinking the situation over first).

While some of these automatic thought responses can help us, others cause us to react in hurtful ways. So how can we possibly acquire the mind of Christ and renew ourselves according to His purpose if we don't really hear the script that shapes our actions? Without good monitoring, we so easily imprison ourselves in patterns of unhealthy thoughts—and likely we aren't even aware of how our thoughts have shaped our reactions! When we don't monitor our thoughts, we risk hurting ourselves—but we also risk hurting the people we love. Dr. Roxanne remembers a man in her counseling practice whose marriage foundered because his wife couldn't escape the prison her own thoughts had created about him:

> A young man in my counseling practice knew his wife felt frustrated with his shortcomings and resentful over their differing parenting styles. He wanted to save their marriage and took her concerns to heart, and he'd invested a great deal of effort into the marriage counseling process. During one session, he turned to his wife and asked, "How do you think things are going between us?"
>
> As his wife began to talk, his tentative optimism turned to despair. Her bitterness was palpable. "You'll never change," she said. "I'm just waiting for the other shoe to drop." No matter what changes her husband made, his wife kept listening instead to her negative inner voice. "We're so different," it was telling her. "This will never work. He's never going to change." Even though the tools he'd gained in counseling helped him make substantial progress toward the behavior she desired, her inner thoughts sabotaged the healing process between them.

You can see from this example that our thoughts are powerful enough to shape our actions—and ultimately our lives—so paying attention to our narrative equips our souls with a stronger, more fortified army to fight against the temptations of our flesh. We'll cover this in more depth further into this chapter, but for now, remember that the process of uncovering your thoughts begins with the ability to notice and hear yourself in real time.

With that in mind, let's pause to pay attention to *this* moment. Tune into your body. How do your shoulders feel? Are they relaxed or tense? What about your jaw—is it clenched? How about your brow—is it furrowed? Are you sitting comfortably? Is your breathing slow and rhythmic and coming from your lower abdomen, or is it coming from your chest? Are you distracted? What thoughts are running through your head? Are you worried about anything? Is your mind wandering? Are you tired? Do your eyes hurt? What's the room like around you? Are you comfortable? What's the noise level? Can you concentrate? Does any unhealthy thought present itself? Do you feel God's peace at this very moment? Why or why not?

We often hear people say they're actually *afraid* to be too mindful—they don't want to think about what's bothering them. However, remember that what's going on within your body, mind, and soul impacts you *whether or not you choose to acknowledge it.* So we ignore these inner voices at our own peril! Dr. Roxanne has a poignant example of this phenomenon in action:

My friend struggled for a time with her relationship with her sister. She had managed to submerge her feelings of frustration—or so she thought. One evening, her sister came over for dinner, and as soon as she walked into the kitchen, she began complaining about nearly everything—from how loud my friend's children were playing to the music she was enjoying. The complaints grated on my friend, who began to secretly wish that her sister hadn't come over at all.

Eventually, her sister said one more thing: "Aren't you going to season that a bit more?" and my friend exploded. It was the proverbial straw breaking the camel's back; emotions of resentment and anger triggered by her sister's words overwhelmed her in a flood. My friend poured out the recording of negative thoughts and frustrations she'd been playing and replaying in her mind for years. To her surprise, her sister just looked at her and began to cry. No retaliation, just tears. My friend felt heartsick. She had exaggerated and overstated things in her angry rant—the way we all do when we're angry—but the damage was done.

Prior to this conflict, neither sister had been aware enough of their building feelings to have the healthy discussion that would have helped them avoid this damaging collision. When we feel strong emotions about a person or situation, and those emotions don't dissipate over time, that's our cue that we should pay attention! That it's time to pause and examine those thoughts and feelings as they unfold in real time, understanding what they mean and why they've occurred. Had my friend noticed her own unhealthy thought patterns brewing beneath the surface, she might have turned those thoughts into prayers, replaced her negative complaints with productive requests, and all the judgment with empathy and grace. It turns out that even her sister had been unaware of her own brewing negativity about her life, which often came out as complaints whenever they spent time together.

It's so easy for us to react without thinking in heated moments. But as we develop a habit of mindfulness, we'll begin to notice when our feelings toward ourselves or a loved one take a negative turn, which allows us to change this inner critical soundtrack by choosing empathy, grace, understanding, and godly love. "My sister is overwhelmed right now with her own emotions," my friend could then say, "and isn't able to articulate what's *really* bothering her. This isn't about just this moment. When the situation calms down, I'll let her know how hurtful her words can sometimes be, and we can both talk about the circumstances that are causing us to feel tense."

What recordings play in your mind about yourself or about the people you love most? Remaining mindful allows us to pay attention to our thoughts *before* their impact.

Perhaps that's why, time and time again throughout the Bible, we hear about the notion of guarding our thoughts. Here are a few examples to carry with you:

- Solomon wrote in Proverbs 4:23 (CEB), "More than anything you guard, protect your mind, for life flows from it." We take Solomon at his word because God calls him one of the wisest men to ever live, and the Book of Proverbs is also known as the Book of Wisdom.
- 2 Corinthians 10:5 says we should bring "every thought into captivity to the obedience of Christ."
- We hear from King David in Psalm 139:4 (ESV) that "even before a word is on my tongue, behold, O LORD, you know it altogether."

Learn to Discern

The church fathers also have a good deal to say about our thoughts—particularly in terms of *spiritual discernment*, which means learning to distinguish healthy thoughts from unhealthy thoughts. Saint John of Damascus considered the virtue of discernment to be "greater than any other virtue."[3] Saint John Cassian said, "Discernment is no small virtue, but one of the most important gifts of the Holy Spirit. . . . It is the greatest gift of God's grace . . . the ability to discriminate between the spirits that enter [us] and to assess them accurately."[4] Cassian considered discernment the mother of all virtues and our guardian.[5] Saint Antony of the Desert said that discernment means "scrutinizing all the thoughts and actions of a [person]," which "distinguishes and sets aside everything that is . . . not pleasing to God."[6] Saint John of the Ladder pointed out in Step 26 in *The Ladder of Divine Ascent* that "discernment is real self-knowledge . . . the spiritual capacity to distinguish unfailingly between what is truly good and what . . . is opposed to the good."[7] It's distinguishing the will of God in all times, from an uncorrupted conscience. And St. John Climacus wrote that discernment gives us the "ability to see how certain actions and thoughts give rise to sin and teaches us how to avoid [it]" as well as the ability to "scrutinize ourselves thoroughly."[8]

We must keep in mind that the practice of spiritually discerning our thoughts requires action on our part. As an active process, it does not occur automatically or without our intention, and it often involves a struggle, as Jesus warns us. So we must remain wise to the enemy that seeks to destroy us and create impediments to following God's will, as Matthew 10:16 (ESV) tells us: "Behold, I am sending you out as sheep in the midst of wolves, so be wise as serpents and innocent as doves." Discernment is one of the tools we have to help us remain wise. Additionally, we can also learn to notice the quality and veracity of our thoughts by becoming aware of possible errors in our thinking as we encounter them.

Avoid Thinking Errors

Thinking errors often hijack our minds. Psychologists call these "cognitive distortions," a term psychologist Aaron Beck made popular.[9] They are mistakes in judgment our minds make when we misinterpret different situations, events, or potential outcomes. These inaccurate thought processes convince us that what we think is true, but in reality, they only serve to make things so much worse. It's like walking into a fun house at a carnival and seeing a distorted image of yourself rather than a true reflection. Our thoughts can have the same effect on us, only we don't actually realize we've entered a fun house! Here are the most common errors to watch out for, as well as some keys for helping us escape these thought prisons!

Extreme (black/white) thinking. This type of thinking involves language such as "always," "never," "all," and "nothing." It's absolutist and doesn't allow for any gray areas. It happens when we believe we're either really amazing or a total failure, or when we can't pursue something God has designed for us because we're too afraid to make a mistake. It also happens when we experience a setback and turn it into a hopeless prediction of defeat, which leaves us feeling worthless and destroyed. Here's a way the error of extreme thinking once played itself out in the marriage of one of Dr. Roxanne's friends:

> A friend of mine felt hurt by something her spouse said to her, and so she shut down, retreating into herself. "I need you to let me in when you're mad," her husband told her. "You can't just shut down when I tell you things. I need you to talk to me instead of

shutting me out." But instead of examining the comment for its actual intention (an attempt at repair and connection), she responded in a way that was informed by a thinking error: "Of course, now this is *all* my fault. I *never* do anything right. It's *always* me who's doing something wrong. I just can *never* make you happy."

Needless to say, her defensive posture, which came out of thoughts like "always" and "never," essentially caused a shutdown of communication and healing. All-or-nothing thinking often inhibits growth in ourselves and in our relationships. A healthier interpretation might be, "I can see that I sometimes do withdraw when I get upset. I get it. I could probably stand to work on opening up. It's just hard to do when I'm hurt, and I get hurt when you complain about something I've done."

In arguments, it's especially tempting to think in black-and-white terms in the heat of the moment, and we can easily receive one piece of feedback as, "I never do anything right." We sometimes apply this to other people as well. "He's *always* so impatient with the kids." "I can't remember her *ever* complimenting me." "This relationship is *never* going to get any better; *all* we ever do is fight." This type of thinking completely blocks the potential for change because we've convinced ourselves that there's *nothing* worth fighting for. It leaves us tormented by feelings of helplessness, bitterness, or hopelessness.

To keep this thinking error from affecting you and your relationships, try to avoid using words like "always" and "never," and replace them with more accurate, honest, and specific descriptions of what's actually occurring. Instead of saying, "We're *always* fighting," try, "Yes, we do fight, but it happens most when we're both stressed, and honestly, much of the time we're happy."

Overgeneralization. Sometimes we draw drastic conclusions without sufficient evidence, which leads to poor decision-making. To understand this concept, read how Father Nick experienced it with a student when he taught college one semester:

> I had an amazing student who was forty-five years old. He was so committed! He showed up early to class, participated in discussions, and was always the first to turn in his papers. Curious about his story, one day I stopped him after class and asked him, "What brings you to this class?" He told me that when he was in third grade, he would talk and act out in class. "I just didn't really like school," he said. He went on to share that he'll never forget his teacher at the time saying, "If you keep this up, you'll never amount to anything."

> Well, those words stuck: His life followed them! He grew up believing he would never amount to anything. Whenever opportunities came his way to make

a change, he would remember those words. He never went to college and had trouble holding down even the simplest of jobs. One day, though, something happened that turned his life around. The owner of a place he worked for saw how hard he was working and said, "You have so much potential; you're bright. You could really go far in this company. If you'd just go back to school and get some more education, I could promote you to upper management."

When my student heard the owner say these things, the stronghold over his life lifted. Though the teacher had cursed him, the owner reversed it. So, you see, sometimes we too can speak to ourselves like that teacher spoke to my student: We can generalize a lifetime of failure from a situation of struggle. In doing so, we overgeneralize, forgetting our worth and underestimating what God can do in our lives.

It helps to keep things in perspective. Recognize that yes, we will meet struggles, but overgeneralizing our failures will never help us become who God has called us to be; rather, it will add another layer of emotion to an already frustrating situation. Now, not only does our current struggle upset us, but we've also added worry about what it means for our life in general, fueling an already charged moment with extra gas. No one is perfect, and we all struggle with something. Don't allow one area of weakness to smear the lens by which you evaluate everything else!

The same holds true for how you view others. If you're rushing to get somewhere in traffic and you pull up behind someone who seems to be taking a Sunday drive without any sense of urgency, you might say to yourself, "Why does everyone in this town have to drive so slow?" But with this reaction, not only do you feel irritated with this particular driver, you're also now upset at "everyone." Again, it's easy to evaluate one annoyance in terms of a broader pattern, but usually these interpretations aren't accurate and will likely only spawn increased intensity and emotionality.

Magnification. Magnification causes you to ignore the positive aspects of a situation or person and magnify only negative details. When we make this thinking error, our minds focus so intently on what's wrong that we no longer feel the joy around us. And when we look at those we love, we often see their weaknesses to such a degree that we can barely see their strengths at all.

Say, for instance, your spouse excels at kicking back and having fun but isn't as efficient at getting things done. Try seeing the beauty his relaxed manner brings to your family, rather than setting him up to fail by expecting him to efficiently manage all the household tasks. Rather, if efficiency is *your* strength, take the lead on the plan to accomplish everything—and let your partner take the lead on keeping things relaxed as you go. Thank each other for the unique gifts you *both* bring to your family and to the world around you. Stay focused on the greater good between you, work together to collaborate as a team, and embrace your differences.

God has equipped us each differently for *His* purpose, not necessarily for *our* purpose. As I Corinthians 12:12-27 puts it, the body of the church has many different members, each with its own unique function. So instead of looking for what you think is *wrong* in someone else, try instead to look for what's *right*—and notice how your actions become part of a bigger plan to build upon those strengths. Interestingly, research supports this idea that when we fill our thoughts with good sentiments, we're less likely to see the bad in someone and are even more likely to give her the benefit of the doubt—even if she does something to upset us.[10]

Jumping to conclusions. Do you ever believe you can predict how something will turn out or how someone will act, before it even happens? Sometimes we jump to conclusions about what people feel or think without ever bothering to *check out* our assumptions. Don't assume you know what your partner is thinking; *ask.* Is he quiet because he's intentionally ignoring you? Maybe he simply had a long and stressful day at work and needs a few minutes to unwind. When your wife asks if you've taken out the trash yet, don't assume she's condemning you because you haven't. Assume the best in people, and test your assumptions before drawing conclusions. When we assume the best in others, we follow what St. Paul in I Corinthians tells us about the keys to a healthy way of loving: love "does not behave rudely, does not seek its own, is not provoked, thinks no evil; does not rejoice in iniquity, but rejoices in the truth; bears all things, believes all things, hopes all things, endures all things" (13:5-7).

Emotional reasoning. Sometimes we think that if we *feel* a certain way, then what's behind that feeling *must* be true. We use our feelings as objective standards for truth and facts. If a certain outcome *feels* possible or likely, we treat that emotion as a fact, regardless of the evidence. But feeling nervous doesn't always mean you're in danger. And feeling betrayed doesn't always mean someone did something to hurt you. Maybe a friend isn't purposely ignoring you, even though you felt her acting distant.

To correct this error in thinking, instead of seeing feelings as facts, try to see them as just a cause for pause. They're a reason to tune in and evaluate further. When we pause instead of react, we can examine the evidence for our feelings and reactions, looking at the bigger picture and keeping everything in perspective. After all, when the smoke alarm goes off in your home, is there always an actual fire? No! Most of the time, it's because a piece of toast has burned in your toaster oven. Calling the fire department every time without investigating first would use up precious resources needed for actual emergencies. So, when you pair your strong feelings *with* objective facts and spiritual discernment, you'll find you can conserve many of your own internal resources you may have otherwise squandered in needless negativity. And in turn, when you cut needless negativity out of your life, you'll be better able to embrace the renewal and inner transformation God has in mind for you!

Catastrophizing. Another error in thinking involves imagining worst-case scenarios. When we imagine the worst outcome, we often assign greater credibility to that potentially negative outcome than actually exists. Have you ever pulled up a stream of texts from someone you haven't spoken to in a while? What did your life look like at that time? Are your worries today the same as they were then? How has God brought you through those times to bring healing, perspective, and peace about the things that bothered you back then? The other day, I (Dr. Roxanne) pulled up a stream of texts from someone I hadn't spoken to in quite a while. At the time, I'd asked her to pray for my dad the night before a major, fourteen-hour surgery to help him battle cancer. As I read my message, I could see the worry in my texts: the uncertainty and the fear of all the "what-ifs." The text took me right back to a time when worst-case scenarios consumed my mind, and I remembered how hard it was to imagine life beyond that point or see how God was going to get us through that day. My mind was caught in catastrophizing, struggling to remember to "let go and let God" work in my life, as I Peter 5:6-7 tells us: "Therefore humble yourselves under the mighty hand of God, that He may exalt you in due time, casting all your care upon Him, for He cares for you." It's amazing how God works in our lives over time to bring us healing and peace about things that once plagued us.

To help yourself through this thinking error, when you find yourself imagining the worst-case scenario, try to also imagine the best-case scenario—and then ask yourself, what's the most *likely* scenario? Remember, *possibility* isn't the same thing as *probability*. Just because something *could* happen, doesn't mean it will. Besides, God has equipped us to handle even the worst situations—He's always with us, even in disastrous circumstances. And eventually, as we rely on Him to renew us and our thinking, either we find a way to fix the problem or our perspective toward the problem changes as we slowly adapt to something we can't change and find a way to reinvest in a new normal. So when the storms of life come your way, lean on the God of peace to get you through the day. Because, you see, peace is not the *absence* of a storm, it's the *presence* of God. As Father Nick would encourage you to remember, Christ is our hope and "an anchor for [our] soul, firm and secure" (Heb. 6:19 [NIV]).

Personalization. This thinking error occurs when we decide that situations having nothing to do with us are, in fact, about us! Let's say you walk into work and your coworker is less than friendly. If you personalize that situation, you might think, "What did I do? It's clear she's upset about something I've done." This thought might throw off your entire day, preoccupying your mind with worry. As a result, you may even begin withdrawing from her, which only adds to the awkward tension. Instead, ask yourself what else might have caused her less-than-sociable mood. Could she have stress at home you aren't aware of? Maybe her child is struggling in school, or maybe her aging mother isn't doing well. Is this a one-time event, or does it seem to happen often? Could something else be wrong?

Keep your mind open to the fact that, more often than not, people's behavior has more to do with them than it does with you. Also, remember that everyone has bad days, and your coworker's mood may be nothing more than that. Plus, even if it is about you, it's up to her to take ownership of her own emotions and bring you her needs. Either way, run your own race—continue to act positively toward her! If it turns out she *is* upset with you, your kindness might soften her heart. If something else is going on, she may even decide to open up to you about her worries, and then you can minister Christ to her and remind her she's not alone in the midst of the sadness and stress. So, although the flesh of our minds can sometimes cause us to take things personally, St. Paul reminds us that the process of growing in our faith requires our willingness to put on Christ in moments exactly like these. "You were taught, with regard to your former way of life, to put off your old self, which is being corrupted by its deceitful desires; to be made new in the attitude of your minds; and to put on the new self, created to be like God in true righteousness and holiness" (Eph. 4:22-25 [NIV]).

Transform Your Thinking—with God's Help

This is the good news about our pesky thought problems! Thoughts are nothing more than interpretations and snap judgments intensified by our own emotions—which is why we must remember to "take captive every thought to make it obedient to Christ" (2 Cor. 10:5 [NIV]), rather than let our thoughts imprison us and lock us into hurtful responses. We can *choose* to make different, more helpful interpretations that keep our lives moving along on the right path, which leads to healing, growth, and renewal. When we slow down, pause, and take some time to consider our thoughts, we can even discover that not all unhealthy thoughts are created equal! Sometimes, an unhealthy thought is completely unhelpful and we need to toss it, but other times, it can serve as a useful source of understanding that prompts healing and repair—*if* we handle it properly. Here's a great example of this at work, from one of Dr. Roxanne's experiences:

> It's such a gift when I get to see someone realize that their thoughts can be windows into the needs of their soul. I spoke to someone years ago, a gracious woman who gave to others more than she ever asked of them. Well, at one point in her life, she experienced one trial after the next. She kept going, managing her own needs while continuing to give to those around her. But one day, everything just came crashing down: It all suddenly seemed like more than she could bear. She felt alone, and she began feeling down about how little others seemed to notice—or care.
>
> Two questions I asked prompted her awareness. "How often do you put yourself on other people's radar? Do you think you've shed any light on your own struggles?" She paused and realized in that moment that, although she needed support, she hadn't really asked for it. She decided to put words to this realization. "It's really been a rough few weeks," she began sharing with friends. When she tried this, a beautiful outflowing of support came in from those who mattered most

to her. She found this a shocking revelation. "People did care!" she said. What seemed like an unhealthy thought, initially, ended up helping her find just what her soul needed most. Without intentional discernment, her initial thought could have led to detachment, distance, and resentment from the very people she treasured and needed most. Thoughts can function as powerful windows into our souls if we take the time to unpack them, listening for what's important, rather than just engaging the feelings they create.

Use the Three Ts

We've discovered three steps that can help us begin to change our thoughts and open ourselves up more powerfully to God's purpose for us. The first step is *tune in to your thoughts*. This step involves learning to notice and examine our thoughts—especially when strong feelings surface. Remember, most of us don't examine our thoughts during the course of the day because we're usually too busy *reacting* to them. In fact, the cognitive behavioral model of human behavior in psychology explains that, while most of us tend to be aware of *what* we feel in any given moment, we have less awareness of the thoughts and interpretations that got us there. So we need to work hard to *tune in* to them. In prayer, at church, when you lie in bed at night, during your daily exercise routine—any time you notice a distracting voice or an unhealthy, destructive storyline developing in the background without your permission, stop and notice it. What plays out might surprise you.

Take, for instance, this moment. Perhaps you find yourself yelling at someone you live with because they've plopped their shoes down in the middle of the entryway again. You notice a sudden impulse to react. Stop! Ask yourself, "Is it the shoes, or am I just tired from doing too much in general?" "Is it the shoes, or do the shoes remind me that I need to enlist more help around the house?" "Or am I still angry about something that happened last week with this same person?" "Is it the shoes, or is something completely different putting me on edge today, and the shoes were just the trigger?"

The best way to reduce unhealthy emotion is to figure out what's making you upset in the first place and put words to it. It could be the issue that triggered you is something entirely different, and irritation can mount quickly if you don't take the time to acknowledge it. So, noticing our thoughts is the first step to changing them through a conscious process of understanding rather than reacting.

The second step you can take is to *test your thoughts*. Remember, left unattended, our thoughts will direct our lives and ultimately shape our interactions with the world. Because our thoughts can mislead us, we have to carefully evaluate them before we engage them. By testing, we discern the will of God, so we need to constantly ask ourselves, "Does this thought lead me toward God or away from Him?"

Because our thoughts don't have power until we give it to them by blindly following them, we can test them by *developing a filter*. After all, we use filters to clean out pollutants in so many other areas of life! We use filters in our cars, for our drinking water, for UV rays from the sun, and even in our dryers in the laundry room. So let's also develop filters to eliminate the impurities in our thoughts! Any thought that doesn't lead us toward love for God and others—and yes, even love for ourselves—is a thought we need to filter out. And we can rest assured that *God will never talk to us in a way that conflicts with His Word or character.*

We can also test our thoughts for thinking errors by heeding the wisdom of St. Paul in Philippians 4:8. Here, St. Paul gives us filters when he says we should fix our thoughts on things that are true, honorable, just, lovely, commendable, and worthy of praise. Do the thoughts you entertain fit these descriptions? When we filter our thoughts through this lens, we have assurance that the God of peace will be with us and that the filters will clear away the pollutants which keep us from seeing His purpose.

So, in the midst of your irritation at finding those shoes in the middle of the floor, test the thoughts that come to your mind: "I'm the only one who ever cleans up around here!" (Is that *really* a true thought?) Or, "With habits like these, the kids will never be able to manage the responsibilities of life." (Yes, this is a false overgeneralization.) Perhaps you're thinking, "What slobs! I can't remember a time when they cleaned up after themselves." (This magnifies the negative and ignores more positive realities.) Or, perhaps you've personalized it and are thinking, "No one cares about how much I do around here!"

Remember, just because we have a thought doesn't mean it's true, and the thought has no power over us unless we believe it. Even thoughts like, "I shouldn't feel this way," can subtly undermine our healing. Instead, ask, "Why do I feel this way?" and, "What do I need?" to help you understand yourself better and recognize and address what's really wrong. Testing our thoughts also ensures we don't just listen to any voice (knowing this is where the devil can get a foothold and lead us without our awareness), so that we instead listen to the one voice of the Person who loves us so much that He gave us life.

When you find yourself in a situation where you need to test your thoughts, try asking yourself these questions:

- "Does this thought help me or make me feel worse?"
- "Where am I headed if I believe this thought?"
- "What does this thought tell me about what I might need?"
- "Am I looking for a solution or just indulging the urge to stew about it?"
- "Is this thought pushing people I love away?"
- "Is what I'm saying even true? Are there any thinking errors I can see?"
- "Does this thought align my spirit with the fruit of the Holy Spirit (Gal. 5:22-23) and the Beatitudes?" (Matt. 5:3-12).
- "If these thoughts were broadcast aloud, would I still be thinking them?"
- "Does this thought conflict with Scripture? If so, how?"
- "Does this thought seek my will or God's will for my life?"

Once you've practiced the art of tuning into your thoughts and testing them, the third step is *transforming your thoughts* and beginning to choose the life-affirming and more Christlike thoughts. As you become more Christlike, you'll experience His renewal and discover His purpose for you in a more and more profound way. As Isaiah 26:3 (NLT) promises, God "will keep in perfect peace / all who trust in [Him], / all whose thoughts are fixed on [Him]."

We can keep our thoughts fixed on Christ by holding on to the right perspective. For example, have you noticed how you often lose your joy over things you won't even remember in a few days or weeks, or how you sometimes alter the course of your life over a single comment? Challenge yourself, when you're upset with others, to use empathy to see life through their lens. Remember, even when Christ was on the Cross, in one of His first statements He said, "Father, forgive them, for they do not know what they do" (Luke 23:34). Looking at what others do—through their perspective—makes forgiving them and loving them easier.

When you're trying to see through someone else's point of view, ask yourself:

- "How might this thought change if I look at this situation from the other person's point of view?"
- "How might it change if I remove my judgment from the situation and insert mercy?"
- "How might I replace my thoughts of resentment with thoughts of empathy and forgiveness?"

- "Can I forgive myself, too, and show kindness to myself in my own weaknesses and struggles?"
- "How can I turn this into an opportunity for healing and renewal, both in my thoughts and in my actions?"

Our thoughts have brought us to where we are today, and tomorrow we'll go where our thoughts take us, too. You see, God has a will for our lives, but in this world, we also have free will. And ironically enough, this "free" will often ends up putting us into a prison of unhelpful thoughts and actions! Yet through His perfect design, God also gave us the *ability* to evaluate those thoughts in relation to who He calls us to be. Seeking the constant renewal of our minds is the ultimate battle of every Christian. As Scripture tells us, "For those who live according to the flesh set their minds on the things of the flesh, but those *who live* according to the Spirit, the things of the Spirit. For to be carnally minded *is* death, but to be spiritually minded *is* life and peace" (Rom. 8:5-6). And as II Corinthians 10:3-5 (NIV) says, if we want to overcome the enemy's power in our lives, we have to "take captive" and make obedient every thought to Christ.

Stay Prayed Up

Consistent, daily spiritual practices help us keep our thoughts healthy by nourishing our spirits and ensuring we don't allow the demands of the world to overwhelm our time and energy. First, try following the First Fifteen method for prayer, Bible reading, and devotional reading that we suggest in Chapter I. Prayer and reading help us keep our thoughts focused on God, and prayer is especially important, as it's our opportunity to connect in gratitude, unload our worries, unpack our thoughts, and ask for God's guidance. It's our chance to lay down our burdens onto God's broad, unbreakable shoulders—and the Bible assures us that when we pray, God listens! If you look for God in earnest, you will find Him when you seek Him (Jer. 29:12-13).

And remember Colossians 3:2? "Set your mind on things above, not on things on the earth." If you don't make time in your day for your thoughts to center on things of heaven rather than of earth, you'll have difficulty renewing your mind because you won't be able to focus on the things that bring you peace! And take note: Prayer doesn't have to be fancy! God doesn't need our petitions to be poetic or in the language of King James English. We just need to talk to Him every day and listen for His voice at work within our souls. You see, prayer isn't to remind God of our existence; it's to remind us of His.

So even beyond your daily five minutes, gradually work toward praying more often, as St. Paul says in I Thessalonians 5:16-18: "Rejoice always, pray without ceasing, in everything give thanks; for this is the will of God in Christ Jesus for you." Notice, as we talk about in Chapter I as well, God wants us to pray continually—not just during worship at church or only when we face difficulties or only for others who have asked us to—but all the time! It might help to listen to music or podcasts that keep you centered on Christ as you journey through your day, or to choose to "like" pages on your social media feeds that speak spiritual wisdom into your life.

Assess Your Environment

Sometimes you may find that your surrounding environment causes your thoughts to stray. Our advice? Get out—fast! Here's a story from our lives about a time when a particular environment proved unhealthy for us. Father Nick says:

> The seas we swim in and the atmospheric conditions we breathe can block our progress as we prayerfully focus on renewing our minds and correcting our thoughts. Several years ago, Roxanne and I went with friends to a Broadway play on tour in our city. We didn't know anything about the play, but we were looking forward to spending time with our friends. However, not even five minutes into the show, we realized it wasn't for us. Every other word was a curse word, and the performers' costumes left very little to the imagination. We both felt uncomfortable, like something was tugging at our souls. After looking over at each other several times in utter disbelief, we decided to slip out and wait in the lobby until the play was over. Neither of us felt right watching the whole play when its themes conflicted with our values.
>
> At intermission, our friends found us in the lobby and asked why we'd left the theater. We shared our

thoughts, but our friends responded, "Come on, guys, you two are being old-fashioned. If you could just get past the cursing and the outfits, the plot is really great."

"That might be true," we said, "but honestly, those things were so distracting, we couldn't actually pay attention to the plot!"

If we strive to be "in the world but not of it," that sometimes means we'll need to remove ourselves from a situation. Our souls are too valuable for us to waste time feeding them on the wrong messages and breathing in the fumes of a toxic environment.

The world encourages us to live by the flesh. Everywhere, a relentless barrage of images, empty promises, and fantasies confront us. Tempting shortcuts promise us lasting peace and happiness. Convenience stores and *fast* food tempt us with *quick* and *easy* fixes after a stressful day. *Happy* hours sell us on the empty promise that *happiness* flows from the outside in, and technology has taken away our sense of peace. TV and the Internet offer to fill our minds with darkness, disrespect, violence, and a corrupted sense of intimacy.

If the mind is the gateway to the soul, what impact, then, do violent acts on TV shows have on us? And have you ever noticed how TV shows portray many marriages as unhealthy, disloyal, or unfaithful? Much of the intimacy depicted on TV takes place outside of marriage. Storylines glamorize extramarital affairs while rarely depicting fulfilled and happy marriages. After enough exposure to these images, we begin to change our standards or become numb to the violence and licentious behavior we view. "Everyone else is doing it. It can't be that bad," we reason.

We heard a story recently where a teenaged boy asked his mom if he could have several friends over for a sleepover. They wanted to watch a movie, but it was rated R. "It only has one bad part, Mom," he uttered.

Feeling pressured, she said, "I guess it's okay."

Later that evening, she returned to the room to feed the hungry teens. She brought snacks and freshly baked brownies, her son's favorite. "Oh, Mom, these are awesome!" he said as they all dug in with delight.

As she walked out, she said, "So glad you like them, son. There's just one thing you should know. I had to go outside and scrape a bit of dirt into the mix since I was out of cocoa, but no big deal. It's just one bad part."

The boys' faces changed. Funny how a different perspective can illustrate faulty reasoning! We wouldn't even think of consuming brownies made with dirt, but we consume messages all day long that fill our minds with the same.

The psalmist reminds us, "I will set nothing wicked before my eyes" (101:3). So when a show or a website conflicts with your values, find the discipline to change the channel or close the tab. That's why the remote control was created; you don't even have to get up from the sofa. Just push the button! Don't feed your flesh or hope your willpower alone will see you through.

We only have one opportunity to live out our lives on this earth—and one chance to make good choices. So we should think long and hard about the thoughts we entertain and the mindset we cultivate! We don't even know if we have another tomorrow—at some point we'll live our last day and then we'll enter eternity. If we want to change our tomorrows, we must renew our minds today, instead of allowing the prison of this world and its temptations to keep us locked away from our love for God and our sensitivity toward spiritual things. Our surrounding environment makes a tremendous difference in whether or not we'll have the discernment to renew our minds and focus on the keys that keep our souls strong.

PRAYER

✠ ✠ ✠

OH HEAVENLY FATHER, we know You've blessed

us with the power of our own thinking. You've given

us the ability to process and to analyze. And with

this great power, we know we can use this ability for

good or bad. We realize our minds will naturally

want to move toward what's unhealthy. We also

realize that our thoughts and beliefs oftentimes

dictate our actions and behaviors: if we look at our

thoughts, we'll begin to see our lives. You share with

us, through the pen of St. Paul in Philippians 4:8-9

(GNT), what type of files we should download for

our minds: those things that are good and deserve

praise; "things that are true, noble, right, pure, lovely,

and honorable" so that "the God who gives us peace will be with [us]." So, we humbly ask You, oh Lord, to help us take in those thoughts that lift us up, while at the same time leaving out those thoughts that keep us from being our best. Empower us to put a "no vacancy" sign on the doors of our minds, so that if a thought doesn't help and challenge us, then there's no room in the inn of our minds for that thought. In the name of the Father, Son, and Holy Spirit; one God.

Amen.

✠ ✠ ✠

FOR DISCUSSION:
THE THREE Rs——REST, REFLECT,
AND RESPOND

1. What thoughts play in your mind when you think of yourself?

2. What thoughts play in your mind about the people you love most?

3. What thoughts do you think during moments that cause you the most distress?

4. Which of the "thinking errors" do you find yourself committing most often in your life? In your marriage? With your family? In your workplace? In your friendships? In regard to your goals and dreams? How can you apply the solutions to address those errors?

5. What was your biggest worry five years ago? Do you still feel the same about it right now?

6. What advice would you give the five-year-old you?

7. What keeps you awake at night, and what is your dominant inner voice like?

8. What is the harshest criticism you've ever received? How does that impact your inner voice today?

9. What do you tell yourself that might conflict with what God says about you? How does it conflict with the messages of Scripture?

10. When you notice strong feelings, what do you hear as you tune in to your thoughts? Are they productive? Accurate? How could you transform them?

Find Victory over Your Vices

I count him braver who overcomes his desires than he who conquers his enemies; for the hardest victory is the victory over self.[1] —ARISTOTLE

A S YOU COME to this chapter, you may be thinking, "But if I renew my spiritual life and my thinking, won't my vices automatically come into line?" Well—sometimes! And creating better spiritual and thinking habits definitely helps. However, vices and bad habits have a *bad habit* of sticking around unless we confront them head-on. The Apostle James references this when he says, "Temptation comes from our own desires, which entice us and drag us away. These desires give birth to sinful actions. And when sin is allowed to grow, it gives birth to death" (1:14-15 [NLT]). Because our vices originate in our urges and desires, if we don't confront them, we fall into temptation because we end up entertaining the very urge we wish to avoid. And how can we be renewed if we entertain our passions and urges? Confronting our vices head-on means that we spend some time first thinking about what our vices are and then make a resolution to work on one or more of them. As you read through this chapter, we encourage you to do just that!

We once heard that the concept of setting resolutions has been around for three thousand years and that we predictably set them at the start of the year. But why do we only set resolutions for improving our lives in January, when it seems that God designed us to constantly seek renewal and growth? As it says in 2 Corinthians 4:16 (ESV), "Though our outer self is wasting away, our inner self is being renewed day by day." Every day as we mature in our faith and our knowledge of Christ, we have an opportunity to be more transformed into His image and likeness. After all, life is a journey, and every stage presents repeated opportunities to escape the corruption of the world and seek a better, more *renewed* version of ourselves. We hear this beautifully put in 2 Peter 1:3-7 (NLT):

> By his divine power, God has given us everything we need for living a godly life. We have received all of this by coming to know him, the one who called us to himself by means of his marvelous glory and excellence. And because of his glory and excellence, he has given us great and precious promises. These are the promises that enable you to share his divine nature and escape the world's corruption caused by human desires. In view of all this, make every effort to respond to God's promises. Supplement your faith with a generous provision of moral excellence, and moral excellence with knowledge, and knowledge with

self-control, and self-control with patient endurance, and patient endurance with godliness, and godliness with brotherly affection, and brotherly affection with love for everyone.

If we're honest, we all have at least one major issue in our lives we need to improve, and improving these things will add to our faith by helping us cultivate better self-control, more moral excellence, and more perseverance. This is why we try to set resolutions! It could be anything from a temper to a more physically debilitating problem like an addiction. Whether we struggle with smoking, drinking, procrastination, over-spending, lack of exercise, or eating too much sugar, vices come in all shapes and sizes. Our world often sensationalizes vices like these, telling us over and over again that they are actually just escapes—that they are tools for happiness and for coping with life's ups and downs. Yet, we know that Christ tells us to "take up [our] cross, and follow [Him]" (Mark 8:34). So if we desire to follow Him—if we wish to fulfill His purpose in us—then we must be willing to look directly at ourselves and find the humility not to defend our behaviors or believe in the world's messages about them, but to confront them, understand them, and change them.

Confronting and understanding first is key: After all, we can't win a fight over what we don't see in ourselves or understand. We need to understand that vices function as a relief valve for our discomfort—a way of overcoming boredom and escaping from bottled-up feelings we don't know how to manage more effectively. And *strong emotions usually lie at the root of unhealthy behaviors*, whether we succumb to overeating when we're stressed, explosive anger when we're mad, or reckless behavior when we're excited. Because of this, Scripture wisely warns us to guard our hearts against strong feelings like fear, worry, anger, unforgiveness, jealousy, and guilt. But why does it warn us so much about these so frequently, and in so many different ways? Perhaps because God knows how easily we succumb to such behaviors and how much they can hurt us and those around us! So, seeking a better version of ourselves must be a resolution we commit to every day, knowing God calls us to constantly renew our minds in Him.

Because our vices often become habits—recurrent and often *unconscious* patterns of behavior—we engage in them without much conscious awareness or intention. In fact, it's often hard to notice these behaviors until *after* they're already set into motion, or worse, after we've already acted on them. This makes them very difficult to change—but it's not impossible! Understanding how our bad habits sabotage us and imprison us in repetitive, unintentional behaviors—and learning how we can develop new habits of thinking and behavior—is an important task as we prepare for an intentional life.

Our habits are an important area to confront in seeking renewal because our bodies and souls are united. That means our spirits can easily become paralyzed by a body that succumbs to weakness. Perhaps that's why, in the Book of Matthew, we hear Jesus encouraging us toward vigilance. Even a willing spirit must remain watchful over the flesh it resides in: "Watch and pray so that you will not fall into temptation. The spirit is willing, but the flesh is weak" (Matt. 26:41 [NIV]). Jesus said this to His disciples after asking them to stay watchful while He went off to pray, but then He found them sleeping in the Garden of Gethsemane on Holy Thursday, the night before His Crucifixion.

Just like the disciples, we all give in to weaknesses of our flesh at times: Our vices are exactly that. And our flesh drives us to continue our behaviors, even when we can clearly see that the result is no longer desirable. Habits usually start out rewarding, but over time, even when they begin to hurt us or block our potential, we somehow continue to repeat them, keeping ourselves from living the type of renewed life God wants for us. How does this happen?

Let's look at our brains for a moment. Recent research has found that our brains can take anywhere from eighteen to 254 days to form a habit, with the average length of time being sixty-six days. Once formed, this habit is stored in neural pathways in our brains in the *basal ganglia*, located in our cerebral cortex—the outermost region of the brain. Interestingly, the basal ganglia help us form habits because they encode the context or circumstance under which a behavior initially occurred and was reinforced. This means that the moment you find yourself in a specific situation (the signal), your brain will automatically remember to perform a particular behavior (automated response). For instance, when we walk into our homes at night (the signal), we automatically reach for the light switch (automated response) because it usually leads to our ability to see. However, most of us will continue to reach for that light switch, even when our electricity is out.[2]

We act out this kind of behavior in many ways. For instance, every day when you wake up (the signal), you may automatically walk into the bathroom and follow a specific routine, in a specific order, without really thinking about it. You walk in, wash your face, brush your teeth, and comb your hair—no decisions, no thinking, and no brain energy required. Over time, your brain has helped you by storing this information as the "wake-up routine" so that the moment you awaken, it immediately retrieves your automatic response. Throughout the day, this automation saves your brain countless hours of cognitive energy. Another example of God's perfect design!

Unfortunately, because we live in a world that tempts our flesh with many unhealthy habits, this automation also means many other engrained, destructive habits may fly under our radar yet still lead our decisions. We remember sitting down to eat with a family friend who would light up a cigarette at the same point during every meal, even though he often talked about wanting to quit. As soon as the server cleared his plate (the signal), he would pull out his box of cigarettes (automated response) and be ready to leave our gathering so he could smoke. This happened because the conserving part of his brain didn't distinguish between an unhealthy habit—like pulling out a cigarette at a certain time—and a more life-giving habit, like staying to connect socially at the end of a meal, which would have been more in line with his values. If we want to seek renewal, we must be able to discern when our conserving brain causes us to continue an unhealthy habit like this. God calls us to notice when we fall into patterns of behavior that threaten to keep us from living the way He intended, as I Peter 5:8 (NLT) says, "Stay alert! Watch out for your great enemy, the devil. He prowls around like a roaring lion, looking for someone to devour." The devil will often do anything he can to bring defeat into our lives, weighing us down with behaviors, passions, and habits that leave us less than whole and move us further and further away from our deeper values.

Be Attentive

The good news is, because of God's perfect design, our brain also has a *frontal lobe*, a dedicated section of the cerebral cortex that's more developed in human beings than in any other living organism. It's responsible for so many things, but most importantly, it's our decision control center. This region helps us make rational decisions based on sound reason. It also helps our judgment, our problem-solving capabilities, our impulse control, and our ability to make plans—all important aspects of managing and changing our unhealthy habits! All we have to do to engage this part of our brain is start paying more attention to *what* we do *when* we do it, and then we can begin to work toward obtaining *what* we want. This helps us make values-based decisions.

Research on behavior change has demonstrated that even something as simple as monitoring and tracking a behavior can help us significantly reduce (or increase) the frequency of that behavior.[3] So, it turns out that the virtue of *attentiveness,* often described by spiritual fathers and mothers, is our brain's key to unlocking the potential for change. Once we become aware of a behavior, our frontal lobe assists us in both thinking through the cost of continuing it *and* calculating the benefits of making lasting change for the better—as well as planning for the steps of change.

The frontal lobe also gives us the ability to examine our habits on a deeper level until we begin to discover the often-hidden needs driving our unhealthy choices. We can also, then, vigilantly notice the situations that trigger our unhealthy behaviors, reminding ourselves of our values and the kind of person we want to become—even in the very moment of temptation! In this process of awareness and intentionality, we realize that ultimately we have other options for how we respond to triggering situations, and we can choose an option more in line with who we hope to become. As Christians, we have a great helper in the person of the Holy Spirit, the Comforter, who is "everywhere present" and "filling all things."[4] With His help, as we examine our habits and begin to make healthy changes to our behavior, we open ourselves up to the renewal God has in mind for us, and we can better see His purpose for our lives!

Take a few moments to consider which of your unhealthy habits you wish you could change. What do you notice about the situation or context surrounding your unhealthy habit—does a particular situation or person activate it? Or does something you see? Does it happen in a certain place or during a particular time of day?

Maybe your unhealthy habit is a short fuse. Then, perhaps stressful situations signal your unhealthy habit is about to arrive. To visualize this, imagine that as you drive home from work, it feels like it's been a long day. You're tired and frustrated by several bottlenecked tasks at the office (the signal). Then someone cuts you off in traffic (the event). If you don't recognize your own emotional state, it's easy to react and give that person a "piece of your mind" (your unhealthy habit) because it just feels right at the time. This results in increased agitation and stress throughout your whole body, causing the following internal reactions:

- Decreased immune response. Research shows you can lose up to several hours of immune system response from just a few minutes of anger.[5]
- Your blood-brain barrier also starts allowing chemicals and toxins to pass through, where normally it would prevent foreign invaders from adversely affecting your brain.
- An increased heart rate, which makes you less able to think, solve problems, or take in new information from listening.

You now arrive home in this state and try to use what little energy you have left to will yourself into showing kindness to your family!

So, did your vice ease your initial struggle or serve to prolong it? You can see from this example that if we don't intentionally recognize our unhealthy habits, the devil can use our bodies and minds against us!

Now, imagine yourself again in the same scenario. Only this time, you notice the signal and think, "I'm stressed. I can feel it. I know when I'm tired and frustrated it's easy to snap! God, please keep me mindful on my drive home; help me to remain calm and patient, and guide my spirit with Your Holy Spirit. Help me to do what works for my values and my overall needs, rather than just what feels good in the moment." Now, when someone cuts you off (the event), they don't catch you off guard, and you can evoke a different, more intentional response: "This isn't worth it. God, help me to keep my peace, not give it away. Give me compassion for this driver who's probably also tired and frustrated and struggling to choose well. Help me remember that reacting to someone else's stress with my stress always makes things worse."

No matter what the trigger, we can retrain our brain to pause and notice what we feel, take inventory of our needs, and ask God to help us choose with intention a more positive action that addresses what our soul truly needs to thrive. So the next time you feel your vice triggering you, stay mindful. Notice it, but don't engage it; engage God instead, and realize you can make another choice. If stress is your signal, rather than engaging your short fuse, choose a healthier alternative: get some space, go for a run, empty your thoughts into a journal, problem solve what you can, open up your Bible, spend time in prayer, take a warm bath, pick up a book, read a devotional, create a soothing environment to engage all of your senses (think lighting, calming music, a scented candle, a cup of hot tea, and a warm blanket), or reach out to call a friend who usually gives you encouragement and wisdom that soothes your soul.

As your brain repeatedly registers a positive result from a new behavior, *a new healthy habit begins to form and will become automatic over time.* Remember, habits on average take around two months to create. And simpler habits like drinking more water require less time to develop than those that need a bit more discipline, like stepping away in the midst of a triggering situation when you have a short fuse. But the more you practice, the more reflexive your new habit will become! God has wired our brains for elasticity, so no matter what we struggle with, we can always return to the drawing board and reprogram our mental computers, altering, strengthening, and renewing our neural pathways through His grace.

More good news: when we perform the new behavior, we actually thicken the myelination, or coating, that surrounds the nerve fibers carrying the electrical signal that fired in response to our new behavior. Think of it like the barriers along an interstate that prevent cars from going off the road. Myelin helps make the neural signal travel faster and helps direct the signal in the right direction. The thicker the myelination around a neural pathway, the more easily and effectively we perform the action that uses that pathway. In other words, the more we practice, the easier it becomes! More of God's perfect design to reward us in our renewal.

Naturally, you have to keep feeding healthy habits in order to make them stronger, while remaining on the lookout for old habits that might seep back in. Keep in mind that the old neural pathway (the unhealthy habit) doesn't completely disappear, so you might experience setbacks. But work at staying the course, and don't give up. God has equipped you with everything you need to become who He has designed you to be!

Resist the Pull of Addiction

Sometimes, what starts out as an unhealthy behavior solidifies and deepens into an unmanageable addiction that imprisons you within it. Addictions are not just habits. They're mediated by a different layer of our brain's intricate working system, making them much harder (but not impossible) than habits to break.

The *nucleus accumbens* is a cluster of nerve cells known as our brain's reward center, and it drives and motivates many of our behaviors. Many types of addictive behaviors increase the level of dopamine in our brain, and increased dopamine makes us feel good. In fact, researchers can actually observe strong changes in brain activity within the *nucleus accumbens* when we indulge in external rewards (like drugs, alcohol, gambling, etc.) or even when we just think about them.[6] Sometimes more dopamine releases in anticipation of a reward than when we act on it. This is problematic because it sets us up to become slaves to the gravitational pull of our addictions! Rewards like these flood us with a strong sense of pleasure, desire, craving, and goal-directed behavior—so we feel a strong urge to repeat the behaviors. For example, even when we are focused attentively on a task, the moment we receive a social media or text notification, dopamine release drives our desire to seek out the reward of opening up the notification. Anytime we come into contact with something we've previously associated with a reward, dopamine is released, making us hyper-focused on checking for and seeking out that reward.

Keeping Scripture in mind can give us a renewed reason to help us resist the powerful pull of addiction. As St. Paul reminds us in the Book of Romans, "Therefore do not let sin reign in your mortal body so that you obey its evil desires. Do not offer any part of yourself to sin as an instrument of wickedness, but rather offer yourselves to God . . . for sin shall no longer be your master" (6:12-14 [NIV]). We must remember, too, that addictions occupy a significant amount of our time and emotional energy, and they alter our goal-directed behavior—but we know as Christians we cannot serve two masters! As Matthew 6:24 (NIV) says, "Either you will hate the one and love the other, or you will be devoted to the one and despise the other." Simply put, we cannot serve God if we let our addictions enslave us. Without confronting our addictions, it becomes very difficult to remain on the path to God's purpose.

If you struggle with addiction, know that while it is difficult to break, it's not impossible. Try asking yourself today, which master do you feed the most in your life? Which master do you spend the most time protecting? Which master is winning the battle over your soul? And know that the master you *feed first* in your life is the one that will *lead* your life, for as I Corinthians 6:19-20 reminds us, "Do you not know that your body is the temple of the Holy Spirit *who is* in you, whom you have from God, and you are not your own? For you were bought at a price; therefore glorify God in your body and in your spirit, which are God's."

It also helps to realize that those struggling with addictions often need professional help to learn how to take their lives back by practicing extreme caution in situations that trigger their destructive behaviors. If you struggle with addiction, remember that guidance is always available. Turn to a trusted mental health professional and seek spiritual counsel. God has a bigger plan and a better life He wants to give you, and as you become free from your addictions, you'll experience His renewing presence in your life in ways you've only dreamed of!

Learn the Difference between Helpful and Unhelpful Guilt

Destructive habits and addictions often cause us to feel guilt, and as a priest and a psychologist, we often encounter people who feel imprisoned by it. One woman told us, "I no longer experience the joy I once did. I watch as my friends carry on laughing and talking like good friends do, and that used to be me, but I just can't get back to feeling that way again. Everything is different now." This woman had battled depression and anxiety for most of her adult life, and after struggling for years to find relief, she decided to enroll in a residential treatment center for a month to see if it would help alleviate her symptoms. After returning home, not only did she feel guilty for having depression to begin with, but she felt guilty for having to leave her family to seek help. Thoughts of judgment and condemnation only filled her with more guilty feelings.

Left unchecked, guilt like this can feel like walking on a treadmill and expecting to arrive at a new destination. We expend a lot of energy, but we don't get anywhere—and we end up feeling imprisoned by the guilty thoughts we turn over in our mind again and again! Remember that the devil constantly battles for our souls and will often use subtle forms of deception to keep us down. Therefore, we must remember the advice of St. Paul when he says in 2 Corinthians 2:11 (NIV) that we are not to be ignorant of his devices, "in order that Satan might not outwit us. For we are not unaware of his schemes." So while guilt can help us, it *can* also very much mislead us—and sometimes it's difficult to figure out which direction our guilty feelings are leading us. So here are some keys to help you distinguish between helpful and unhelpful guilt.

Helpful guilt alerts us if we have strayed (as we all do at some points in our lives) and urges us to make an adjustment to get back on track. Guilt is only useful if it does this. For instance, say you blurt out something hurtful in a moment of anger, and you immediately feel guilt. It's helpful because it alerts you to the fact that there's something you regret and need to repair. *Helpful guilt is a sign we've done something that doesn't sit right within our soul,* and it gives us the opportunity to change direction, return to our faith, and seek forgiveness through renewing our souls in Christ.

Once you've repaired something that came out of helpful guilt, it's important to forgive yourself and move on! God has given us all the gift of hindsight, not so we can judge ourselves but so we can grow from our past mistakes—because *life is just a series of opportunities that teach us how to live more like Christ.* So, if you find guilt dragging you down and locking you into unhealthy thought patterns despite your repentance, it's not serving it's intended purpose and could even have the opposite effect on your life. *Rather than teaching you how to live more like Christ, it then begins teaching you to stop trying, leaving you helpless and more distant from God.* So we must carefully discern where our guilt comes from and what effect it has on us.

How do we know whether our feelings of guilt are helpful or not? Try this simple test: If your guilt is helpful, it will provoke a change in direction to make your path straight (Heb. 12:13). You'll find something you can do to make the situation right again, and you'll feel like your spirit has just won a battle over a temptation of the flesh. On the other hand, unhelpful guilt leaves you directionless, without a means to make things better—either because you've already changed direction or because it wasn't in your hands to begin with. Dr. Roxanne remembers experiencing this:

> One evening, feeling tired already, I walked into the kitchen to begin preparing dinner. I noticed what felt like sticky sand beneath my feet, and I saw it on the counter too. "What's this? It's everywhere!" I thought. I started wiping it up but noticed I was only

smearing it all over the counter! Someone had clearly already used my sponge for another mess!

I went to the pantry to grab sugar for the brownies I'd planned on making, but the sugar was gone. "What? I know I had sugar!" I thought. I immediately called for the kids and asked, "Do you guys know what happened here?" Our daughter jumped at the chance to share! With enthusiasm, she showed me her new skin care line. "Mom, look what I've created! I'm going to sell it, and I've already typed up the ad for the newspaper I created at school."

"What are you even saying?" I said. Undeterred by my question, she went on, "My friend and I have started a newspaper—I write, she delivers!" At that point, I lost it. "Don't you know that would probably never work?" I said. "And look at the mess you've made. Did you even think about asking whether or not you could use up all the sugar?" Her enthusiasm quickly turned to tears, and I felt like a punch to the gut had knocked the breath right out of me.

But did I stop? No! I kept going, somehow thinking I could trust my jumbled-up feelings to lead me into a better place, without pausing to think things through. Out came more of the same, as if reading the same paragraph back to her would produce a different effect—one that would help her better understand my frustration or enlighten her in some way. Sadly, it only hurt her more.

"Mom," she said, "I did try to clean up all the sugar, but I guess the honey just got the sponge all sticky. I'm sorry." Why didn't that feel satisfying to hear? My confused feelings suddenly made sense. I had switched from feeling mad at her to being mad at myself. Going on and on, I was only working out *my* feelings on her, at her expense. Guilt set in.

As the mom—and a psychologist—I was supposed to be the perfect picture of love, patience, gentleness, and mercy. What had I done? I had taken the joy of a freely creative spirit filled with ambition and drive (God's design) and shamed her into thinking, "What's wrong with me; why do I ruin everything?" I had taken a "still learning" teachable moment and turned it into a "you should know this by now" condemning moment.

Was my guilt appropriate? Absolutely. Should it teach me something about how to nurture my daughter and how I can better handle moments like these? Absolutely. Should I grow from it? Absolutely. Should it linger? Absolutely not. My guilt taught me to channel her creative ambitions and spirit's desires within boundaries that make sense for living with others. So, I repaired. "Here are the times you can use the kitchen when it won't conflict with preparing dinner," I said. "Please ask first if you want to use something that might run out." And, "Here's how to handle cleaning up something you've never dealt with before. It's hard to clean up honey!"

My guilt also helped me remember that I'm not the potter, only God is. As Isaiah 64:8 (ESV) says, "But now, O LORD, you are our Father; / we are the clay, and you are our potter; / we are all the work of your hand." So I added, "By the way, I'm totally impressed by your creativity, resourceful nature, drive, and ambition. I would never have thought of something like this at your age. God has big plans for you." Guilt helped me integrate what I need into who she is and who God designed her to be.

The next time you notice yourself nursing feelings of guilt, pay attention to what goes through your mind at the time. Do your thoughts pull you closer or farther away from God's will for your life? Does your guilt provoke a change in direction, or is it just keeping you idle in shame? Remember, *any thought that results in feelings of worthlessness, helplessness, and hopelessness doesn't come from God; instead, try to empathize with your struggle.* There's usually a reason for every transgression, and making sense of why it happened might breed self-compassion and forgivenesss. Besides, most people respond better to encouragement than to criticism, and you're probably no different. Don't set yourself up for a fight-or-flight reaction by yelling internally. After all, has a screaming child ever respond better when you scream back at her? Neither self-condemnation nor complete avoidance will lead to finding God's peace in our hearts.

Forgive Yourself

Sometimes guilt lingers longer than it should. If we refuse to forgive ourselves for something we've struggled with—either intentionally or unintentionally—essentially we say that our transgressions require a bigger price than what Christ has *already* paid for us. Yet what does Scripture say? "He *was* wounded for our transgressions, / *He was* bruised for our iniquities; / The chastisement for our peace *was* upon Him, / And by His stripes we are healed" (Is. 53:5).

Additionally, if we labor under a heavy burden of guilt, God promises us a way out! "Come to Me, all *you* who labor and are heavy laden, and I will give you rest. Take My yoke upon you and learn from Me, for I am gentle and lowly in heart, and you will find rest for your souls. For My yoke *is* easy and My burden is light" (Matt. 11:28-30). We can also remember that God forgives and forgets: "I have blotted out, like a thick cloud, your transgressions, / And like a cloud, your sins. / Return to Me, for I have redeemed you. / Sing, O heavens, for the LORD has done *it!*" (Is. 44:22-23). And if God forgives and forgets, who are we to hold on? Remember, God can't give you the keys to renew your life if you won't let go of the prison of guilt you've created for yourself!

If guilty thoughts plague you, try this. Observe your thoughts as they move in and out of your mind, like clouds in the sky on a windy day. See them, but don't judge them. Just allow them to come in and go out without spending too much time on them. Recognize that just because a thought has entered your mind, it doesn't mean it has to stay there—nor does it mean it's true. That's worth repeating: *Just because you think it doesn't mean it's true.* Although we can't control whether a thought pops into our minds, we can control whether or not we feed it. If we choose not to give it attention, the thought will eventually leave us. *Remember, what we feed will thrive, and what we starve will die.* Take a deep breath; ask God to help you receive His grace and move on from your guilt, seeing yourself through His eyes.

And also remember, in your mistakes you're not alone. All throughout Scripture people made catastrophic mistakes but learned to accept God's forgiveness. Moses, for instance, had a terrible temper and often acted out of his anger. But there came a point in his life when he realized that God's call was more important than his shortcomings or his guilty past. And how about Peter? He denied Jesus three times, even after seeing Him walk on water, heal the sick, raise the dead, and perform countless other miracles. He even told Jesus that he would never deny Him—only to then deny Him in the midst of Christ's suffering (Luke 22:61). Later, Peter played a key role in founding the church (Matt. 16:18); God's forgiveness made him a new man. Or how about the Apostle Paul? He grew up persecuting Christians, even admitting, "For I am the least of all the apostles. In fact, I'm not even worthy to be called an apostle after the way I persecuted God's church" (1 Cor. 15:9 [NLT]). God not only forgave Paul, but He then sent him into the world to share with others the new life Christ offers to all who put their trust in Him. Paul would go on to become one of the most prolific contributors of the New Testament: he went from being a murderer to a great missionary.

Finally, keep in mind that Christ called the devil the accuser (Rev. 12:10-11), and the devil is constantly trying to imprison us in our minds. We can block his influence and suggestions by filling our minds with Christ-centered thoughts so that there's no room for wallowing in the past. When you catch yourself listening to an inner voice of condemnation and shame, we encourage you to recognize that those thoughts are *not* from God. Refuse to accept them and remember that, when we turn toward God, we are redeemed and renewed. Christ has swept away all our past mistakes and keeps no record of our sins. Our mistakes are not bigger than the price Christ has already paid for us all.

Forgive Others

Since Christ keeps no record of our sins, we should do the same for others! But we often hold on to grudges and refuse to forgive—which keeps us from experiencing God's renewal. We all know we *ought* to forgive and keep a calm, virtuous, and kind disposition, but we struggle because our emotions don't naturally lead us there when we feel hurt! And while anger can help teach us what we need to know about our own emotional landscape, when anger combines with other forces, it *can* misguide and derail us. So we can see the struggle to forgive as a collision of three forces: anger, tunnel vision, and judgment.

This collision system causes us to stop seeing the whole picture—and the whole person. So rather than seeing our anger for what it is, and trying to identify why we're so upset, we concentrate on the offender. This, in turn, causes us to lose our ability to see the person as someone who has both positive and negative traits; instead, we unconsciously assign the label of "all bad." Our judgment then provokes a negative cycle of hostility and blame that causes us to focus completely on the offense while no longer seeing the person. Here's an example of this cycle at work, from Dr. Roxanne:

A woman recently awoke after an incredibly telling dream where, while she was driving on a highway, the driver in front of her unexpectedly slammed on his brakes and came to an abrupt stop. She didn't have enough time to stop or even slow down. With her children in the car, her life flashed before her eyes and she thought, "This is the end." Yet, all of a sudden, she saw an out, made a sharp turn to her right, and veered off onto the shoulder onto a clear, wide path. Magically, it seemed, she was saved by a split-second decision. But as she continued talking, the dream began to make sense: Her marriage had recently caused her to feel sad and desperate, and she wished she could find a way out. She didn't know how to repair her marriage or where to go in her desperation.

External stressors had been suffocating their relationship for months, and she felt tired and didn't have many resources left to tolerate her husband's intensity, which was often negative and sharp. Her children, though stressful at times, she could handle: She expected their grumpiness, as they were still learning how to self-regulate. But having to manage her husband exhausted her—with his dark moods, short temper, and sharp tongue. She didn't know how to mend whatever was bothering him, plus she had enough on her plate without having to manage his stress, too.

Apparently, her husband had never managed his own needs well. "Stress just eats away at him," she said. He generally had good intentions, but poor self-awareness, and others typically managed his care—especially her. He also tended to push on full speed ahead, despite signals of extreme fatigue, and he couldn't see his short temper telling him to set better boundaries or take on less. He needed to take more responsibility for finding ways to relax and better care for himself emotionally and physically, but he didn't know how. His body needed rest; his mind needed peace. And as stress continued to mount in his life, sadness mounted in hers, and her thoughts filled with negativity and judgment. The climate in the household had become hostile.

When she shared her dream with me, I couldn't help thinking it sounded like a parallel to her life, so I asked her, "Could your marriage feel like this too, like it's about to derail in a way you fear you won't be able to come back from? Maybe you're searching for the off-ramp that will save it."

She admitted, that yes, something had to change; that the longer she stayed in this mode, the worse her soul felt. "I just can't keep going with my thoughts so consumed with negativity," she said. So I asked her, "What needs to change?" Recognizing that she couldn't change her husband, she said, "My peace. I know it's mine to keep, and I haven't been keeping it. Today, I choose to keep it."

"What do you need to do to keep your peace?" I asked. Without flinching, she said, "I need to forgive him." That decision began a process of forgiveness and healing. If she noticed negativity within herself, she replaced it with the words "stay positive." She remembered mercy. She tried to think back to her husband's innate goodness and do things that helped her maintain her joy. She did kind things for him. She began to let go of trying to manage something that wasn't in her hands, and in doing so, she learned to lean on God. She prayed for God to give her husband the peace that only His Spirit could provide, and she prayed for God to help her remain at her best, even if her husband wasn't. She controlled where she allowed her thoughts to take her, and she chose to stay present with her children and at work, allowing herself to experience joy in these other aspects of her life, rather than letting her thoughts rob her of moments that could provide renewal.

In the toughest moments, she would go for walks when the household felt stressful. "God, fill me with Your positivity, and bring my husband the peace only You can provide," she would pray on her walks. It was a choice, and she chose well. She sought forgiveness and simultaneously began seeking joy, and she let God do the rest.

Then, one day, out of nowhere, her husband came over to her, after not talking much for a week, and began rubbing her back. He asked her to take a walk and began crying as he explained all that was consuming him. It was the relief valve he had been needing to press but hadn't realized it. Sometimes our own behavior can block others from seeing themselves. But now, he had seen himself and began opening up, saying, "I know I've been short lately. I'm sorry." Suddenly she felt compassion again. The connection was back.

We hear all the time that healing is hard and forgiveness is a process, and while we agree that this is true, we must remember that forgiveness is *also* a choice, and the process doesn't actually begin until we make the choice to forgive. This is an active and intentional change that takes place in our hearts, minds, and souls that sits right with our salvation. Forgiveness is always the right choice.

How about you? Where do your thoughts go when someone wrongs you? Do you react angrily when you feel someone has treated you unjustly? Do you simmer in negativity or allow judgment to consume you? When these moments happen, we often feel righteous indignation. Our mind attaches itself to the wrong, and just like trying to bead a necklace with a knot in it, we get stuck. Our thoughts get stuck, our body gets stuck, our heart gets stuck, and we just don't want to let it go. But, have you ever truly asked yourself why? "Why am I holding on to this? Am I going to teach the other person a lesson? Will she better understand her wrong if I punish her through holding on to anger? Will he decide to be a better person?"

We'd often like to believe we can change others by withholding our forgiveness, but this never really works—and you've likely experienced that yourself! Ultimately, only God can bring about change in an offender. Our only mission is to seek God's renewal and live our lives filled with His grace, mercy, love, and compassion; and yes, this still remains our mission even when we are hurt. Forgiveness isn't an option, it's a command—as Luke 6:37 (ESV) puts it: "Judge not, and you will not be judged; condemn not, and you will not be condemned; forgive, and you will be forgiven." Colossians 3:12-13 (NIV) also has important words for us on this subject: "Therefore, as God's chosen people, holy and dearly loved, clothe yourselves with compassion, kindness, humility, gentleness and patience. Bear with each other and forgive one another if any of you has a grievance against someone. Forgive as the Lord forgave you."

Consider, too, how God has already forgiven us to a much larger degree than we will ever be called upon to forgive another person. As C.S. Lewis once put it, "To be a Christian means to forgive the inexcusable because God has forgiven the inexcusable in you."[7] If our job is so much easier, then it should be a cinch. Right? Unfortunately not! Our human flesh desires to hold on to grudges as hard as possible. Father Nick recently came across this illustration that demonstrates our unwillingness to forgive so vividly:

> I read the other day how certain cultures have an interesting way of capturing monkeys. They build a large wooden box with a small hole on the side, and in the middle of this box they put some peanuts. They then put the box in a tree. After a while, a monkey will approach the tempting food cautiously. Soon, though, his desire will overwhelm him, so he'll thrust his hand inside and grab the peanuts. The problem is that now, when he holds the peanuts, his fist is much bigger than the hole, and no matter how hard the monkey tries, he's unable to remove his hand *with* the

peanuts inside. Soon the hunters approach the monkey. With his keen hearing, the monkey hears them approaching and knows he's in danger, but he can't make himself let go of the prize. Even to the point of capture, he will still hold on to the peanuts.

Here are a few ways you might find yourself holding on to your own peanuts in life. First, maybe you are an *avoiding person*—someone who disconnects emotionally when he's hurt and decides, "That's fine, I'm just going to shut down and give her the silent treatment. I will stay in my own world, paying no attention to the person who hurt me." While this may feel like a good solution, all the while, you aren't truly moving on. You just continue simmering internally.

Then, there's the *passive-aggressive person*. If this is you, you want to lob bombs from a distance or talk about the person who hurt you in a negative way. Or you might want to just do whatever you can to undermine that person—all from a distance.

There's also the *accommodator*. Accommodators get the name because they do just that: They accommodate the offender—often for years—tolerating hurtful behavior because it just seems "easier." But is it? Pretending on the outside like everything is fine often has its downsides in the long run, because you may detach little by little without really noticing. But over time, your pain grows so large that one day you can no longer contain it, and you suddenly give up completely on the situation.

Or how about the *angry reactor*, who simply refuses all of the above! If this is you, you struggle with strong emotion, often finding yourself on a hostile battleground without a ceasefire. You may find it hard to contain yourself, instead screaming and yelling in response to hurt.

Which is best, you might ask? Well, none of them, really. With each of these dynamics, the person who has hurt you never really has to look in the mirror. The best-case scenario is the "offender" either gets what he wants and becomes increasingly more difficult to deal with over time, or he gets a rise out of you and gets to point his finger back at your behavior as the reason he hurt you to begin with! What's left, then? How can we operate best in a situation that might seem hopeless?

Like that monkey, we could evade capture if we would just let go, but instead we choose to hold on and thus become captured and controlled by our unforgiving spirit. Yet when we refuse to forgive, we don't destroy the other person, we destroy ourselves: It's not possible to feel at peace when we "hold on to our own peanuts." When we remain stuck in the past, we miss out on experiencing the peace that God has created for us in the present. We simply can't draw closer to Christ or grow in our faith if we remain chained to yesterday's hurts and disappointments.

Scripture says, "And then *many* will be offended, will betray one another, and will hate one another" (Matt. 24:10). So we know that since we live in this world, we will experience betrayal and we will also feel hatred toward other people at times. We will face people who offend us, and we will offend others in return. But if we want to experience God's renewal, we must deal with our unforgiving hearts. How do we do this? First, let's look at a few common myths we tend to believe about forgiveness that may hold up our motivation to forgive:

If I forgive, I let the offender off the hook. Since we can't change others, and we can't change the past, the effect of our forgiveness on the offender isn't our concern! Forgiveness isn't about the other person, and it doesn't mean the offense didn't hurt us or that it wasn't wrong. Yes, the offense was a big deal, but the only way to regain our own emotional health is to forgive and move on, because the one thing we do have control over is *how we move forward.* We need to do what it takes to move forward in such a way that the offense doesn't stop *our* life of purpose. Forgiving someone will not change your past, but it can create for you a whole new future—and forgiveness doesn't release another's soul; it releases yours. So leave the rest to God! As Romans 12:19 (GNT) says, "Never take revenge, my friends, but instead let God's anger do it. For the scripture says, 'I will take revenge, I will pay back, says the Lord.'"

If I forgive, I have to tolerate unhealthy behavior. When we forgive someone in our hearts, we have no obligation to let her back into our lives if she will continue to mistreat us. Forgiveness simply means we've let go of the bitterness that resides in our hearts—it doesn't mean we should compromise our self-respect in any way. In fact, we must put up boundaries when we encounter people who behave in unhealthy ways. The Bible tells us we shouldn't use willpower to maintain a relationship with someone who hurts us because, whether we like it or not, the people around us influence us. "Bad company corrupts good character," I Corinthians 15:33 (NIV) says, and God calls us to flee from people who seek to compromise us spiritually and to "test the spirits to see whether they are from God, because many false prophets have gone out into the world" (I John 4:1 [NIV]). God also calls us to flee from anyone who calls himself a believer but is sexually immoral, greedy, an idolater or slanderer, a drunkard or a swindler (I Cor. 5:11-13). He even cautions us to be wary of those who are hot-tempered and easily angered, or "you may learn their ways and get yourself ensnared" (Prov. 22:25 [NIV]).

We like to think of relationships as existing on a bookshelf. Those on your top shelf have proven their goodness to you: they labor in love and possess the fruit of the Spirit. Top-shelf relationships allow you to let your guard down in a way that doesn't result in compromised values. These people respect your boundaries, value the same things you do, and you can be completely yourself with them without fear of judgment. When you walk away from them, you have more joy or peace than you had before, and they seek the good rather than relish in offense. Safe relationships remind us of God's goodness and bring us closer to Him and His purpose for us because of the peaceful positivity they bring to our lives. They remind us not only of who we are, but also of all we could become. They are people who, even without our assertion of our values, will protect those things we hold dear, as they live according to the same values.

As relationships experience turmoil, you may find certain behaviors make you feel less safe emotionally; this indicates you should move them down a shelf. Second-shelf relationships are still helpful. Maybe you enjoy the way the person makes you laugh or find their opinions helpful in a work setting, but you can't trust them with your innermost heart and the vulnerability of your soul. They don't hold all of your same values. Third-shelf relationships include people you associate with but don't grow from. Then, bottom-shelf relationships are spirits we must maintain vigilance with, being careful to not compromise ourselves around them. In most situations, you won't need to remove people completely from your bookshelf, unless they possess characteristics God has warned us to flee from.

If I forgive, the other person has to forgive also. We shouldn't make our forgiveness contingent on another person's willingness to forgive. In general, we choose forgiveness because of our relationship with God, not because of our relationship with the offender or the offense. In order for us to offer forgiveness, we don't even need to speak to the person who offended us. It's enough to forgive the person in our heart, as we do with those who mistreat us—then move on! In any case, whether we forgive in person or only in our hearts, we have no control over the offender's response, as Romans 12:18 (NIV) reminds us: "As far as it depends on [us], live at peace with everyone." It's not our job to take ownership of someone else's repentance or to demand reconciliation. We can only control our *own* behavior—what depends on us—and forgiveness allows us to move more deeply into God's renewing love for us. Remember, regardless of whether people apologize or acknowledge their offense or not—God calls us to forgive them anyway. Forgiveness doesn't mean waiting on someone to say they're sorry, but rather praying as Christ did for the two criminals crucified with Him in Luke 23:34 (GNT): "Forgive them, Father! They don't know what they are doing." And much of the time, when we forgive, it helps to remember that others may not truly know what they have done to us. They may lack perspective or the skill set necessary to handle things better, or they may have experienced a less-than-ideal upbringing. Regardless, our prayer remains: "Help me to do my part in letting go."

If I try to forgive, I won't be able to. The enemy of our soul sometimes convinces us a particular offense is so great we can't possibly forgive the offender. But we can't forgive using our own power in any case, no matter how terrible the offense; however, we *can do all things through Christ* when He strengthens us (Phil. 4:13). The health of our soul depends on this. And remember, we know that forgiveness isn't impossible—but that doesn't mean we'll always find it easy. Forgiveness takes time, but the journey doesn't begin until we actually make the decision to forgive.

If I forgive, I'm getting the short end of the stick. Actually, our lack of forgiveness doesn't destroy the other person; it destroys us! We think that when we hold on to our anger and grudges we somehow punish the other person, yet we

CHAPTER 3: *Find Victory over Your Vices*

don't really punish her at all—we punish ourselves. Research has shown that forgiveness is linked to reduced anxiety and depression, restoration of positive thinking, improved self-esteem, greater capacity to cope with stress and find relief, as well as fewer physical health symptoms and lower mortality rates. Forgiveness also improves our emotional well-being because it decreases stress and negative rumination.[8] Additionally, Bob Enright, a psychologist at the University of Wisconsin who's at the forefront of studying forgiveness, believes that the toxic anger that comes from holding on to our hurts in deep and lasting ways makes us tense, anxious, and fatigued. He says that when we choose to forgive, we let go of toxic anger and therefore can improve our overall sense of well-being, even strengthening our immune system response again.[9]

Now that we've debunked these myths, here are some practical steps you can use to begin the difficult but necessary journey of forgiveness.

Pray for them. God calls us to pray for the people who have hurt us, as Christ says in Matthew 5:43-44 (NIV): "You have heard that it was said, 'Love your neighbor and hate your enemy.' But I tell you, love your enemies and pray for those who persecute you." The person may not ever respond to God, and her heart may never change, but yours will, because it's impossible to hate people when you're praying for them. Also, as you pray for her, remember to look at her offense through a lens of empathy: Attempt to reframe the offense in ways that neutralize your anger. This will increase your own ability to feel compassion and love and may even help you understand why the person did what she did. It doesn't mean what she did was right. It doesn't mean we agree with it. It just means we understand the "why." Recent research has even found that something as simple as saying a prayer for the person who offended you correlates with exhibiting less retaliatory behaviors like doing something to even the score.[10]

See the person underneath. As empathy shows us, more often than not, when people do things that hurt us, they don't strive to hurt us on purpose. They know not what they do! The offense usually happens because they don't know how to manage their *own* feelings in that moment, or in life in general—and plenty of people lack self-awareness about that. The truth is, *people who hurt you usually have a deeper story beyond that hurtful moment or their hurtful nature, and it doesn't typically involve you!*

To understand this idea better, let's dig into it a little more deeply. Scientists and faith leaders alike generally accept that we're all born with the innate ability to feel compassion and altruism toward others. Then why do we find it so hard to feel this *supposed* natural emotion when we're angry at someone? It's as if compassion gets turned off like a light switch the moment we feel offended or hurt. So if most of us find it this hard to react with compassion in heated moments, imagine how impossible it might be for someone who never developed the ability for compassion and benevolence in the first place! Researchers[11] and spiritual leaders[12] say this is why some people seem to be naturally aggressive or otherwise offensive. Allegedly, compassion development is really no different than language acquisition: we're all born with the ability to develop this skill, *if* we're in an environment that nurtures it. So, simply put, chances are high that hurting people were once hurt themselves.

Once we understand this, we can find it a bit easier to see the person underneath the behavior, which in turn helps our ability to forgive them. Compassion still isn't easy, though, so we have to call on every ounce of empathy we can find within ourselves to see life from the other's vantage point. It helps to remember, here, that choices must lead; feelings follow. Choose to unstick your mind by resisting the urge to stew: it only leads to tunnel vision. Rather, choose to "set your minds on things above, not on earthly things" (Col. 3:2 [NIV]). Try focusing your attention on other aspects of your day or your life, and concentrate on other positive relationships in order to renew your spirit. And also, keep choosing to depersonalize the offense, keeping in mind it's really not about you.

Pay attention to your own narrative. Because we follow a narrative in our mind that explains everything we experience, when someone acts in a hurtful manner toward us, that explanation begins almost instantly, and it plays a large role in determining our reactions. The narrative tells us whether we should take the offense personally and whether the offense was intentional. It assigns motives, and before we know it, we've decided what kind of person the offender must be because of what he did or said. Our narrative can even tell us that the other person doesn't deserve our compassion, which only validates our own righteous position and keeps us locked into a vicious cycle of unforgiveness.

As we journey through life, if we want to return back to the "goodness" that God intends for us, we need to learn to let our choices transcend our moment-to-moment reactions, putting compassion at the forefront of our interpretations. Our narrative is an essential part of the journey toward forgiveness. Try practicing compassion with the same kind of discipline you use to accomplish other challenging goals.

Bless them. The word *bless,* according to the *Oxford English Dictionary,* comes from the Greek word *eulogeo* and the Latin word *benedicere,* both of which mean "to speak well of, or to praise."[13] They are used in Scripture to translate the Hebrew word *brk,* which means "to kneel down," or "to bless." Generally, blessing someone means to praise, to celebrate with praise, and to cause to prosper. So if someone offends us or is set against us, as Christians, God calls us to speak well even of our enemies, as Jesus reminds us: "But I say to you who hear: Love your enemies, do good to those who hate you, bless those who curse you, and pray for those who spitefully use you" (Luke 6:27-28). And in the Book of Romans we also read, "Bless those who persecute you; bless and do not curse" (Rom. 12:14 [NIV]). So, God calls us to ultimately help anyone who offends us to prosper; at the very least, we should not harm them or wish them ill. Again, our choices must lead here, because our feelings will certainly not support our efforts in this direction. To act opposite to our feelings, we must fix our minds on God, trusting Him to lead us, rather than focusing on the problem and trusting our feelings to lead us. Father Nick has a great example of this in action from early in his career as a priest.

When I first graduated from seminary, I once led a youth group of several hundred kids in Boston, Massachusetts. I hadn't learned to delegate yet, and not only would I lead the lesson using different programs and illustrations, I would also set up the tables and make sure the food was ready for them. I was busy!

Every Wednesday night a young woman's mother would drop her off about thirty to forty-five minutes early. The young woman would park herself in the very last row, where she would fold her arms and cross her legs to signal her indifference. Clearly, she didn't want to be there. Most of the teens in our enthusiastic youth group loved our stories and activities. But not her! About halfway through my talks, she would start creating a little commotion in the back. This went on week after week until I'd had enough. One week, anticipating that she would come in about forty-five minutes early as usual, I prepared to confront her. It was time, I decided, for a "come to Jesus" talk, and I had my speech ready. "What's your deal? If you don't want to be here, then don't come," I planned to say.

Yet something happened as I started walking toward her. About five feet away from her, I heard the voice of the Holy Spirit say beseechingly, "No, don't do it!" So instead, I surprised myself by saying, "You know what I love about you?" As the words tumbled out of my mouth, I thought, "This isn't the right speech!" But I continued: "You are the most consistent person in our group." Her surprised expression spoke volumes. I added, "Not only are you here every week, but you're the first person here, and I want you to know that means a lot to me." I walked away, again saying to myself, "That wasn't the right speech!" Yet that night, she began to give her heart to Jesus.

Had I cursed her or reprimanded her, she might never have darkened the door of the church again. Instead, she and I have stayed connected, and more importantly, she's still faithful in her love for God. That's the power of choosing to act opposite to our feelings when they call us to condemn someone and instead allow God to use the moment for a blessing that they may truly need! The Book of Ephesians reminds us that every word that comes out of our mouths either builds someone up or tears her down (4:29), so we need to use our words intentionally. We can also remember what the Apostle Peter said: "Don't repay evil for evil. Don't retaliate with insults when people insult you. Instead, pay them back with a blessing. That is what God has called you to do, and he will grant you his blessing" (I Pet. 3:9 [NLT]). Blessing others is part of our powerful protection plan to keep ourselves from becoming bitter, hateful, and focused on ill will.

Don't repay them. Too often, when someone hurts us, we want to retaliate. Yet, that doesn't help the other person see the wrong he's done. Instead, when we choose to do the *right* thing, the offender is more likely to recognize his offense. We always say, don't get in the way of someone else's mirror! God may be working in his life through that very moment of hurt, and we only get in the way of that work if we repay evil for evil. The Bible confirms this when it says:

> Repay no one evil for evil. Have regard for good things in the sight of all men. If it is possible, as much as depends on you, live peaceably with [every-one]. Beloved, do not avenge yourselves, but *rather* give place to wrath; for it is written, "Vengeance *is* Mine, I will repay," says the Lord. Therefore "If your enemy is hungry, feed him; / If he is thirsty, give him a drink; / For in so doing you will heap coals of fire on his head." Do not be overcome by evil, but overcome evil with good. (Romans 12:17-21)

We must remember here that God tells us, "I will take care of it. You don't need to avenge: I will do that." Judgment belongs to God alone, and the *only* way for us to overcome evil *is* to do good.

Wipe the slate clean. If you've ever reconciled your bank statements, you know it's important to bring the balance to zero. It's no different with forgiveness, and we need to wipe the slate clean even when someone doesn't apologize. When we don't get an apology, we must remember that admitting wrong requires a certain level of humility and ego strength not everyone has developed. And for these people, apologizing proves challenging because it poses a threat to their entire self-worth, which they have delicately based on infallible expectations of themselves and probably others. So again, we must move on, because if we don't, we may put our peace and our lives on hold for an apology that may never occur.

How about if someone *does* admit fault? Wiping the slate clean means we embrace their attempt at repair by letting them know they owe us nothing. Sometimes when others do recognize their wrongdoing and apologize, we still struggle with accepting that apology, and we instead feel tempted to make them pay for their wrongdoing. Yet, letting go and moving on is an important step toward wiping the slate clean. Remembering what God has already done for us can help us accept apologies. If God can forgive us, how can we withhold our forgiveness from others? Consider this story of wiping the slate clean:

> On the night of July 28, 1984, a masked man entered Jennifer Thomson's house and assaulted her. The twenty-two-year-old college student had gone to bed early in her off-campus apartment, and as she slept,

a man shattered the light bulb near her back door, cut her phone line, and broke in. Through brave and clever distractions, Jennifer escaped him and fled to the police station, giving them an accurate description that their artist turned into a sketch composite. They swiftly identified the man as Ronald Cotton, an employee at a restaurant near the scene.

Although Ronald insisted on his innocence, the police arrested him, and he spent eleven years in prison. Eventually, however, in a stunning turn of events, another inmate in Ronald's prison admitted to the crime, and Ronald was released. Jennifer, now approaching middle age, heard about this and went to visit Ronald. "I started to cry immediately," she remembered later. "And I looked at him, and I said, 'Ron, if I spent every second of every minute of every hour for the rest of my life telling you how sorry I am, it wouldn't come close to how my heart feels. I'm so sorry.'

And Ronald just leaned down, he took my hands . . . and he looked at me, he said, 'I forgive you,'" Thompson recalled. "'Jennifer, I forgive you. I don't want you to look over your shoulder. I just want us to be happy and move on in life.'" Ronald Cotton had spent 4,015 days in prison for a crime he hadn't committed, and yet during those years he had learned how to be a free man.[14]

This story illustrates so perfectly how we can wipe the slate clean and free both the person who has wronged us and ourselves. So let's remember to "forgive and forget" as we journey through this life—no matter what the offense. We all have vices we struggle with, and forgiving both ourselves and others as we work to overcome them is necessary for experiencing God's renewal and working out our purpose in Him according to His will!

PRAYER

✠ ✠ ✠

OH HEAVENLY FATHER, as we seek to renew
ourselves in Your goodness, please inspire us to have
the humility to identify the vices that keep us locked
away from Your victory. Help us also to overcome
the guilt of our past mistakes, remembering that You
have paid them all in full and that You came into
this world to save us. We also remember that you
continually forgive us no matter what we do, so let
us then take on that same level of forgiveness in our
interactions with others, and although our emotions
will tell us otherwise, let us be led by our faith. Help
us to find the ability to forgive, as we know that love
embodies forgiveness, and You call us to love others

the way You have loved us. We know that without

You, none of this will be possible and that with You,

we can do all things.

So, heavenly Father, the Comforter,

the Spirit of Truth,

Who is everywhere filling all things,

Treasury of blessings and Giver of Life,

Come and dwell in us. Cleanse of from

every stain (vice),

And save our souls, Oh gracious Lord![15]

✠ ✠ ✠

FOR DISCUSSION:
THE THREE Rs——REST, REFLECT, AND RESPOND

1. What are your vices?

2. What signals have you noticed that clue you in to your vices?

3. What are the consequences of your vices?

4. What are your greatest reasons for wanting to overcome your vices?

5. What is something you struggle with feeling guilty about? Have you forgiven yourself?

6. What is one step you could take to let go of that guilt?

7. If you've held on to guilt, how has that impacted your life?

8. Is it harder for you to forgive yourself or to forgive others?

9. Who do you need to forgive?

10. What's one Scripture you can claim that will help you as you practice forgiveness toward others? What's one you can use as you work toward forgiving yourself?

CHAPTER FOUR

Turn Your Trials into Triumphs

So we do not lose heart. Though our outer self is wasting away, our inner self is being renewed day by day. For this light momentary affliction is preparing for us an eternal weight of glory beyond all comparison, as we look not to the things that are seen but to the things that are unseen. For the things that are seen are transient, but the things that are unseen are eternal. —2 CORINTHIANS 4:16-18 (ESV)

WHILE OUR VICES can keep us from fully experiencing God's renewing power, trials we encounter as we live and work out His purpose for us in the world can also threaten to do so. Since our vices come from within, they may seem easier to change and control. But trials come from outside of us, and we often have no control over them whatsoever! Still, we *can* use our trials to bring us closer to God and His purpose for us, because even though we can't control the trials we go through, we can control how we respond to them. If we respond to trials in unhealthy ways by withdrawing, sinking into despair, acting out in anger, allowing fear to lead us, or seeing them as signs that God doesn't care for us, we keep ourselves from experiencing the very renewal we need in order to move through those trials. Instead, we must work to *transform* ourselves through our experiences—seeing them as opportunities for growth and for learning how to depend on God. We must work to remain our best selves as we encounter trials, which means figuring out how to endure them without letting them define our lives. Only then can we stay strong in Christ and continue to pursue His purpose for us.

Accept That You Will Experience Times of Drought

The first key to coping with trials and not allowing them to rob us of God's renewing presence is to accept that everyone experiences hardship. Life is unpredictable, and we all face our own seasons of drought. And these seasons often come on very suddenly: One moment everything's fine and we don't have a worry in the world. And the next, life has thrown us a dramatic turn and we now feel the weight of the world on our shoulders. We plan our days and weeks, and we even plan the hours within the day, yet life can so quickly change our plans and what we see as important. Maybe the phone rings and it's a family friend calling to tell us she's getting divorced. Or maybe a severe storm destroys part of our house, or we suddenly receive news of a medical scare from a family member. Whatever the case, these kinds of crises can throw us for a loop and even make us feel that God is suddenly far away from us.

One of life's unpredictable moments happened to us in 2009. In April of that year, our second child, Gabriella, was born, joining her older brother George. What a joy she was! During this time, our church was growing, our families were healthy, and our marriage relationship was strong. The wind was at our backs: we enjoyed a season of plenty, feeling God's blessings rain down all around us!

But just five months later, our lives took a sudden turn. One morning, our phones began lighting up with streams of text messages. Father Nick's then nineteen-month-old nephew Andrew had contracted a possibly deadly virus and now had pneumonia on top of it; his condition was steadily getting worse, and his prognosis didn't look good. The doctors had suddenly given him only a 10 percent chance of pulling through. "We need you now," Father Nick's sister Stephanie said. In that moment, Father Nick felt a sinking feeling in his stomach. Just like that, dread had laced our season of plenty. That light and airy feeling that had encompassed our lives only moments before had now shifted to heaviness and worry. After spending five weeks in the hospital, including three weeks in the ICU and two weeks on a ventilator, the situation finally resolved, and Andrew is now a happy and healthy twelve-year-old boy. But it was such a reminder for us of how suddenly these times of drought and trial can come upon us. It can happen to all of us, because we exist in a fallen world, which means no one is immune to the experience of pain, sorrow, and suffering. When we learn to accept the inevitability of these seasons of drought, we can more readily move through them in a way that doesn't make us lose our footing.

An experience Father Nick had on a missionary and humanitarian trip to Turkana, Kenya, in the spring of 2014 so perfectly illustrates how these seasons of drought can come on—but also how they don't last.

After a long period of travel, our vehicle finally pulled up to the village we had come to visit, and I immediately saw the poverty. The people lived in mud huts, wore sparse clothing, and appeared emaciated and malnourished. We parked, and as we exited the vehicle, the children of the village ran up to our group yelling the word "*matta, matta.*" Our translator told us *matta* meant "water"; the children were begging for water to drink. To see these young children hungry and crying out for water was heartbreaking—and many of them appeared the same age as our own children.

A few seconds later, the chief tribesman, along with the entire tribe, walked up to us. His eyes looked weary and tired: they were eyes of despair and desperation. He shared with us that the village had not had rain for over a year and that his people had gone without food and water for several days. He said, "We have prayed to our ancestral gods for food and water, but they have not responded. They must be punishing us, and now my people are dying from hunger and thirst. If this Jesus Christ that you speak about is such a great and powerful God, then tell Him to let it rain tonight. If He can make it rain, then I, along with the entire village, will become followers of this Christ you speak about."

Although I trust in God and His goodness, I confess that in that moment my head filled with voices of doubt. Silently I questioned, "What if it's not God's will to bring rain today? What if these people don't get the water they need to survive?" After all, this entire desert area had not seen rain in more than a year. Despite my uncertainty, we gathered the tribe, held their hands, and prayed in a circle, "God, You are an awesome God. You are the all-powerful, all-knowing, and merciful God, and You have the ability to let it rain here today. If it's Your will, let it rain for these people." We continued to pray for a while, and then we simply waited and hoped, but nothing happened. The tribespeople were uneasy and losing hope. For them, the possibility that "our God" would bring them water faded quickly as darkness fell upon the village, bringing another night they would go without.

When I awoke at 6:30 the next morning, I'd never before felt so disappointed to see a brightly shining sun. My shred of hope was quickly fading. The morning felt especially hot—probably over a hundred degrees—and there wasn't a single cloud in the sky. I thought to myself, "How will these men, women, and children endure yet another day without water?"

Then, something extraordinary happened. Something we couldn't have orchestrated or imagined. Suddenly, dark clouds from every direction began to form right over the village. The dark blue clouds didn't match the landscape of harsh sun. A few moments later, lightning, and then the booming sound of thunder shook the earth. The people stared in amazement as the skies opened and it began to rain. And it didn't just sprinkle, or mist. No, the rain came down in buckets, as if we were standing under Niagara Falls. Before we knew it, a river of water flowed right next to the village. The tribesmen were so thirsty, they lay down on the ground and opened their mouths to let the precious, life-giving water flow in.

Then a moment I'll never forget happened. Afterward, they stood up and cheered, dancing, praising, and honoring their new God, Jesus Christ. That day, more than seventy people chose to begin their journey toward knowing Jesus Christ. The drought was over.

Refrain from Blame

While we find God in the rain, and we rejoice and praise Him when the rains finally return, is God to blame for our droughts? No. While our trials do often test our strength, perseverance, character, and sometimes even our faith, *they are not tests from God.* God doesn't inflict pain or sorrow on us, and one of the easiest ways to get derailed on the path toward renewing our lives in Christ is to blame Him for our trials. Rather, pain and sorrow result from the fallen world we live in and the imperfect ways we, as humans, approach our interdependent existence.

In short, every decision we make as fallible human beings has implications for our world and the lives of everyone in it. From war to job loss to abuse and neglect to the misuse of power to poverty and greed, the collective trickle-down effect of our free will affects everyone. God has designed us this way so that we learn to need each other and to count on one another! As such, He also spent a lot of time teaching us how to best care for each other, instructing us to "love [our] neighbor as [we] love [ourselves]" (Mark 12:31 [GNT]) and to "carry each other's burdens" (Gal. 6:2 [NIV]). But since humans sometimes make selfish and hurtful choices, many trials we experience indirectly come out of the choices other people make. Sometimes people set out to harm others, but other times our trials stem from a person who makes an oblivious choice rather than a purposefully hurtful choice—such as when someone chooses to drive while under the influence of alcohol and ends up striking another car.

In many ways, we count on other people to choose well when we decide to go out into the world, because in large part, our lives really do depend on the integrity of other people's choices. Every day we trust others when we drive to work, ride a bicycle, enter into relationships, put our trust in people we love and hope they don't hurt or betray us, start a new job and expect not to lose it—or even when we use certain products promoted as safe. Yet in this fallen world, we have no guarantee that the decisions others make won't affect our health, safety, or emotional and physical well-being.

We don't have to look far in order to find people making choices out of greed, selfish ambition, pride, and other temptations of the flesh that lead to intentional or unintentional devastation in another person's life. We even see entire industries (run by fallen people, of course!) making decisions that shortchange the welfare of individual lives. How many lawsuits happen because companies knowingly promote agendas and products that could compromise our physical health, but they choose to do so anyway for the profits they could yield? Only years later do we see the collateral damage of such misplaced priorities and decisions that end up resulting in disease and human suffering.

So, no, it's not God who causes our trials and afflictions; it's the collective damage of the forgotten virtues and fallible choices of humankind. Every day God asks us to go out into the world and love one another and to remember that our choices have implications not only for our lives, but for the lives of others.

Remember That Jesus Suffers with Us

Even when we manage not to blame God for our trials, we may still doubt God's renewing power or, worse, His very existence when we have to deal with extreme circumstances. It's not uncommon to find ourselves saying, in these moments, "God, You abandoned me. Where are You? Why have You let this happen to me?" When we think these things, it can help us to remember that Christ understands! Christ was fully God, yet fully human, and He suffered as we suffer: He understands what it feels like to do so. This means we're never alone in our suffering, so we can always call on Christ to help us. Father Nick recalls a time of suffering he experienced, which brought this point home to him in such a real way:

> For ten years, I worked as a youth director both in Boston and in Jacksonville, Florida. Within ministry, you develop bonds of friendship that you treasure for a lifetime, and one of these relationships I had was with a teenager named Elie. He was the type of person who lit up a room when he entered, he had so much joy and charisma. He also loved God and His church very much, and he was known for always being a voice of encouragement. I remember hearing how he counseled a young lady who was being bullied at school: he told her how God had fearfully and wonderfully created her in His image.
>
> Several months after I had become a pastor of my first church, my ministry was growing, people were coming to Christ, and life was good. That is, until I received a phone call that took the wind out of my sails. "Father Nick, brace yourself. I have some terrible news," my friend said. "Elie has tragically died." I stood in silence, frozen, unable to utter a word. I asked, "What? Are you sure?" She replied, "Father

Nick, I'm so sorry to give you this devastating news." I couldn't believe what she was saying! It felt like time had come to a standstill.

At the funeral several days later, I still felt confused and bewildered, and Elie's friends came to me with the most common question in a crisis. "Why?" they asked. "Why Elie? Why now? Why would God take him?" I felt no different. In my mind, I went through a litany of "why" questions, but what I kept coming back to was the example Christ's Crucifixion gives to us.

Although we often refer to the Crucifixion of Christ as "Good Friday," there was really nothing good about it for Christ. It was good for us, but not for Him! He had to endure mocking, people spitting in His face, whipping, nails, the crown of thorns, and ultimately death. But in His Crucifixion—His pain—He taught us how to deal with the darkness we must endure in this life, sharing how He, too, felt fearful, alone, abandoned, and rejected, when He cried out, "My God, My God, why have You forsaken Me?" (Matt. 27:46 [NIV]). Christ wanted us to know that even though He's the God who breathed the stars into their courses, He can still relate to us in all our struggles.

So God certainly understands our trials, and while Christ acknowledged shortly before His death that "here on earth you will have many trials and sorrows" (John 16:33 [NLT]), He also in the same verse reminds us that we can find peace in Him because not only does He understand what we go through, but He has already "overcome the world." So our trials are no greater than what He's already done for us through His Crucifixion and Resurrection, and we can also "take heart" that He has overcome the darkness of this world, and He ultimately promises us a better and more perfect life with Him someday in eternity. When we pray for a loved one who doesn't get better; when we pray for healing in a relationship, but it doesn't heal; or when life just keeps presenting us with droughts, we can take comfort in remembering His Resurrection. Because of this, we're not living for this kingdom but for the heavenly Kingdom.

Keep on Praying

While we remember that Christ suffered just as we do, another key to experiencing God's renewing presence as we move through trials is to *keep* on praying. And as we pray, we ask God to renew us, strengthen us, and remind us of His plan and purpose as we experience this season. It's easy to remain faithful during seasons of abundance—to be grateful, to trust in Him, and to believe in God's goodness—but when we encounter trials, it's hard to see the light of God's continuing presence through the darkness of our difficulties.

We experienced this several years ago when both of our fathers got sick around the same time. We'd taken our kids to Disney World on vacation when, halfway into our trip, a family member called to tell us that Father Nick's dad had just suffered a massive seizure and was unresponsive. She asked us to get to the hospital as soon as possible, and hearing the anxiety and urgency in her voice, we knew the situation was dire.

Upon arrival, the nurse brought us into a special waiting room where we joined other family members to wait for the doctor. Father Nick's mother was crying, and the other family members looked panicked. When the doctor arrived, he took one look at her and said in a cold and unsympathetic voice, "Ma'am, check your emotions at the door. Your husband has a very small chance of pulling through, and we need to make some decisions." Needless to say, this didn't make any of us feel better or help us think more clearly. Father Nick felt something welling up on the inside of his soul and rather indignantly said, "Sir, you might be the doctor on this earth, but we worship a heavenly doctor. Give us a moment to pray."

One week later, things got even worse. Dr. Roxanne's father, the picture of perfect health, was admitted to the hospital for a routine hernia repair. Shortly after, Dr. Roxanne's mother called her at work. Alarmed, yet composed, her mother explained that the doctors had inadvertently discovered cancer, and it was everywhere. "They suspect he has about four to six months to live," she said. Dr. Roxanne could scarcely process the news. "Feeling chills rush down my spine, the panic set in. I was tense and filled with anguish," Dr. Roxanne says. "I remember just wishing I could release the tension and angst in my body as I drove an hour and a half to get to them. I tried to breathe deeply and roll down the windows, but nothing helped. I just remember praying."

It was hard to believe how fast life could change, seemingly all at once. Healthy only days ago, our families now faced two very rare forms of cancer, both accidental discoveries. Our lives turned upside down, and we'd lost that feeling of ease we'd previously felt. The darkness felt smothering at times, swallowing up any light, as we kept uttering, "Lord Jesus Christ, Son of God, have mercy upon us." We found ourselves cycling in and out of trusting whether God really was with us and had a plan for it all, then being back in His comfort, then slowly feeling swallowed up again by our doubts, asking questions like, "What's happening?" "How is this even possible?" "Nothing about this makes sense." It felt impossible to keep going, and everything seemed to move in slow motion. We had to slow down, to settle into the grief and remove ourselves from the daily rhythms of our normal lives for a while. Yet, in intuitively moving away from the world, we can now see how much that opened up our souls and hearts to feeling God's presence, reminding us that yes, God is close to the brokenhearted and "saves those who are crushed in spirit" (Ps. 34:18 [NIV]). Even in our darkest hours, God is truly with us, and He sticks around, waiting patiently for us even as we fumble in our prayers and in our attempts to return to Him.

Have Patience

Even though God waits patiently for us as we struggle to find Him in our trials, we ourselves find patience so difficult, even in the most normal, everyday circumstances. Sometimes just waiting for a table at a restaurant or for an elevator to arrive seems to push our capacity for patience to the very limit—so trying to exercise patience in situations of high stress isn't easy. And it's in the waiting that the temptation to doubt God's presence in our lives becomes real. Examples from the Bible of people who remained faithful under trial without knowing how their story would end can help us learn how to remain faithfully patient. Joseph, for instance, waited years to experience his freedom after his brothers betrayed him (Gen. 50:20). David waited for many years and had to overcome numerous obstacles before being anointed king of Israel (Ps. 40:1), and Job waited for relief through more suffering than most of us can even imagine (James 5:11).

These biblical characters understood the principle that even though things may not seem to change fast enough for us on the outside, that doesn't mean God isn't at work on the inside, renewing us, healing us, and making us stronger. And as we read these stories, we see that God used the waiting to teach them and prepare them for good. They all developed character traits they would need to fulfill a greater plan. They learned to trust God, and they ultimately learned greater virtues like forgiveness, patience, reconciliation, and humility. They learned, as St. Paul said, to "rejoice in [their] sufferings, knowing that suffering produces endurance, and endurance produces character, and character produces hope, and hope does not put us to shame, because God's love has been poured into our hearts through the Holy Spirit who has been given to us" (Rom. 5:3-6 [ESV]).

So maybe the gift of patience is that we learn not to focus so much on what happens *to* us but on what happens *within* us, trusting that preparation occurs through it all. After all, we know from the Book of James that going through trials helps our faith develop and grow into its maturity (1:2-4). It also helps us to remember that God does not inflict our pain, but He finds a way to use it for our good: " 'For I know the plans I have for you,' declares the LORD, 'plans to prosper you and not to harm you, plans to give you hope and a future' " (Jer. 29:11 [NIV]).

Keep in mind, though, that having patience doesn't mean we just stand by and watch life happen. Of course, we should continue to do what we can to improve our circumstances, but only while also trusting God is at work within us and for us, working behind the scenes on a bigger plan. And although we can't see all the moving parts and how it all will fit together in the end, we can remember that "faith is confidence in what we hope for and assurance about what we do not see" (Heb. 11:1 [NIV]). Knowing that we can only see our circumstances from our vantage point, we must remember that God sees the whole picture. God sees the growth that's necessary for us to live our lives in the fullness of His will, and as we wait, He prepares us, strengthening us and pruning us in ways we don't yet know or understand. We can trust God as we wait because, as the prophet Isaiah says, " 'My thoughts are not your thoughts, / neither are your ways my ways,' / declares the LORD. / 'As the heavens are higher than the earth, / so are my ways higher than your ways / and my thoughts than your thoughts'" (Is. 55:8-9 [NIV]).

So, let's try to choose in these moments not to engage in the type of despair that prompts questions like, "Why me?" Let's ask, instead, "What now?" "What can I learn from this?" *Sometimes being patient in the waiting doesn't mean that God changes our situation; sometimes it means He changes us through our situation.* Maybe we learn how to have a deeper relationship with God or how to rely more on Him through the experience of our trials. Or perhaps in the waiting, God calls us to help invoke a change in someone else's life. Dr. Roxanne recently experienced at a conference how being patient in the waiting ended up benefitting another person:

> Upon arriving at the airport for a conference, a lovely woman picked me up, and after we made a few other stops to pick up others, we started toward the conference location. I certainly felt eager to arrive, get settled, and continue preparing for my talk, but first we decided to grab a quick cup of coffee. But then, as she turned into the parking lot, the steering wheel suddenly locked up. Thankfully, she exerted enough control to actually direct it into a parking space! As she went into the shop, I got out my phone and researched what could cause a steering wheel to lock up. Although it looked like we probably shouldn't keep driving the car, because we all felt anxious to get to the conference, we decided to chance it. After all, we weren't that far from our location.

Well, the steering continued to get worse and worse. All the while, I just hoped and prayed we would make it to the conference center so I could settle in. All of a sudden, we happened to pass by a mechanic on the right. "Let's pull in," I said.

We all piled out of the car, and while the mechanic worked to diagnose the problem, we waited. As we talked among ourselves, the mechanic asked us about the conference, and we shared with him a little about our faith. He then told us about a trial he was going through in his own life, and tears came to his eyes as he spoke. We all stopped and listened as he shared with vulnerability and transparency. Moments later, our new ride had arrived, but just as we were about to leave, he said, "This might sound like a strange question, but would you ladies mind saying a prayer over me?" So, we all gathered and prayed over him. Afterward, he looked up and said, "Thank you. I didn't realize how much I needed that." His last words as we exited left footprints on my heart: "I think you guys coming in here today was probably more for me than it was for you." One thing I realized in that moment was that sometimes, in our hurry to get to where we want to be, God diverts our paths, using our circumstances as opportunities to work through us and for us—not only for our own good but for the good of those He places along our path.

Another thing our own trials have taught us is that God's timing, the "right time," is not always "our time." Thinking back to the drought in Kenya, the chief tribesman and Father Nick wanted it to rain the night they prayed, but it didn't. When we first learned of what happened to our dads, we wanted things to resolve quickly, but they didn't. And yet God had a purpose for all of it: for allowing the waiting, the process, and the struggle. We learned that things don't always happen on our time frame *or* in the ways we expect; we also learned that with God's help, we *could* handle it. Father Nick has noticed this lesson, about how we *can* handle things, in action in our own backyard:

> I love working in the yard! I often write sermons while I'm out planting flowers, and I love reading about the different types of trees in the Bible and how God often uses them to teach us a lesson. Did you know that, according to some studies, the Bible references thirty-five different types of trees? In Psalm 92:12, God compares the way His people flourish to a palm tree. Why would He do this? Well, have you ever seen the news after a hurricane or tornado? Perhaps the only thing still standing after the storm is a palm tree: Every building could be decimated, but the palm tree stands strong. Even with winds howling at over one hundred miles an hour, the palm tree remains firm because of its root system. Every time wind bends them to the point where they look like they will snap, the root system, which isn't

that deep, begins to grab more soil, creating a stronger system. As the storms come through, the palm tree finds ways to get stronger. It gets stronger in the waiting! In much the same way, when the winds of life try to push us down, even though we may not know when the storm will end, we must continue to be patient, letting the roots of our faith ground us and strengthen us through it all.

So, what can we do to remain patient and steadfast on the journey? One thing is for certain: it helps to sometimes get out of our own heads, because we can lock ourselves into tunnel vision as we overthink our circumstances, playing through things over and over again even though we have no new information to process. We've found it helps us to avoid overthinking if remain active in our daily lives. We try to look for things to devote our energy to—things that bring healing and comfort to our spirits. When we attach ourselves to aspects of our lives that bring us meaning, it helps us more easily endure the wait. How can we remain productive in our waiting? Here's an illustration from Dr. Roxanne:

> At my father's last birthday, I remember asking him for a nugget of wisdom: something he'd learned through his life's journey. "Life is like a mountain," he said. "Never stop climbing until you reach the top." He said this during one of the most treacherous stages of his battle with cancer. Yet his message was clear: No matter how hard something feels, no matter what

comes your way, keep living, keep pursuing, and keep climbing. One of the ways he did this was to complete what would become his seventh and final book.

Looking back, I wonder, how did he keep climbing? He did it by continuing to use what God gave him to contribute meaningfully to the world: in his case, through writing and publishing. By attaching to something meaningful, he found a powerful source of encouragement that kept him patient on his own climb, that gave him the purpose, power, and conviction to push ahead amidst his own pain.

To help yourself keep going in your own climb, consider these questions: What keeps you pushing forward in your difficulties? What gives you meaning and a sense of purpose? What gifts has God given you to contribute to this world in a meaningful way? What drives you? What helps you more easily endure the wait during your own trials? Maybe it's something as simple as sitting down to write a card that encourages someone else in need or offering compassion to someone struggling with a similar situation. Whatever your gifts, remaining connected to your passions, purpose, and convictions even amidst your trials can be a powerful source of encouragement as you remain patient in the waiting.

Finally, having hope also helps us remain patient. Looking back at my own dad's journey, I (Father Nick) realize that hope helped him wait patiently, as Romans 12:12 (GNT) says: "Let your hope keep you joyful, and . . . patient in your troubles." My dad lived by those words every day, even on his worst days. No matter how trying his circumstances, when you asked him, "How are you doing today?" he would always say, "I'm okay; I'm better than most!" And then he would always follow it with, "God is with me. How can anything be against me?" He maintained this attitude throughout his entire battle with cancer, never complaining about his circumstances, no matter how difficult.

What about you? Do you feel hope and keep your joy when you go through trials? Though it's hard to be patient and have hope, remember that God is always there holding you in the palm of His hand, rooting you to the ground in the midst of the storm.

Seek God First

When a crisis comes barreling in on the shores of our hearts, the key to staying strong is to anchor our souls to Christ *first*, renewing ourselves in Him *before* we do anything else. Yet all too often, we spend hours thinking and fretting about how to resolve our situation before we ever talk to God. We fall into the trap of believing that we *alone* can solve our problems and that we *alone* have the power to calm our storms. We often don't turn to Him until we're on our knees after a great deal of heartache and frustration, when we find ourselves broken, alone, and afraid. Yet in reality, the way we *begin* something often dictates how it all turns out.

Jesus Himself modeled this notion of seeking God first in His own life, on the night before His Crucifixion. He knew

what He had to endure and that it would be His ultimate
trial. Yet, while in the Garden of Gethsemane, what did
He choose to do? He went to His heavenly Father and *He
prayed* (Matt. 26:36-46). He knew every detail of what He
was about to face: the humiliation, the shame, the betrayal,
the disgrace and rejection, the whipping and scourging—
and still, *He prayed first.* Now, it's interesting that the word
Gethsemane means "the place of crushing." It got the name
because the harvest of olives would be laid down upon a hard
surface there, and then a large stone would be rolled over
the olives to crush them.[1] So there Jesus was, in the place
of "crushing," knowing that in just a few short hours, He
would experience a physical "crushing" of His own body.
He even prayed so hard and felt so much agony that "His
sweat became like great drops of blood falling down to the
ground" (Luke 22:44). How does this happen? Though
this medical anomaly is relatively rare, under the pressure
of extreme conditions, the blood vessels that surround our
sweat glands can constrict and dilate to the point of rupture,
which allows blood to flow into the sweat glands.[2] Have any
of us sweated blood during our trials? Likely not—but Jesus
did, and the Bible says He "fell to the ground" and prayed
that He wouldn't have to suffer the pain ahead of Him. "*Abba,*
Father, . . . everything is possible for You. Take this cup from
me," He prayed. In terrible anguish, He longed for relief
from His suffering, but He still said, then, "Yet not what I
will, but what you will" (Mark 14:35-36 [NIV]). Here, we
see Jesus' humanity—His fears and worries—yet in the very
next sentence, He obediently entrusts Himself to the will of

God, submitting fully to God's ultimate plan for His life. Even in the midst of His own terrible pain, He showed us what it looks like to "seek first the kingdom of God and his righteousness" (Matt. 6:33 [ESV]).

What about you? Have you brought your trial to God? Or are you still trying to control it, manage it, and resolve it all on your own? One of the ways we can go to God *first* is through prayer and seeking stillness, as the Psalmist David says: "Hear my cry, O God; / Attend to my prayer. / From the end of the earth I will cry to You, / When my heart is overwhelmed; / Lead me to the rock that is higher than I" (Ps. 61:1-2). In effect, King David was saying, "God, I can't do this on my own. Bring me under the shelter of Your wings. Lead me to a place of stability and security, something strong enough to stand against the crashing waves that overwhelm me. Give me wisdom from above and give me strength beyond my own." When we approach God as our starting point to handling trials, we handle them better. And our prayers are less about coming to God and filling Him in on all the breaking news and more about taking a moment to remember that we're not alone: that we have someone who loves us, comforts us, and strengthens us. Someone we can hand it all over to, knowing He will give us what we need to withstand our trial.

Take note that many times throughout Scripture, when people approached Jesus for healing or help, He often first told them to "have faith." For example, in the Gospel of Matthew, a father asks Jesus to help his demon-possessed son, whom the disciples had been unable to help. Here,

Christ *first* deals with the faith of the father and the disciples, and only then does He heal the son. He says, "How unbelieving and wrong you people are! How long must I stay with you? . . . Bring the boy here to me!" (Matt. 17:17 [GNT]). Essentially, He rebukes His disciples not because of the size of their faith but for thinking they could do everything on their own, by their own understanding and power, forgetting that they need Him. Christ then heals the boy, and the disciples wonder why they weren't able to heal him. Jesus answers them, "Because of your unbelief" (Matt. 17:20). In the telling of this same story in Mark, Jesus says that "only prayer can drive this kind [of demon] out; . . . nothing else can" (9:29 [GNT]), pointing out once again, "I can do what you can't" and making a clear differentiation about the object of our faith. The disciples had put faith in themselves instead of in God. This reminds us to stop trying to do everything all on our own and instead remember to bring our worries to Him.

How else do we seek God first? By reading our Bibles. In Chapter 1 we mentioned the saying, "dusty Bibles lead to dark lives." When our Bibles just sit on a shelf collecting dust, we find it even harder to hear God's voice of comfort, His words of hope and assurances of strength. Without His Word, our soul wanders around aimlessly, alone and without direction, as if in a dark and unfamiliar land without a compass. Remember from the Psalms, God wants his Word to be for us "a lamp to [our] feet / and a light to [our] path" (119:105 [ESV]). God's Word anchors us to His promises, mercy, and love for us. "Do not fear, for I am with you,"

He says. "Do not be dismayed, for I am your God. / I will strengthen you and help you; / I will uphold you with My righteous right hand. . . . Do not fear; / I will help you" (Is. 41:10-13 [NIV]).

Reach Out to Others

Reaching out to God during trials is essential, but we also need to reach out to others around us, as Galatians 6:2 (NIV) commands: "Carry each other's burdens, and in this way you will fulfill the law of Christ." Our family and friends not only offer needed support during times of trouble by helping us carry our burdens, they also heap blessings upon us, further demonstrating that God's renewing power sticks with us even through hard times. While in the middle of the darkness of trials, we often have difficulty seeing the blessings that still come our way, but when we can acknowledge them, it will help us get through trials with our spirit intact.

We all need support at different times, in different ways. Even Jesus Himself needed support! On the road to His Crucifixion, when He was forced to carry His enormously heavy Cross, He'd been so beaten down and mistreated that He couldn't carry it the whole way. He ended up falling under its pressure and weight. A man named Simon came and helped Jesus lift up His Cross. From this example, when we feel the weight of the world on our shoulders, Jesus shows us we don't need to carry it alone. We encourage you to look for that support and to be open to it and accept it. In our experience of both giving and receiving support, we've found true joy in being able to bring comfort to those who need it. We once heard someone say, "When you refuse to accept the help of others, believing you are a burden or an inconvenience, you take away the gift they receive in giving it." And, isn't that so true? It feels good to give!

An experience we had when our children were young truly opened up our eyes to the blessings and support other people give us during times of trouble. We had scheduled a trip to Spain to celebrate our ten-year wedding anniversary. It was our first vacation alone together since having our two children, and we'd had our plans in place for over a year. We felt so happy to be getting away! But two days into our blissful trip, we received a phone call from home. During a bad lightning storm, a bolt of lightning had struck our home, hit a gas line, and caused a massive explosion. Our entire house had suffered major damage as it was enveloped by flames. We arrived home from vacation to an uninhabitable house in need of complete reconstruction. Our possessions and our place of peace were now destroyed. Our children, then three and five, struggled to understand why they couldn't go home and sleep in their beds or see their toys. We found shelter in a hotel, but we only had to remain there for a short time, as one of the many families who supported us arranged for us to live in their home for nearly a year as we rebuilt ours.

Their support was just the beginning, as God's light shined through from so many directions during this time. We had the blessing of our amazing church family, our own families, and wonderful friends. And it was interesting how each person played a uniquely different role in offering support. Some offered their hearts and good, listening ears. Others gave physical support by bringing meals or donating clothing and toys after the fire. And when our fathers were both ill, some traveled distances both near and far to physically be present with us and provide companionship when we felt isolated and alone during and after long hospital stays. Their support brought us the comfort, love, companionship, laughter, and joy we needed during very difficult and trying times. Dr. Roxanne still remembers one moment in the very beginning of her dad's battle with cancer when she reached out for such support. This time, she reached out to her husband:

> I remember picking up the phone because I felt scared, worried, and alone on my drive to Gainesville shortly after learning of my dad's sudden diagnosis. Father Nick said this: "Roxanne, God is with us. Whatever happens, we'll deal with it together. Let's just take one day at a time." Those words stuck, and to this day, I live them. I was so comforted by his words, yet I still wonder, were they really *his* words? Could God have given them to me, reminding me, through my husband, of what He needed me to know? I knew then that I wasn't alone. My husband would walk with me, and God would be with me through it all. It was just a few words—so simple, yet so powerful. Sometimes what we need the most is just so hard to find from within.

Surrender to God

When we allow God and others to help us during times of trouble, what we're really practicing with this is *surrender*. The word *surrender* means to "yield power" and "control" or to "give oneself over to something."[3] And in order for us to "give ourselves over" to anything, we must have trust. The Bible says, "Trust in the LORD with all your heart / and lean not on your own understanding; / in all your ways submit to Him, / and He will make your paths straight" (Prov. 3:5-6 [NIV]). You see, trust means having faith even when you don't know how things will work out. It means believing that God can help us solve our problems better than we can on our own. Father Nick shows us how trust works with this illustration:

> When Roxanne returns home from the grocery store, she loves to pick up all the bags at once to avoid going back and forth to the car. And trust me, we always have a lot of groceries, so this involves a lot of bags! I always know when she arrives, because I hear the bags of groceries hitting against the door as she tries to open it with her hands completely full. I always run to get the door for her, and in her predictable and routine way, she says, "Hey, honey, can you grab these?" As she hands them over to me and the blood returns again to her hands, I always think, "How in the world was she holding all of these at once? They're so heavy!" It makes me think of how we often carry

around in our hearts more weight than we can bear, with our many worries and stressors.

To experience how this feels, try something with me: Hold out your hands before you with your palms facing down. Now, close your hands in the form of tight fists, still facing down. Imagine placing all the things that worry you the most right now inside your fists. Keep squeezing your fists tight as you think about everything that weighs you down. Then, take a moment to really own your feelings with transparency and vulnerability, asking yourself questions like, "What's keeping me up at night?" "What have I been trying to resolve?" Once you know what stresses you're holding, then turn your fists right-side up. Next, slowly open your palms and imagine letting go of it all, allowing it to flow up to God as you hand it all over to Him. That is what surrendering looks like. It's releasing everything you can't control to the God who turned a Crucifixion into a Resurrection.

When we surrender our troubles to God, we acknowledge that He can do what we cannot—that He can help us in mind, body, and spirit, renewing us so that we feel lighter as we give up our burdens to Him. We need to remember that "God will supply every need of [ours] according to his riches in glory in Christ Jesus" (Phil. 4:19 [ESV]). Father Nick experienced this so vividly during that time when his young nephew was sick nearly onto death:

As my nephew, Andrew, battled the H1N1 virus, we sat in the waiting room all day long, just waiting for visiting hours to open. One night while we waited, a woman walked into the room holding a basket of snacks, and she offered one to each person in the room. She said she was from a local church and she wanted to provide some "nutrition for the soul," not just for the body—so inside each snack was a piece of paper folded up and glued to the wrapper. When I opened mine, it read, "Starve your fear, and feed your faith." This message struck my heart. It was, in fact, just what I needed to hear: it was the food for my soul I didn't even realize I needed. Yes, I could do my part to help my nephew, visiting, offering support and encouragement to the family, gathering as much data as I could to help the family speak with the doctors, but I also needed to remember not to let my fear drown me in the process and to know that ultimately, I couldn't control anything, no matter how hard I tried. I knew then that I needed to surrender my fears to God and trust in Him.

What about you? Are you trying to control a crisis that's out of your control? Do you spend morning, noon, and night dwelling on that trial? We suggest that if you hold on to a worry for more than fifteen minutes, that indicates you need to surrender it in prayer. Lift up your worry and turn it over to God because, you see, fear and faith can't both be in control at the same time; one will naturally take the lead.

Remember, God promises that "in all things [He] works for the good of those who love him, who have been called according to his purpose" (Rom. 8:28 [NIV]). And when we believe He's there with us in the midst of our crises, we find that He brings meaning to our circumstances, as 2 Corinthians says: "God is able to make all grace abound to you" (9:8 [ESV]).

Now, we know it isn't easy to let go of control. But when you worry or get anxious over your circumstances, do you really remain in control? The word *anxious* derives from the Latin root word *angere,* which means to feel tormented or strangled.[4] Perhaps that's why St. Paul tells us, "Do not be anxious about anything, but in every situation, by prayer and petition, with thanksgiving, present your requests to God. And the peace of God, which transcends all understanding, will guard your hearts and minds in Christ Jesus" (Phil. 4:6-7 [NIV]). Here, St. Paul confirms that trying to handle everything on our own can torment us, and the more we surrender, the more we'll experience God's promise of peace. Dr. Roxanne experienced this as she watched her dad die of cancer:

> Throughout my darkest days, I always felt God right there with me, holding my hand and answering my prayers. He kept letting me know in so many little ways. And as my dad neared the end of his journey on this earth, I found myself living in almost constant prayer as I realized just how little control I actually had in this life. Amidst my many prayers was always,

"God, please don't let him suffer." All I could hear in my own mind was the phrase "I can't handle that" and the word "intolerable."

I kept praying, confident that God would walk with me, knowing He had never left me, remembering all the times He had delivered us when we prayed. And in the end, in his final days, my father *did* suffer. And yet, I *did* what I thought I couldn't do: I walked through it with him, right by his side. And in the end, although I contended with helplessness, I acted with an unanticipated strength that could have only come from God. There I was, walking a path I never thought I could walk, providing comfort I didn't think I could stomach. In our darkest times, we remember that although life doesn't always turn out the way we hope, we're never alone, and God hears us, and He will give us the strength to do immeasurable things we never thought possible. He has equipped us for these very moments.

Now, as I look back, that whole time feels surreal. My dad is no longer here; his battle has ended. And I wonder, why *did* he suffer? But I also realize, it wasn't until he suffered that we all truly surrendered: that we began to accept what we had refused before. Until he suffered, we were never really ready to say goodbye. I now know that God stayed right there with us, holding our hands, keeping His promise that "when you pass through the waters, I will be with you; / and through the rivers, they shall not overwhelm you; / when you walk through fire you shall not be burned, / and the flame shall not consume you" (Is. 43:2 [ESV]).

Let's remember, also, Christ's ultimate example. As He was about to breathe his final breath, He said, "Father, into your hands I commit my Spirit" (Luke 23:46 [NIV]). So even Christ committed Himself, or surrendered, to God! And when we, too, surrender in the face of our own trials, we free up the longing of our souls to be held by God, in the warmth of His embrace. It's in Him that we find the comfort to endure our trials.

Acknowledge and Accept What Comes

Before we can surrender our trials to God and open ourselves to His renewing power, we must first *acknowledge* and *accept* what's happening to us. Sometimes we find it difficult to accept what life throws our way, and we'd prefer to avoid our reality rather than face our trial. But we can't work our way through a trial without acceptance—denial will only bury the problem, which certainly will work its way out of us at some point in unhealthy ways. Instead, we need to practice "radical acceptance." Psychology researcher Marsha Linehan coined this term while developing a treatment approach for people who struggled with managing intense emotions.[5] To practice radical acceptance, we must let reality permeate our present awareness so we can figure out how to live with it. Acceptance *does not* mean we agree with our circumstance, or that we like it, nor that we've given up trying to move forward. It simply means we acknowledge what's happened without adding judgment, which worsens it. This involves not looking at things as good or bad, okay or not okay—but rather, taking a stance of "it just is." Acceptance doesn't take away all the work we have to do or the painful emotions that *naturally* occur with any trial. But *through acceptance, we take the first step necessary toward moving forward and actually dealing with the problem.* Radical acceptance also helps us lessen the pain of our experience because we *stop judging* it and *start responding* to it.

When we refuse to accept our circumstances by fighting reality or judging it as "wrong," it only intensifies our pain and delays healing. This might happen when we refuse to talk about it or when we say things like, "This is horrible" or "I can't stand it." And yet, the reality of our problem remains. Suffering results from the pain of our trials *plus* the non-acceptance of our circumstances or the refusal to cope. Having feelings about our difficult circumstance is normal, but judging them, or ourselves, only leads to more complicated emotions and gives birth to secondary problems.

It's also essential in our trials that we learn to make room for our emotions, accepting them as they come. Whether we lose our home to a natural disaster, endure a divorce we don't want, have a medical scare that turns out to be real, or suffer the agony of our children choosing the wrong path, we cycle through many, many emotions in the middle of our trials as we struggle to accept life on terms that aren't ours. Grief and sorrow are very real and present emotions that surface once the shock of a trial subsides, and emotions like these don't vanish just because we banish them or try to will them away. They don't go away just because we proclaim, "I'm strong." Rather, they just continue to eat away at us in less obvious ways.

I (Dr. Roxanne) will never forget listening to one of my clients share her emotional experience during a trial she faced. As a strong woman in her mid-forties with a strong faith, she could command a room with simply her presence—and one thing that stood out to me was how positive she remained while doctors tried to diagnose her mysterious symptoms.

She came in for an appointment with me after several months of tests, only this time, she seemed somewhat different: she talked without her usual upbeat and animated style. "It's cancer, and it's not good," she said to me. She explained that the doctors recommended aggressive treatment, since the cancer had already spread to so many places. Still, she displayed her usual tenacity: "I'm going to fight this," she said.

As she went through the treatments, she tried to keep it all together. She stayed upbeat with family, coworkers, and friends at church and kept trusting in the Lord. Yet, one day she said to me, "You know, I know I'm supposed to be strong. I get it. I'm supposed to think positively, to trust and have faith, but

I really don't know how to do that when, truthfully, I don't feel any of those things. I just feel afraid. I end up pretending all day long to everyone, and when I come home, I break down into tears when I'm finally alone."

Many of us manage our trials in this same manner, by living two lives: one where we pretend everything is fine and the other where our heart screams out in pain and agony. Perhaps part of the reason we do this is because people who love us say well-intentioned yet ultimately unhelpful things to us during our trials like, "Be strong," "Have faith," or "Stay positive." Does this happen because they believe we shouldn't feel weak, sad, or afraid? Or does our discomfort make them feel uncomfortable? Sometimes when someone says, "It's all going to be okay" or "Just stay strong," they really mean, "I'm having a hard time witnessing your pain, sadness, and affliction because I can't take it away." The world also pressures us with messages that say, "*Move on* from negative emotions," and it tries to provide us with quick fixes. Yet, telling someone to "stay strong" is like telling a panicking person to "relax" or "calm down." One thing we know for sure: If she could, she probably would!

We all *want* assurances. We all *want* to feel positive, but sometimes the situations that life brings just don't allow us to feel that way. Trials overtake our peace, tranquility, and sense of normalcy. *Nothing* about life feels normal during a trial, yet life keeps moving. And all the while, people expect us to participate in the usual social graces, such as congratulating our friends and coworkers in their seasons of abundance, while at the same time we notice that constant pit in the bottom of our stomach. Our light heart and authentic joy feel like distant memories of a past we can no longer reach. Agony, fear, and disbelief now cycle through us and accompany us everywhere we go. We endure life as if we're walking alongside the edge of a cliff, holding our breath, just looking for a place that feels safe. It helps us to remember that these reactions to our trials are normal!

God gave us emotions for a reason: so that our feelings could help us better understand where life demands our attention most and what we might need in order to cope with it. And we can't avoid our feelings; we have to deal with them at some point. While it does take time to sort out what we feel, the goal is to not be *alarmed* by them but *informed* by them. Ultimately, feelings teach us something about the situations we face. Just as embarrassment informs us that we've acted outside the realm of how we'd like to see ourselves, worry and fear mean we perceive a threat toward something or someone we love. Sadness signals that we've lost something we value. When we make room for our emotions, we begin to understand what's wrong and what we might need to make it right. Our feelings may remind us that we need a hug, a listening ear, a word of encouragement, or a prayer from someone who can put words to what we struggle to say. We can't prevent feelings from coming on, but we can control what we do with them once they arrive.

As we work toward accepting our feelings, it also helps us to consider what types of things human beings tend to feel during a trial, which include, among others, loss, grief, and sorrow. Confusion can accompany sadness as we wonder, "Is this real?" Waves of shock, numbness, and disbelief can quickly shift into anger, fear, anxiety, and even despair. We sometimes even experience a general feeling of intensity throughout our bodies that we can't identify with a particular feeling or explain with words. People also commonly experience anxiety about other areas of their lives that the trial did not even directly affect. All of this is normal! As you cycle through your emotions during a trial, try to identify them and let yourself feel them fully—and try not to get caught up in expectations about how you believe you *should* feel or the way you *should* react. The truth is, everyone reacts differently to loss. There's also no "normal" time period for someone to adjust to loss, and though our feelings typically diminish in intensity over time, dealing with them is an important part of the process.

Accepting your feelings means acknowledging that they sometimes come up in ways and at times you don't expect. It might happen while you're sitting at work in front of your computer or while you're making dinner for your family. It might happen when you're watching a Netflix show and something reminds you of your trial, or it might happen while you're singing a hymn at church. The feelings may even get triggered by something that seems completely unrelated to your trial, and they tend to come in waves and often unexpectedly, hitting at random times. However, we can also intentionally open ourselves to them for a period of time. Setting aside an allotted amount of time to fully feel our feelings can help the process along.

No matter what your feelings or when they arrive—whether at planned or unplanned times—remember the principle of "radical acceptance" and don't judge them as good or bad, right or wrong. People often tell us they feel guilty if they laugh at something or if they have moments of joy during a trial, but it's normal to get distracted by enjoyable moments in life. The part of you that's beginning to move forward may experience moments of joy or temporary laughter, and yet the very next moment you may find yourself again weeping with despair. But whatever your feelings, allow them! And don't complicate your experience by judging yourself with self-talk like, "I shouldn't" or "I should" or with questions like, "Why do I feel so sad?" "Why don't I feel sadder?" "Why am I angry?" or "Why am I still upset?"

Let's remember, too, that letting our grief out is actually healthy! Tears provide us with release and relief. God placed this relief valve within us to allow the intensity inside us to flow out. Even our Lord wept over the death of His friend Lazarus (John 11:35), and Scripture tells us that Jesus was "despised and rejected by men, / a man of sorrows and acquainted with grief" (Is. 53:3 [ESV]). Since He has experienced everything you will ever experience, Jesus can be your best friend in times of shock and sorrow. Throughout the Bible, God even encourages His people to look to Him in their grief. King David wrote about this when he said, "From the ends of the earth, / I cry to you for help / when my heart is overwhelmed. / Lead me to the towering rock of safety" (Ps. 61:2 [NLT]). King David wrote most of the Psalms, the Bible's hymnbook, and in many of them he reaches out to God and worships Him in the midst of his sorrow—and when he does so, God heals him.

On the other hand, sometimes our sorrow can overwhelm us to an unhealthy degree. When sorrow turns into longer-lasting suffering, it can rob us of a life that makes sense. If your life starts to feel dark and hopeless and you begin to question whether you'll ever move past the weight of your sorrow, or if you feel totally alone and start to isolate yourself, these could indicate that your grief is becoming unhealthy. Isolating leaves us more alone with our dark feelings because we then have nothing to distract us and nothing to contradict our reasoning; we only have hopelessness as we validate our own suffering. If sorrow runs rogue and begins to dominate our lives, it can rob us of the life God intended us to live, and if left unchecked, it can stand between us and our purpose and can keep us from Christ's renewing presence. King Solomon reminds us that there's "a time to weep and a time to laugh, / a time to mourn and a time to dance" (Ecc. 3:4 [NIV]), so if you feel unrelenting sorrow that doesn't ease with time—if you can't seem to get back to the time of dancing and laughing—that means it's time to reach out and ask for help. In this way, our feelings can give us clues about how our soul is truly responding to whatever upheaval we face, and they can remind us that we need to seek God's healing presence that will surround us in our brokenness.

On the other hand, many of us only feel comfortable with the laughing and dancing, and we'd rather avoid dealing with the flip side of these emotions. We may worry that if we let strong emotions in, they might never go away—but we need to remember that no emotion lasts forever. Feelings always pass, and they do so more quickly when we give them a voice. If we let our emotions run their course, like waves in the ocean they will rush in, rise to hit their peak intensity, and then begin to fall with diminished intensity. We all return to our baseline at some point, once our emotions run their course. But if we move through life attempting to avoid our strong emotions, we might not deal with them in ways that help us heal.

But Guard Your Thoughts

As we've seen, trials have a way of threatening to break us, filling us with so much worry, sadness, agony, and fear we can't think about anything else. We go to bed and wake up in the morning thinking about our worries, tossing and turning all night. During the day, even in moments of distraction, our minds can revert our attention back to our circumstances, reminding us of the problems we face. And there's no greater win for the devil than when he steals, kills, and destroys God's purpose for our lives by afflicting our minds during our trials. It's the perfect chance for him to swoop in because we're most susceptible to his misguided direction during these times, as our unhealthy thoughts cause us to question ourselves: "I could have done more in caring for my loved one." "Why didn't I see the signs that this was going to happen?" "Why didn't I make her go to the doctor?" "What if I had been home?" "What if I'd gotten that report in sooner? Maybe I'd still have my job."

"What-ifs" are completely unproductive and can hijack our true need to sit with the feelings that accompany unanticipated changes in our lives. They distract us, prolong our healing, and complicate it with unnecessary self-condemnation and added grief. We do this also with the "why" questions. "Why didn't I spend more time with them?" "Why didn't I tell them what I wanted to tell them?" "Why wasn't I more . . .?" "Why didn't I do more?" "Why didn't I see this coming?" "Was it something I did that I'm now paying for?" In truth, we don't always understand the "why." As Christians, we sometimes think bad things shouldn't happen to good people, but the only thing God promised us was that He would always be with us. So when you find yourself getting caught up in the "why," remember there's often no satisfying answer to that question. And getting stuck there will do nothing more than keep you stuck.

What do we do, then? Well, as St. Peter tells us, we must "be alert and of sober mind. Your enemy the devil prowls around like a roaring lion looking for someone to devour" (I Pet. 5:8 [NIV]). This scripture stresses how important it is to watch over our thoughts. The battlefield of spiritual warfare exists in the mind, where the devil uses our reasoning and the arguments we make to ourselves about our situation as a platform to launch his attacks, and he tells us lies that subtly corrode our spirit with messages like, "Things are only going to get worse." "You should have done more." "You should have seen this coming." "What's the point of maintaining hope?" "God isn't listening; you're in this alone." We also must strive to avoid the kind of absolute thinking the devil pushes us toward: "I can't live with this." "I will never find joy again." "My life is over as I know it." We must strive to discern which voices we allow to lead us, especially when we feel weak. Dr. Roxanne says:

> I remember so many worry-filled moments over the last several years while our fathers battled cancer. One day in particular sticks out in my mind. I stood in my father's hospital room praying for answers— for good news—and felt so overwhelmed and afraid. As usual, I monitored all his lab numbers and read and researched everything I could to make sure the doctors didn't miss anything pertinent to his care. I remember I felt so overwhelmed because so many things were going wrong. "God, please give us hope," I prayed.
>
> At that very moment, a knock on the door interrupted my prayer. We didn't expect anyone, so I cautiously opened the door to an African-American woman who looked to be in her late fifties or early sixties. She said, "Excuse me, ma'am, I know you don't know me, and I don't know you, so forgive my intrusion, but my sister is being discharged from the hospital today after a medical scare. We feel God granted us a miracle today. And I have no idea why you all are here, but as I was passing your room, I just felt God telling me that you're in desperate need of prayers. Can I give you this little book of prayers for

healing that I used when I prayed for her? Maybe it will help you."

She spoke with conviction and comfort, as though she was an old friend who knew exactly what I'd been thinking, and I felt like she had wrapped a warm blanket around my soul. After making that statement, she left before I could even say anything back to her. In that moment, I felt God swoop in to remind me that in my worries, He hears me, and that I didn't have to fight this battle alone. The Greek word for Holy Spirit is *paraclete*, which literally means "advocate" or "helper" and one who comes "alongside" us.[6] What a perfect description of what we need most in our trials, and a reminder that God will send His Holy Spirit to walk alongside us in our toughest moments. "I know the Lord is always with me," Psalm 16:8 (NLT) says. "I will not be shaken, for he is right beside me."

Fight Your Fears with Faith

Life is full of scary situations like the one Dr. Roxanne experienced with her father, and if we let our minds operate in isolation as the only system interpreting our situations, not only do we make room for the devil to slip in, but we also allow our trials to immobilize us. Certainly, we will experience fear, but we need to temper our fear with faith. *You see, renewing our minds as we walk through trials doesn't require an absence of fear, it requires the presence of God.*

Fear isolated from faith breeds four responses:

- Fight: We become aggressive and angry toward ourselves, our situation, and other people we see as threatening.
- Flight: We look for a way out. We try to avoid the threat or remove ourselves from feeling it or dealing with it altogether.
- Freeze: We become immobilized by our situation and can't respond. We essentially shut down.
- Fright: We become consumed by the fear in our minds, obsessing over the same unproductive thoughts and worries. We might get stuck in the ruminating cycle of "what if" or "why me": "Why is this happening to me?" "I won't be able to handle it." "I can't stand it."

In any of these circumstances, fear can easily debilitate us, leaving us in a state of internal unrest. And because fear and anger are really just two sides of the same coin, in our darkest times, fear can provoke us to anger, mobilizing our fight response. Consider the normally docile husband who suddenly yells at the nurses on a hospital floor when he requests pain medication for his wife (who's been screaming in pain), and they tell him, "You'll have to wait. We have other patients." His heightened reaction of anger and impatience actually masks fear. He's afraid! The threat he wants to confront and heal is his wife's pain, discomfort, and agony. I can certainly remember how quickly my (Dr. Roxanne's) fear

shifted into anger one day when an ambulance rushed my
dad to the emergency room.

My mom and I followed along in our own car and
waited in the waiting room for what felt like an
eternity. Every ten minutes, we'd check in with the
receptionist, asking, "Are we able to go back to his
room yet?" At one point, I could literally feel the
fear building within me as I thought of all the possible threats: How little my dad understood about
his own medical situation, how he wouldn't be able
to answer all the nurse's questions, how afraid he
must feel, and how much he relied on us to comfort
him during times when he felt most afraid. Charged
by my thoughts, I walked up to the security guard
after about forty minutes and said, "I really need to
get back there to help my dad. The doctors won't
have a clear picture of everything that's going on if
I don't."

The security guard, probably just doing his job,
stated, "You can't go back there yet without permission; it's policy rules. I'm sorry, but you'll have to sit
down and just be patient."

"Be patient?" Hadn't I already been patient? "But
sir, please! My dad won't know the first thing about
what to report about his condition, and he's hard
of hearing." Unaffected by my pleas, the guard just

continued to repeat the same phrase as if I had offered no new information.

Now pushed into a corner, my fear had transformed to anger, prompting me to fight back with a level of intensity I wouldn't normally have. Suddenly, I was no longer talking—it was my fight response. I said, "May I please see your badge?" I took a picture of it and let him know that if he didn't let me through, not only would his superior hear from me, but I would hold him personally responsible if anything happened to my dad as a result of his negligence. The receptionist finally had compassion on me, likely because she was watching me unravel right before her very eyes, and called out, "Let her through!" My heart dropped as I darted in, rushing to his room. I broke out in a cold sweat, and my usual low blood pressure and slow heart rate skyrocketed. It took time to compose myself again as I searched for him while trying to slow my breathing.

When I got there, my dad's eyes lit up as if seeing me for the first time in months. "What took you so long?" he said. "I've been asking for you and your mother. I don't know how to answer everything they're asking me."

"Yep," I thought, just what I feared. Albeit justified in that moment, my anger *had* led me, and probably in isolation of trust in God and effective reasoning. Thinking back, I know now that God was with me as the receptionist took pity on me, opening the doors to let me through.

The anger we feel during trials can prompt us to attack, blame, judge, or otherwise become intolerant of others. We may also get angry at ourselves, blaming ourselves for our circumstances, thinking, "I could have done more to prevent this." We can even find ourselves mad at God, asking, "Why, God, are you allowing this to happen?" But in these scenarios, we aren't feeling true anger. No, we're responding to fear, to a threat we're facing that we don't know how to move through. And our fear and anger are really only reminders that we value life, health, prosperity, and happiness—and trials threaten all of these things. When we cultivate this kind of anger, it can lead us to withdraw from the greater world and from loved ones and others whom God may place along our path to offer us the support we need. So if we don't understand our anger, catch it, and deal with it, our trials can easily leave us alone, afraid, and in anguish.

Others of us in the midst of a trial don't find ourselves fighting or angry—no, we simply want a way out. We try to escape it, engaging in thoughts that deny our experience, like, "This isn't happening." Or we minimize it: "It's not really that big of a deal." "I'm fine." Or we shame ourselves: "It's my fault I'm in this mess." These thoughts all have one thing in common: they invalidate what we feel. But we can't run from the hurt or discomfort that trials bring. We can't wish our feelings away. These thoughts just indicate that our minds want escape routes because the threat feels like more than we can handle. The trouble is, fleeing doesn't work; rather, it makes an already difficult or painful situation worse by prolonging it through denial, invalidation, or adding judgment. Getting comfortable with feelings long enough to understand what they mean isn't always easy, but judging them or wishing them away will never make things better.

Although fight and flight are both instinctive responses that God has equipped us with to help us survive certain threatening situations, unfortunately, these impulses, just like the freeze response, can easily get activated in all the wrong situations. Then, rather than protecting us, they hurt us. For instance, freezing can help when our lives are in danger, because it gives us a moment to assess our situation so that we can decide whether to flee or fight. Think of someone holding you at gunpoint, or an animal that has pinned you down; in these moments, freezing may be an adaptive response. But, when we face our own trials, the freeze response can be less adaptive. Rather than helping us evaluate our next steps, it often simply paralyzes us and lingers longer than necessary. We begin restricting our breathing, and we feel helpless because our situation overwhelms our capacities so that we can neither flee nor fight. Fortunately, we can fight the freeze response. When you feel paralyzed by a fearful situation, try taking a few deep breaths. Especially when we exhale slowly, we can stimulate the vagus nerve, which regulates our rest response, putting the parasympathetic nervous system back in charge to slow our heart rate and decrease our blood pressure. This will allow us to unfreeze and move forward in the process of dealing with our circumstance.

Lastly, many of us face trials in a state of debilitating fright, thinking of all the things that could go wrong and having thoughts like, "I won't be able to endure this" and "I'm afraid of my own fear taking over." Worry can overwhelm us to an unhealthy degree, immobilizing God's purpose in our life. This is why St. Paul says in Philippians 4:6-7 (NIV), "Do not be anxious about anything, but in every situation, by prayer and petition, with thanksgiving, present your requests to God. And the peace of God, which transcends all understanding, will guard your hearts and minds in Christ Jesus." When worry overwhelms us, it can take hold of our attitudes, our energy, and our thought life, stepping in like bad company on a long and tiresome journey. Worry adds pressure to an already overwhelming situation, invading our minds and telling us things like, "Things are only going to get worse" and "You know you won't be able to handle it." It's important to remember that worry often overestimates possible terror or difficulty while simultaneously underestimating our ability to handle it. Ultimately, worry distances us from comfort and hope and makes us forget the times when God *has* come through for us.

Some say, "Well, worry makes me better prepared for what might happen, so I'm not surprised when it does" or "It gives me more control." But does it, really? Research from the National Science Foundation has found that up to 70-80 percent of our thoughts are actually negative, and 95 percent are repetitive.[7] Why? Because as humans, over time we learned to pay more attention to negative experiences than positive ones as sort of a protective mechanism to keep us safe from all the very real threats that exist in the world. What we need to realize now, though, is that we ultimately feel exactly what we think because our thoughts give birth to our emotions. So when we worry, we feed the fear that threatens to overwhelm us.

We find it interesting that the Greek word for worry is *mérimna*, which literally means to "divide" or "separate"[8]—an apt description of how we unravel when we dwell on unhelpful thoughts. And doesn't worry feel like it does exactly that? Tear us apart? And it destroys our energy for greater things, leaving us paralyzed by fear and separated from God's renewing presence and healing comfort. So why do we still listen to all of its negative and repetitive chatter? In addition to having a more sensitive radar for negative thoughts, we also have a tendency to see and hear only what confirms our beliefs. That's right—once we believe something, we're more likely to seek out information to confirm that belief while simultaneously disregarding other information to the contrary. This well-studied phenomenon is known as "confirmation bias."[9] Human beings don't like inconsistencies in what they believe. This works well when it comes to following our values but not so well when it comes to worry and fear. Further, because our beliefs, thoughts, and feelings intertwine with one another, many of our feelings—like worry—are not very susceptible to reason. So, if we worry about coping with our divorce or a recent job loss, we might find ourselves suddenly attaching to all the stories of people struggling in similar situations while selectively not tuning in to stories of people who found new rhythms and a new normal.

We also remember the story of the Israelites who feared the approaching Egyptians, and how Moses told them to stand and watch the victory God would accomplish: "Moses said to the people, 'Do not be afraid. Stand still, and see the salvation of the LORD, which He will accomplish for you today. For the Egyptians whom you see today, you shall see again no more forever. The LORD will fight for you, and you shall hold your peace'" (Ex. 14:13-14). When we've done our best, this story reminds us to let God do the rest. And God specifically commands us numerous times in the Bible to "not be afraid." In fact, "Do not be afraid" is the most common command in the Bible, appearing over seventy times in the New International Version—and that doesn't even include variations like "fear not" or "do not fear." With these, God reminds us that we don't fight our battles alone, since what usually follows is His promise that He will never leave us, that He will deliver us and help us with His peace and His renewing strength. As Isaiah 41:10 (NIV) says, "Do not fear, for I am with you; / do not be dismayed, for I am your God. / I will strengthen you and help you; / I will uphold you with My righteous right hand."

Differentiate between Productive versus Unproductive Worry

Yet sometimes, even when we know God is with us and we remember His deliverance, we still worry about the circumstances we face. And here's an important note: Not all worry is unhealthy. Some worry is productive, because it prompts us to address what's actually within our control. But we'll need to discern the difference between productive worry and unproductive worry.

How do we know if a worry is productive or not? If a worry leads to a productive next step that can improve our situation, this indicates it's probably a *productive worry.* Productive worry motivates us toward action. It gets us moving in the right direction toward doing what *is* within our control, rather than what *isn't*—for example, seeing a doctor when we feel sick, wearing a seat belt to avoid injury, studying for an important exam, or taking precautions when we see a wild animal.

On the other hand, *unproductive worry* has no foreseeable solution. Sometimes we've done everything we can in a situation, and yet we still keep replaying the same outcomes in our head. This moment signifies a crucial crossroads. Remember, the devil often likes to play in our thought life, and he will continually sow seeds of doubt if he believes it will destroy our ability to live toward something greater. He will play on our seesaw of unproductive worry, the swings of anxiety, and the slides of negativity. Let's not give the devil a foothold in our thoughts by allowing unproductive worry in!

As we consider our relationship with worry, we must keep in mind that our attitude during trials plays a major role in how we experience them. And although a situation itself may not be in our control, *we can choose how we respond to it.* If we can't change a situation, then we must change our attitude toward it because *our interpretations, our reasoning, and our story can either help us thrive or just barely survive.* Dr. Roxanne remembers this playing out one day as she drove home with our children:

> During another hard day amidst the battle against cancer with both my father and father-in-law, I felt overcome with worry, though I didn't say much about it. I must have been a bit quieter than my normal, chatty self, not realizing this showed some level of worry or stress. But children live in our subconscious, in the things we don't share aloud; truly, we can hide little from children! Suddenly, my son said, "Look, Mom, over there—it's a rainbow. It's so light, isn't it? Do you see it?" I looked, but I couldn't see it. He kept insisting it was there. "Mom, look again."
>
> "But I'm driving, George. Not now," I said. Then, all of a sudden, I saw it—so faint I barely spotted it, but I saw it. I said, "I do see it, George." And he said, "Mom, that's God. Just like it's *hard* to see that rainbow, God knows it's hard for us to see Him sometimes. But that doesn't mean He's not with us." From the mouths of children, sometimes we hear such profound truths.
>
> Surprisingly, at the same time a song came on the radio that repeated this chorus: "He is with us, He is with us / always, always." I just smiled and thanked God for that moment, for reminding me yet again of His presence. For letting me know once again that I don't need to "worry about tomorrow, for tomorrow

will bring its own worries. Today's trouble is enough for today" (Matt. 6:34 [NLT]). How true that is in any trial we face: take one day at a time.

When we worry, we must remember that how we worry will affect our bodies in a powerful way. Remember the vagus nerve we discussed earlier? This very large cranial nerve originates in the brain and carries sensory information between the brain and the rest of the body about the state of our organs. Therefore, it controls our bodily responses in relation to what we experience. So, when the body is not under stress, the vagus nerve sends signals to slow the heart and breathing rates and increase digestion. But in times of stress, we get the opposite effect. Interestingly, because the vagus nerve connects the mind and the body, the signals can go both ways. So, messages from our conscious mind can travel through the vagus nerve and let our organs know whether it's safe to rest or whether to prepare for a threat. That means that the way we worry and what we tell ourselves in our conscious mind (our self-talk) become very important if we don't want our bodies to exist in a state of alarm. The key to self-talk in any scary situation is to not be unrealistically optimistic—we simply won't believe it! We must speak to ourselves in plausible, convincing ways and with a level of confidence that allows our brain to signal the body that it's okay. Here are some examples of helpful self-talk:

- This feeling will pass.
- I won't allow worries to keep me stuck in my head. I will try to stay present.

- I will deal only with today.
- I will allow people to love me in my toughest moments.
- I know God is with me.
- Things will ultimately get easier than how I feel right now.
- I will be stronger in some way because of all this.
- God will give me the strength I need to handle whatever comes my way.
- I know God will use this to mold me, shape me, and strengthen me. His plans are for my good.
- God loves me. He hears me. He is with me. I am never without Him.
- "I can do all things through Christ who strengthens me" (Phil. 4:13).
- The God who is within me is greater than anything that comes against me.
- This is uncomfortable, but I can handle it.
- I will feed my faith and starve my fear.
- If I put this in God's control, it's never out of control.
- Just breathe.
- Sadness doesn't have to turn into suffering.

Care for Your Body

Our nervous system reacts so efficiently to threats in our environment that it spurs us to take action even before our brain can fully process whether our reaction is reasonable. This threat response, as we spoke about previously, is biologically necessary for us to survive danger that could hurt us, because it allows our attention to narrow and gives us short bursts of energy that prompt our desire to take immediate defensive action. This system helps us dodge a car in oncoming traffic, avoiding an accident even before our minds have fully finished processing the incident. So, in the face of threat, our brains are wired to take action without too much time for thought.

However, as we experience prolonged stress—the type that often accompanies our trials—our threat response causes changes in our body that don't work well for the moment. When our muscles tense up, our heart rate and blood pressure rise, and our breathing becomes faster, shorter, and more shallow. These things should propel us to action. However, if these responses happen when our body is in a resting state, we instead feel anxiety, discomfort, and restless agitation. Sometimes we can even feel panicky without understanding why. These reactions can surface any time, even when we simply think about our situation or must confront something associated with it. Because these bodily reactions feel so uncomfortable, many of us begin to fear our own body's threat response.

Additionally, because our bodies have primed us for action, sleep becomes difficult. Yet, we need sleep so much that, in otherwise healthy people, chronic sleep deprivation alone can result in signs of clinical depression that reverse when sleep returns. Our appetite changes too, as prolonged stress affects our digestive system, causing stomachaches, indigestion, and nausea. Stress also makes our muscles tense up, which over time can cause pain and tightness, prompting tension-related headaches, jaw pain, and teeth grinding, as well as knots and spasms in our neck and back. We also tend to lose our energy and motivation to care for ourselves. With all this internal angst and intensity happening within us, it's easy to understand why many of us can become unreasonable, easily agitated, and anxious during times of trial.

In any trying situation, our physical bodies can react just as strongly as our minds and emotions, sabotaging our efforts at coping well *if* we don't intentionally care for them. And unfortunately, when under stress, our bodies simply don't send us the usual regulatory cues to eat, sleep, and rest, as our nervous system works in overdrive. Without these regulatory functions, we set ourselves up for prolonged feelings of angst, so we need to remember that it's not *what* we face but *how* we face it that can make or break the direction our lives ultimately take.

When we make efforts to maintain our body's physical well-being, it shows its appreciation by helping us better regulate our emotions. It also decreases tension, stress, and anxiety. It helps our brain solve problems during our trials rather than react to them, and we feel calmer, more in control, and more capable. It clears up our foggy thinking and improves our attention and focus. It even improves our immune response to keep us healthier. But even though we know we should care for our bodies, many of us find ourselves hardly eating or eating too much, forgetting to hydrate, and unable to sleep or sleeping too much during difficult times. Then, as a result of feeling "off," we may complain of having little motivation to go out and do anything, resigning ourselves to the couch because we "just don't feel like" doing anything else. So in order for our bodies to help us amidst our trials, our choices must lead, and our feelings follow. We can't rely on "feeling like it" in order to do the things our bodies require.

Though caring for our bodies involves many things, we suggest two behaviors that are fundamental to our survival in a trial: physical exercise and the reset breath. These two behaviors provide a foundation for putting the right parts of our brain back in charge to help us deal more effectively with whatever trials we face. They also help mobilize our inner angst and restlessness and release them from the body, which gets rid of the residue left over from our amygdala's response to stress. When we exercise and reset our breathing, we put our prefrontal cortex (the rational brain) back in control, giving it the power to switch off our heightened emotions and bring us back to a more calm and centered state. Our prefrontal cortex keeps things under control when we feel out of control, so it's essential that we give it what it needs to regain the control it seeks. Then we can return to the feeling of, "Okay, I can handle this."

Studies on the benefits of physical exercise show that exercise improves our mood, our energy, our outlook on life, and our general mental health.[10] When we exercise, we feel the benefits both physically and psychologically. Not only does exercise allow us to breathe more deeply, release feel-good brain chemistry, bring down our blood pressure, and calm our heart rate, it also helps us clear our mind, open our hearts to renewed hope, and lift our spirits. Physical exercise can be anything from taking a walk to going for a run to working out with weights, whether outside, in your home, or at the gym. Even cleaning your house or dancing around the kitchen with your child counts! The idea is simply to move. How, when, and where you move is up to you. If you've never exercised before, we encourage you to consult your doctor and try to start small—perhaps just going for a short walk after dinner each night. If you used to exercise but simply haven't prioritized it in a while, know that it's absolutely essential in helping you cope. Schedule it like you would any other essential appointment! In time, you'll begin to reap the benefits of a renewed sense of peace.

When the fire struck our home, we had to relocate for a year, and in our new community, we had access to a gym. At first we didn't use it much, but over time, as the stress mounted, we began taking turns going to the gym. The instantaneous relief it brought made keeping up with it easy! It became a necessary part of the day for both of us, and we began protecting that time in the morning, planning for it and helping each other out in order to make it happen. The more often we got moving, the better we felt. We would walk into the gym tired, burdened, and stressed and walk out energized, more positive, and more accepting of what we had to deal with that day.

We both also use the reset breath practice often throughout the day, especially during times of increased stress. To engage the reset breath, you'll want to take a few seconds to practice this skill at several different points throughout the day. This is very different from trying to sit and breathe deeply for a prolonged period of time, which can sometimes make people hyperventilate. No, the reset breath is just one large breath that resets your physical body and your soul. Try it now! Sit back comfortably in your chair and take one deep breath from deep down in your abdomen. Breathe in slowly for three counts, then hold your breath for one count, then exhale nice and slow for four counts. On the exhale, let your shoulders fall, unclench your jaw, and allow your facial muscles to relax. Pay particular attention to anywhere you tend to hold tension, and let your entire body release it on the exhale. Do this once, or at most twice, then allow your breathing to return to normal. This exercise is often enough to undo the shallow breathing that perpetuates anxiety and stress, and it can help reset our physical bodies.

Generally, we encourage you to stay active, setting small goals every day for basic self-care. (See the "Tend to Yourself" chapter for lots of good ideas!) And when you do anything with self-care in mind, keep it simple but engage your full attention. When you walk outside, for instance, observe nature, listen to the birds, and notice the way the sun feels on your skin. This brings your awareness to the present moment so that you can't keep cycling in and out of frenzied thoughts that are negative and repetitive. Make sure to consider, also, basic self-care that your stress might have caused you to neglect, and make a plan for it that's simple to follow through on, like, "Today I'm going to brush my teeth and shower before I do anything else." Many times, in the midst of a trial, we don't feel like taking care of ourselves in even the most basic ways. Just keep remembering that choices lead, feelings follow.

Find the Meaning in Your Suffering

Trials tend to put us on a spiritual roller coaster: We know God is good, but how can we reconcile our situation with that goodness? We know He sees and hears us and promises that His plans are for our good, but we also struggle to make sense of our circumstances in light of His promises. The gap between *our* pain and *His* goodness breeds the question: "Why do bad things happen to good people?" In our experience, the trials we've gone through have provided us with many benefits in the long run—even when we couldn't see the possibility of that in the short term. They deepened our faith and our compassion, and they shaped so many aspects of our character in ways nothing else could have done. Also, the gratitude we feel for "normal days," for health, and for the gift of human life has certainly increased. And the virtues of patience, fortitude, humility, trust, and service to others result from our most trying times. Even our ministry together was, in many ways, born out of our years of struggle.

What we now see that we couldn't always see during our trials: It was God who gave us the strength to handle days we thought we couldn't handle. It was He who brought us the blessing of hope and renewal every time we grew weary. It was His glory that was revealed to us when we prayed and He answered our prayers in so many ways along the journey. It was He who surrounded us with His light through the love and support of others when we had literally nothing left inside to keep us going. It was He who really *did* use it all for our good. It was He who was with us through it all.

The blessings: When our house caught fire, we feel blessed we weren't there when it happened. The police report said that when the lightning struck, an explosion occurred right in the kitchen, around dinner time. If we'd we been home, we might not be alive today. And miraculously, the material items in our home we *could* replace were lost, and the ones that we *couldn't* were somehow spared.

Shortly after the fire, our son experienced trouble with his breathing. A series of tests discovered his little body chose this way to react to the drastic life change, something that, at such a young age, he couldn't put into words or figure out how to express. His reaction, along with the loss the fire brought, prompted us to slow down—another blessing! We let go of trying to fix everything at once and began concentrating instead on what mattered most: each other.

As for Father Nick's dad, he went to be with the Lord some two-and-a-half years after his initial diagnosis. The question remained, "Why would God save him earlier and then take him a short while later?" Yet, the doctors look back now and say they never expected him to pull through the first seizure, much less have the years that he did. We also realize now that his life-threatening seizure, which felt so scary in the beginning, was actually the blessing that allowed the doctors to find the cancer lurking beneath, giving us the opportunity to treat it and have more time with him.

We can also see his testimony now. Throughout his sickness, he talked openly about his faith with nurses, medical aids, doctors, and hospital staff. They all learned about Christ through him, and he always gave God the glory for how blessed he felt to still be in the fight. So, did God grant him more time so we could be with him longer? Or did God save him so that he could use that time to share his story of triumph and bring the gospel to others? It's hard to say.

One thing I (Father Nick) do know for sure, I've grown so much in this journey. I've grown as a pastor, a father, a husband, and, most of all, in my relationship with Christ. And now, when I minister to others, I can relate to their struggles from a very real place. My empathy comes from a deeper and much more personal level, now that I've experienced firsthand the pain, suffering, and ultimate death of someone I loved and respected so much. Prior to my suffering, even though I wanted to help others by offering kind words and prayers, the truth is, I didn't have the scope of experience I needed to truly connect to their struggles. We received such tremendous love and support through all our trials that truly became foundational to our ability to keep pushing on. And now, we can offer that fullness of love, support, and compassion to others as we hear so many stories similar to ours. Accident? No, we don't think so. Each chapter in our lives always seems to prepare us for another. We have connected to friends new and old who need *our* support during their struggles—support we can better give now because of our own season of drought. And we were even able to write this book because of our experiences with our own trials. What we have now come to understand is that because of our trials, there is more beauty, love, and authentic compassion that envelops our world today. Through our trials, our ability to feel compassion has grown a bit closer to its potential; in short, we're all only as good as the scope of our own experiences.

Our trials also helped me (Father Nick) discover more deeply how Scripture sustains and renews us in our trying moments. I learned more and more to not be afraid and discouraged, because God promises "He will never leave [us] nor forsake [us]" (Deut. 31:8 [NIV]). I also learned how to rely more on God's promise of eternal life. I find comfort especially in coming back to verses like this one in 2 Timothy 4:18 (NIV), "The Lord will rescue me from every evil attack and will bring me safely to his heavenly kingdom." So, my father went to be with the Lord, and yes, I miss him. Yes, I would love to talk to him once more. And yes, I would love to hold his hand one more time. But I know that because of what God did for us, we haven't lost him forever.

How does the story end for my (Dr. Roxanne's) father? Well, although he went to be with the Lord some three years into his battle, I can look back and remember that even though doctor after doctor told us there was "no real, meaningful treatment" available for his condition because it was "too rare for standard treatment, and his disease was much too far along," through God's grace we found meaningful treatment anyway. In fact, we found a surgeon renowned for these types of surgeries who felt confident he could offer treatment. He gave us so much hope and positivity and lifted my father's spirits! We believe God led us to him, as he wasn't local and didn't work at a world-renowned cancer center; rather, a couple conversations with the right people just happened to lead us to the right person.

It was a destination surgery, but it extended my dad's life by years. Looking back, we also realize the gift of his hernia repair, which helped the doctors find the cancer to begin with, granting us time with him we never would have had. Doctors said if they hadn't found the cancer and performed the surgery, he would have only lived a few months at best. Each extra day was a blessing.

I can now see God's hand in all of it. At the beginning of my dad's diagnosis, his publishers had just commissioned him to write his seventh book, a project he felt humbled by and excited about because of the type of contribution it would offer his field. I remember him feeling so torn as he looked up at the surgeon and asked, "What should I tell the publisher? Will I have enough time?" Looking sympathetically back at my father, the doctor said, "Only God knows that answer. But if you want to write it, then you should tell them you'll do it." Knowing how important this book was for my dad, we all wanted to see him write it. We all prayed, "God, please grant him the time he needs to complete this book, if it's Your will. It means so much to him." We continued to pray this very same prayer throughout his battle. And in the end, against all prognostic indications, my father lived just long enough to complete his book and see it published. He passed away only days after signing original copies for his most beloved colleagues. I can see God's presence from beginning to end.

Finally, remember our sick nephew? He pulled through his sickness and is now a vibrant little boy, full of love. Doctors still call him a medical mystery. To this day, he talks about

Jesus all the time and is a walking example of sharing the light of Christ with anyone he meets.

In any crisis, there can be both danger and opportunity, so when we face a crisis, we can choose to look at it either through a lens of destruction or a lens of opportunity and growth. It's our choice. And although we had many moments during our own difficult times when we wondered, "Why is this happening?" we also never felt closer to God than in our four years of affliction. We once heard it said, "You will never know that God is all you need until He is all you have." And this says it best. God yearns for us to be closer to Him, to rely on Him, and to realize that apart from Him, we can do nothing (John 15:5). And sometimes, it's our very pain and affliction that allows us to do just that. We surrender our control, draw nearer to Him, and put our trust in Him because we realize how much He loves us and how little control we actually have in this life. We give all our attempts at control over to Him and rest, finally, in His love for us as we "trust in the LORD with all [our] heart and lean not on [our] own understanding" (Prov. 3:5 [NIV]).

PRAYER

✠ ✠ ✠

OH HEAVENLY FATHER, I take this moment during my day to tell You how much I love You and thank You. I thank You for all You've done and continue to do for me. Everything I am and hope to be is because of the wealth of Your grace. Lord, as I journey in my life, I know that no matter how much faith I have, it won't keep me from experiencing droughts. Today, I have these struggles on my mind (list the trials in your life). I ask You, Lord, to guide me through this season of drought. Help me to remember the times You delivered me from trials in the past. Give me the understanding to keep the right perspective on my problems, and remind me that You always have me in the palm of Your hand. Give me the wisdom to accept Your will and to accept that Your ways are not my ways, and Your thoughts are not my thoughts. Help me to always know that even though I live *in* this world, I am not *of* this world. I'm not living for this world but for the world to come because You have "overcome the world" (John 16:33 [NIV]). Help me to turn my trials into triumphs, this test into a testimony of Your goodness. In Your mighty name I pray, Amen.

FOR DISCUSSION:
THE THREE Rs——REST, REFLECT, AND RESPOND

1. Do you toss and turn at night, thinking about your trials? If so, what plagues you? How do you explain your situation to yourself?

2. Do you spend a large portion of the day thinking about your concerns? Where does your mind take you? Are your worries productive or unproductive?

3. Would it help to empty your worries on paper or to a trusted friend? When was the last time you did that? (See the "Tend to Yourself" chapter for complete details about the "brain-dump" exercise.)

4. In what ways do you currently take care of your mental, spiritual, and physical health?

5. How do you anchor your physical body and health during a trial? Do you stay active?

6. How do you anchor your mind during a trial? What helps you keep moving forward?

7. What do you feel right now about the circumstance you're facing? Have you accepted your feelings? Or do you feel your pain has turned to suffering?

8. Name one thing you can do to help yourself as you journey through your trial: read your Bible, start a devotion, exercise, reset your breathing, get your thoughts and feelings on paper, accept social support, take time to eat right, etc.

9. Have you surrendered your trial? What might you need to do in order to truly surrender?

10. Have you accepted the circumstance you face? If not, what might non-acceptance be costing you? Joy? Purpose? Peace? Energy? Relationships?

11. How are you staying connected to God during your trial?

12. What could you do to be more patient while you wait for things to get better?

13. Have you ever experienced a time in your life when you lost hope? What helped you regain your hopeful perspective?

14. Make a list of all the difficult times you've faced in your life. Looking back, how did these seasons of drought turn out? Can you see blessings now that you couldn't see then?

15. What Scripture from this chapter do you need to hold on to the most?

16. What three tips for taking care of yourself could you commit to doing out of the following list?

- Reach out to supportive people who give you life.
- Listen to music that calms your body and soul.
- Get out of the house for a walk.
- Get help making the small decisions that stress you out.
- Engage in regular exercise, even when you don't want to.
- Get enough sleep.
- Address things that weigh heavily on you.
- Decide what you need to do to make a negative situation more bearable: In other words, make a plan of action.
- Challenge some of your behaviors that worsen your situation, like crawling into bed to sleep the day away, avoiding friends, or deciding not to exercise.
- Take time for a reset breath.
- Take time to pray.
- Decide not to overschedule yourself—just because it *can* fit into your day doesn't mean it *should*.

- Simplify your life: Let go of what doesn't have to get done.
- Ask for help! And allow the support that comes.
- Recharge daily as needed.

CHAPTER FIVE

Tend to Yourself

Better to have one handful with quietness / than two handfuls with hard work / and chasing the wind. —ECCLESIASTES 4:6 (NLT)

I N CHAPTERS 2 through 4, you've seen how taking steps to challenge your thinking, manage your vices, and more easily endure your trials can all equip your soul for growth and spiritual progression. In this chapter, we take a look into caring for another part of ourselves, something so essential that without it, we risk sabotaging our efforts at renewal in every other realm. When we learn how to tend to ourselves, we protect the very things that restore us most, and we develop a foundation for our flesh that better protects our soul's renewal. Yet, all too often we hear that taking time for *self-care* is often confused with being *self-ish*. But tending to our own needs only makes us *more* well-equipped to be vessels of light and to support those around us. And truthfully, self-care will yield whatever return on our investment we seek. When we take the time to care for our physical bodies, with the intention of protecting the very vessel that houses our souls, we yield a return that helps us more readily bring

God's light into the world around us. After all, if we don't renew ourselves, we simply won't have the spiritual, mental, emotional, or physical energy to go out into the world and share His renewing power with others.

When our daughter was just six years old, she made the most amazing observation about this concept. "Mom," she said, "when I feel tired, all the 'good stuff' just goes away. It's like I can't remember all the ways I know I'm supposed to behave. And I want to, but I just can't." From the mouths of children, God often sends us such honest truths! We all experience how it takes a little more effort to do the right thing when we feel tired, hungry, or are otherwise running on fumes—and when our body distracts us like this, it's so much harder to stay open to God's renewing presence in our lives. Self-awareness is the key to noticing our body and learning to listen to it. If we pay attention to our body and really hear the messages it gives us, we can better act on what it needs *before* the "good stuff" goes away. So rest when you need to rest, plan for eating so you don't miss a meal, exercise when your body holds tension, and seek the quiet company of soft music and a good book when you're overwhelmed. God designed us with everything we need to thrive, if we just pay attention. In turn, when we thrive, we're better able to live in God's loving renewal and put that "good stuff" out into the world to truly make a difference.

God's renewing presence in our lives allows us to discover our true purpose in the world, and Ephesians 2:10 (NIV) reminds us that indeed, God wants us to live according to His purpose: "For we are God's handiwork, created in Christ Jesus to do good works, which God prepared in advance for us to do." God knew what He wanted for us, even before He made us—isn't that amazing? And He has a plan for each of us. But, if we aren't careful, we can let the world imprison us with burdens and responsibilities, depleting our reserves and leaving us with nothing left to devote toward that greater plan. We once heard it said that "an overwhelmed schedule will always produce an underwhelmed soul," and when we give more to the wrong things, we tend to give less to the right things.

Dr. Roxanne has noticed the importance of self-care in her own life as she's encountered recent challenges, both large and small, that threaten to wear her down:

> At this point in my life, I think I've finally realized the powerful importance of living life through the lens of what makes us whole. You see, we're all born with a wholeness of spirit, mind, and body, but these things require our intentional nurturance and routine maintenance. It's hard to get through the challenges of life without caring for every part of that wholeness, in a way that helps us function at our best. Over the last few years, Father Nick and I have experienced a lot of challenges: challenges that have brought us to our knees, that have pushed our emotions to the limits, and that have left our minds cycling in and out of stress and worry. Those difficult seasons certainly took a lot of our attention, but then, we also have normal everyday life, where demands run high and our internal reserves often run low!

The other day was an example of normal life for me, though it certainly had its blemishes. Yet, it unfolded with a level of peace that allowed me to handle the difficulties as my best self. "Where did that peace come from?" I thought. Did it come from the extra ten minutes I took to connect my spirit with God in prayer before I physically got out of bed? Or from putting on my running shoes and heading outside for some exercise? Did it happen because I listened to my favorite, uplifting music that always fills my soul with positivity and encouragement? Was it from praying again during my run as my thoughts flowed freely, and then returning for a relaxing shower? Or from taking the time to prepare a decent breakfast? I guess I would say it came from the collective nature of all of it! *Nurturing my whole being at the start of my day helps me manage the challenges that are sure to come my way.*

So, how did the rest of my day go? Well, one child got a stomach bug. Our dog left me a glorious present on our brand-new carpet, and a glass canister shattered from my other child's kind attempt to make me coffee. Add to this a dead car battery and finding one of last year's Christmas gifts that we obviously never sent—it's all in a day's morning!

I wonder how that day would have gone if I hadn't attended to my needs before it all unfolded. Truth is, no matter how great our intentions, if we don't work to create internal peace for ourselves through self-care, then we often lack the motivation, energy, or feel-good chemistry to actually follow through on those wonderful intentions. When we care for ourselves, we use the equipment God has given us to thrive. *We use our will to get us closer to His.*

Now, put on your own running (or walking) shoes, and let's find out more about how we tend to deplete ourselves as we navigate the fast pace of contemporary life. Along the way, we'll also discover some keys to help us escape the "rat race" and instead "run with endurance the race that is set before us" (Heb. 12:1 [ESV]).

Free Yourself from Chronic Exhaustion

Did you know that people currently average less sleep each night than the average a hundred years ago?[1] Wealthier, college-educated Americans work longer days than they used too, also.[2] So some of us are working longer hours on less sleep! Why do we do this? Many of us have bought into the lie that "more is better, and better is best." So sometimes our decisions are motivated by a desire to acquire wealth and possessions, as recent studies have shown that more than half of Americans spend more than they earn.[3] Or we may want novel experiences, status, or success at work. But our motivations aren't all self-focused. Sometimes good causes drive our decision to overwork, and we may will ourselves to push on through exhaustion in order to do those good works from

Ephesians 2:10. But whatever the underlying motivation, we're a nation of overextended people! And often, we don't even realize how much we're doing until we end up passing our family members on the way to the "next thing" like ships passing in the night.

Our chronic exhaustion impacts our spiritual, emotional, and physical health. In fact, *stress occurs when we operate for too long at the edge of our capacity.*[4] If we ever hope to experience God's renewal on a daily basis, we need to break out of this prison of chronic exhaustion and begin taking better care of ourselves. Does that sound like selfishness? Not if you look at your body as a temple God created to house your soul, as I Corinthians 6:19 (NIV) says: "Do you not know that your bodies are temples of the Holy Spirit, who is in you, whom you have received from God? You are not your own." Our bodies and minds don't belong to us; rather, they are the keys to releasing God's love into the world. We need to prioritize taking care of them so He can work through us. It's the same reason why, on planes, flight attendants tell us that if the cabin loses pressure, we should place the oxygen mask over our face before we help others. Yet, more often than not, the world doesn't slow down long enough for us to even put our own oxygen masks on.

God certainly understands our circumstances today, and He promises that when we're tired and overwhelmed, He will give us rest, as Jesus says in Matthew 11:28-30 (NIV): "Come to me, all you who are weary and burdened, and I will give you rest. Take My yoke upon you and learn from me, for I am gentle and humble in heart, and you will find rest for your souls. For My yoke is easy and My burden is light." All He asks is that we take His yoke instead of struggling beneath the yokes we've created for ourselves. When we take His yoke, we lighten our burden, as the yoke Jesus refers to here is the piece of wood farmers would use to attach oxen side by side, which made plowing more efficient and smoother.

What happens when we don't heed the invitation of Christ to take up His yoke? We pay a heavy price. For one thing, we lower our ability to resist temptation: Whenever we feel stressed and overworked, we find it harder to say "no" to sin and are less able to bear the fruit of His Spirit—whether that is gentleness, patience, self-control, or kindness (Gal. 5:22-23). Being depleted affects our choices every day, knowingly and unknowingly, and makes it harder for us to live the way we intend. For instance, try connecting deeply with your spouse or child when you feel you've already spent your energy somewhere else. Try being merciful or compassionate when you're moving in several different directions at once, trying to accomplish a to-do list that's far too large for your day. Try being tolerant and patient, rather than critical, when someone upsets you when you already feel tired or stressed. Even something as simple as lack of sleep can alter our moods, leaving otherwise emotionally healthy people irritable, angry, negative, and less tolerant of stressful circumstances.[5] What we sometimes don't realize is that physical exhaustion is God's way of warning us to slow down. And if we fail to heed the warning signs our body provides, we end up doing a disservice to ourselves and to all those around us.

Research has even proven that a link exists between chronically high levels of stress and the onset of major depression.[6] How can we be a light of God's goodness in the world if we're doing so much that we no longer feel our own light shining from within?

When we buy into the modern myth that if we just work longer hours and push ourselves harder, we will accomplish more, our Lord reminds us that even He repeatedly took time away from work in order to rest. In Mark 4:35-40 (NLT), we hear about Jesus choosing to depart from the crowds, even knowing He still had work to do: people to heal and lessons to teach. And yet He chose to get into a boat and cross to the other side, and as the boat went out, "Jesus was sleeping at the back of the boat with His head on a cushion." Jesus slept when he needed it, even during a storm that alarmed his disciples!

Our purpose in life isn't "to do a lot of things"—it's to do a few things and do them well! We can't be good at everything, and we shouldn't be involved in everything. Prolonged stress from trying to do too much not only hurts us emotionally, it actually causes decreased productivity. In their book *The Distracted Mind: Ancient Brains in a High-Tech World*, professors Adam Gazzaley and Larry Rosen explain why the brain wasn't actually designed to multitask. The book asserts that multitasking affects our productivity and accuracy. Their research explains that when we try to do too many things at once, "our prefrontal cortex is the area challenged the most, followed by our visual areas, auditory areas and our hippocampus" (responsible for memory). It says that when we engage in one task at a time, with complete focus, the prefrontal cortex actually works in harmony with other parts of our brain the way it was designed to. Yet, when we try to manage several things at once, it forces the left and right sides of our brain to work independently. The researchers suggest that this process of splitting our attention leads to mistakes and decreased productivity. Even something as simple as responding to a text while also writing an email requires us to take in new information, which reduces our original focus. Once interrupted, our focused stream of thought takes time to reset as we try to re-engage our thoughts and "re-create all the elements" of what we were initially focused on. So, while we often *think* we can simultaneously process two tasks that demand our attention at once, this research suggests that we often don't do so very successfully and end up missing important information or wasting time trying to get ourselves back on task.[7]

So, not only should we not try to do too many things at once, we also shouldn't work more hours than we can handle. A study by professor John Pencavel of Stanford University found that our productivity per hour declines drastically when we try to work more than fifty hours per week. He found that after fifty-five hours, our productivity drops so much that it's not worth working at all, and that people who work seventy hours a week actually produce the same amount of work as those putting in only fifty-five hours. Our goal, then, is to exert energy and mental focus where it counts, to focus our energies and attention on one thing at a time, and to let go of trying to fit in every insignificant task and demand that comes up.[8]

If we don't renew our bodies and minds and instead live in a state of chronic exhaustion, we end up relying on good intention and willpower alone to keep the "good stuff" going. We rely on good intention and willpower to love others well with patience, gentleness, and self-control. We rely on them to keep giving to others in need even when we have nothing left to give and feel hurried and frazzled. But studies show that feeling hurried affects whether or not we will even notice someone in need—let alone stop to help them. So all the good intentions and willpower in the world won't help us show God's love to others if we haven't taken care of ourselves—if we let our busyness get in the way of renewing our bodies, minds, and spirits in God!

Don't Fall for Counterfeit Self-Care

So now that we know we need to take care of ourselves, how exactly do we do it? Do we do it with things like treats and shopping trips and fancy vacations and a glass of wine at the end of the day, as the world would have us believe? I (Dr. Roxanne) saw an image on television today of what looked like a tantalizing dessert, and the caption that followed said, "This is happiness." I thought for a moment, "Is that really happiness?" Well, perhaps. The first bite for sure, and maybe the few that follow—especially if you're hungry! After that, we've likely reached our level of peak happiness about the taste of the dessert and continue eating only out of rote compulsion. Research shows that the first bite releases the most dopamine (our feel-good chemical), and then the dopamine actually decreases with every bite afterward.[9] The point is, the happiness boost fades quickly. Then we return to our lives again, and all the same stressors are still there! So the treat was nothing more than a short-lived change attached to a long-term promise. We're not sure this is what God intended.

While many things bring us temporary happiness, real self-care leads to long-term joy and isn't about salt baths and chocolate cake—or any other fleeting indulgence. Self-care also doesn't mean indulging in our bad habits and addictions in order to counteract our stress. These things only imprison us in a cycle of unhealthy practices! As we discussed in Chapter 3, sometimes when we try to meet our needs, we become stuck in a destructive vice in a misplaced notion that it will increase our well-being. Surprisingly, many of our self-medicating addictions really do begin as responses to legitimate needs, but this doesn't mean we should try to justify them. Addictions and bad habits will never lead to lasting joy, only that temporary happiness that decreases with every subsequent "bite." Rather, think of real self-care this way: *Ultimately, it's about making the choice to build a life that better supports our ability to put on the character of Christ.* Do our habits and addictions and temporary indulgences do this? The answer is obvious!

We can only achieve lasting joy by constantly striving for renewal: spiritually, emotionally, and physically. Because true joy happens from the inside out, this requires making time regularly for all the things that keep us happy and balanced: that means devoting quality time to cultivating our relationships with God and other people, spiritually discerning our thoughts, and caring for our body's basic needs. Only then do we find the type of true inner peace we crave most and that can help us through any circumstance.

Because our nature is made up of both flesh and spirit, we must also be mindful that division can undermine our wholeness. We hear in the Gospel of Matthew that "every kingdom divided against itself will be ruined, and every city or household divided against itself will not stand" (Matt. 12:25). So our ability to live for God's Kingdom can be weakened by our own flesh, which constantly feuds against the spirit, seeking division and separateness. If the body works against the soul, our power weakens; likewise, if the soul constantly has to battle against the body, its power weakens. Therefore, when we care for ourselves, we must attend to our wholeness so that as an entity in Christ we stand unified in both body and mind, and we minimize the likelihood of their rebellion against the efforts of our soul.

Understand Your Own Needs

In 1943, renowned psychologist Abraham Maslow created his Hierarchy of Human Needs, a psychological theory describing five motivational factors.[10] In this pyramid, he arranged our needs hierarchically, with basic lower-level needs (like physical needs for food and safety) at the bottom and higher-level needs (like a sense of belonging or living a meaningful life) at the top. Maslow asserted that much of our behavior is motivated by whatever need we're trying to fill, and that it's harder to focus on higher-level needs if our lower-level needs aren't met first. So, our behavior will always be driven by the lowest-level need that isn't met.

Let's expand on this to see more clearly how the pyramid functions. At the bottom of the pyramid, Maslow put our very basic *physiological* needs for air, water, rest, shelter, and food. He saw these needs as important parts of human survival—our body can't survive without them! We can't do much else if we don't meet these needs first. For example, if we miss a meal or don't get enough sleep, the body cannot function optimally, and we realize rather quickly the truth of Maslow's pyramid, since without food and rest we become irritable, less talkative, and very cloudy in our thinking.

Next in the pyramid, Maslow shows our need for *safety*. We all need to feel physically safe from the elements and from danger; we all need to feel secure in our health, general well-being, and finances. When these needs are met, we experience a feeling of order, predictability, and control in our lives. Safety and security come both from our family and society. Having a sense of law and order in society and growing up with emotional and physical security from our families gives us freedom from fear and so allows our minds to open up to higher-level needs. When we don't experience that sense of safety, our brains remain activated toward threat avoidance and self-preservation, and behaviors become narrowly focused on seeking reassurance, safety, and protection rather than creatively seeking our life's potential, personal growth, and purpose. Think of someone who has lost their job, someone living in a war-torn country with civil unrest, someone who has lost their home in a hurricane, or a child being raised in an abusive home.

Once we've satisfied our basic needs for safety and biological survival, we start to direct our behavior toward the higher-level psychological needs of *love and belonging* and then *esteem*. To meet our needs for love and belonging, we seek friendship, affection, intimacy, and emotional connection with others. We achieve esteem with behavior that brings us self-respect, dignity, independence, achievement, value, and respect from others. In this stage, we frequently master certain skill sets, learning more about what we're good at.

Maslow places *self-actualization* at the top of the pyramid. This is what Christians might call discovering our true purpose in life. Once we've fulfilled our lower-level needs, we can direct more of our energies toward fulfilling something we find meaningful and that gives us a sense of purpose. Whether that means becoming the best spouse or parent we can be, contributing fully in our workplace, creating through literature or art, or serving in a broader community or global setting, at this stage we've embraced our innate strengths and God-given gifts and have learned to use them in our world to promote goodness. Our accomplishments now help us feel a sense of worth according to who God has made us to be. So, now the question we must ask ourselves is, "How do we expect to reach God's potential for our lives if we don't tend to our other, more basic needs along the way?"

Pay Attention to Stress Signals

As we keep emphasizing throughout this book, we must develop self-awareness in order to fully experience God's renewal—and paying close attention to our bodies is part of this. When He created us, God placed a system of signals within our bodies to indicate when our needs aren't getting met at the various levels of Maslow's pyramid. Our bodies send out distress signals, and we can catch them if we listen! Here's an example Dr. Roxanne has from her life:

> We ourselves are no strangers to a busy life, and we struggle with slowing down. The other day, as I reviewed my to-do list, I entered that very familiar feeling of exhausted excitement. Though I'm a list-maker by nature, and I normally feel quite energized by conquering my to-do list, this day felt different from most. The balance of my excitement about getting things done was overwhelmed by the anticipatory exhaustion of actually doing it. I felt more apathy than energy, more dread than excitement, and more scatter than focus.
>
> Nothing on my list sounded like something I could start, so I noticed this and decided to listen. What did I hear my body saying? I couldn't tell for sure what I felt exactly, or what I needed, but I noticed my eyes were dry and tired, and my motivation and internal reserves felt depleted. I decided to lie down on the couch and curl up, without even a book (my usual

favorite pasttime). As I lay there, a feeling of calm washed over me, and each passing moment brought a stronger sense of well-being. After a while, my daughter walked into the room and lay down next to me. We didn't say much, just existed together there, in the moment. With each passing minute, I felt more and more relaxed, more relieved, more revived and energized. I started to feel renewed. Eventually, she began talking, and I just listened. I had no other agenda—even though I had so much still to do—no pull or interest in even turning anything she said into a teaching moment or a lesson. She shared so many things, and I noticed myself fully able to attend to her, to truly hear her and just enjoy that moment with her. Before long, my son joined us, and then my husband. It was as if our busy life from only moments ago stopped briefly to allow the peace *inside* our souls to come alive and envelop us. It was a true connection. A real moment. It just felt good.

The next day, my son said, "You know what I just asked God for? I asked Him for more moments like yesterday, where we could just be in the moment with each other." What a realization of what truly matters and of what our bodies need in order to allow our souls to thrive. Our souls, our families, our lives are all gifts Christ has given us, and when we stop to renew our bodies, Christ's Spirit fills the moments where we once felt empty.

You can see, then, that in order to feel renewed and energized for the day ahead, Dr. Roxanne needed to listen to that lethargy she felt when she looked at her to-do list. Here are some other good signs from your body to heed: You've felt your mind racing all day. You feel exhausted and don't want to do anything. You have trouble sleeping at night or want to sleep all day. You eat too much or feel unable to eat at all. You lose your desire to socialize or find you don't enjoy connecting with people as you normally would. You have a hard time concentrating on any one thing. Your muscles feel tense throughout your back, shoulders, jaw, or brow line. You clench your teeth at night. You feel sick to your stomach or carry around a general sense of restlessness, agitation, or irritability from having internalized your struggle.

If we don't pay close attention to the signals our body sends us, we don't intervene to interrupt these stress signals, and permanent feelings of tension become uninvited guests that settle in. It's a biological phenomenon, as well as an emotional one! Chronic stress from pushing ourselves past capacity for extended periods of time can cause our hypothalamus to signal our adrenal glands to release damaging stress hormones that weaken our immune systems and create an array of physical problems, from heart disease to high blood pressure. Even our blood-brain barrier, which normally serves to keep out toxins, opens up and allows foreign toxic bodies into our brain during heightened times of stress.

Chronic stress can also destroy our relationships and lead to a cascade of emotional problems like depression and anxiety. We get stuck in the exhaustion, the sense of helplessness, worry, and dread, and the feeling of being all alone, and these things begin to take a serious toll on us physically and spiritually. God's message to us is clear: overworked vessels carry souls that simply have less to give. Here's a great analogy from Father Nick that illustrates this concept:

> We can liken dealing with stress to holding a glass of water. If we hold a glass of water long enough to drink it—while walking around at a dinner party, for example—it's not much of a burden. However, holding that same glass of water for a whole day would likely be very uncomfortable. Likewise, if we had to hold that glass of water for several days, or a week, a month, or even longer, our arm would eventually go numb and feel paralyzed. The longer we live with unresolved stress, the heavier and more burdensome it becomes, until we feel paralyzed.
>
> On the other hand, when we care for ourselves physically, mentally, and spiritually—especially during trying times—we don't give stress a chance to take up residence in our soul and prevent us from fulfilling God's plan for our life.

In the next sections, we'll cover a few tactics for mind, body, and soul that can help you practice self-care in a healthy way.

Slow the Pace and Create Some Space

Scripture tells us that God wants us to *slow the pace and create some space*—not only for Him, but for our families and the people He brings across our path each day. He wants us to have time to engage with them, to hear them, and to love them. *And to do that, He wants us to take care of ourselves in the best possible way.* Let's see this in action for Dr. Roxanne:

> The other day, I realized that although my daughter was speaking to me, I hadn't really heard her. Although I looked at her, I couldn't tell you what she was wearing. I only noticed the demands that weighed on me. My focus was on managing the current moment and planning for the one to come. Well, I must have paused long enough to realize my distracted state. I noticed my tight shoulders, my clenched jaw, and my fatigued back—typical stress signals for me. I also remembered that story from the Bible about Mary and Martha that reminds us of how Christ desires nothing more than for us to literally "sit down" and connect with Him and to the people He has placed in our lives (Luke 10:38-42). So, I looked over at my daughter, stopped what I was doing, and asked her to repeat what she had just said. I also admitted that I hadn't truly been listening as I should have.
>
> As I focused on her, suddenly I noticed her desire to connect: Her eyes lit up; her tone of voice changed.

She had so much to share! I noticed her joy, her excitement, and her passion. I saw the light color in her beautiful brown eyes, her rosy cheeks. Her cute little outfit she'd worked so hard to pick out that morning. She'd just been vying to reach me amidst the busyness of my day.

Just like I couldn't hear my own daughter when she stood right in front of me, sometimes the many demands and distractions pulling at our attention overwhelm us to the point where we can't even hear our own soul. In these moments, not only do we not make time for God, we don't care for ourselves—and subsequently we aren't able to care for others.

You can see from Dr. Roxanne's example that our family struggles with busyness just like everyone else! We often wish we had just a little more time in our day to get everything done *and* make time for the things that matter most. Many days are so task-focused we feel like mice on an exercise wheel, going through the motions, doing what each subsequent moment demands of us without any intentionality or contemplation. When we live like this day after day, how can we make room for taking care of ourselves? How can God break through to us with His renewing presence?

Try this simple exercise to take your busyness pulse: Take a few moments now to list what you've done so far today. Then look the list over carefully. Are you able to say, "I'm doing exactly what God intends for me to do"? Or are you listening instead to a world that keeps pushing you for more: more money, more work, more responsibilities, more busyness? It's easy to rationalize our busyness to ourselves, saying, "This has to get done! Let me just send one more email, one more text; let me just take one more quick look at social media, attend one more meeting."

Now, make another list: This time, write down a few things you *could* do today, or even just one thing, to slow down enough to care for yourself and allow God to break through. Then, try pausing at various moments throughout the day to ask: "Does what I'm about to do contribute to the well-being of my soul?" "Is it something that 'must' occur?" "How am I doing?" "What do I need right now?"

Remember, *God calls us to live our lives more by design than by default,* so if you make a point to "check in" during your typical busy routine and reflect on your true priorities, you can break free from unimportant tasks and more actively choose what makes the most sense for your peace and well-being. This process is a key to making intentional decisions rather than following the rote routine life so frequently demands. To do this, take an honest look at what you can delete from your "have to do" list or put off for another time. Even altering your to-do list in some small way makes space for more rest and renewal, and doing so can help you learn to step away from commitments that don't contribute to your service to God: it's those things that wear us out unnecessarily! In this process, we learn to say "no" to the more menial tasks and rigid expectations we get caught up in, with our tendency to try to "do it all," "be all things to all people," or our attempts to "please everyone." When we try to do it all, we miss out on important parts of God's plan because we haven't taken care of ourselves well enough to keep ourselves open to His voice. Yes, things have to get done, but responsibilities shouldn't dominate our lives. Here's an experience Father Nick once had that drives these points home:

> I once attended a seminar on time management where the featured speaker talked about adding margins back into your life. He defined margins as the space we create in between our responsibilities to help us rest, and he began by asking the audience to raise our hands based on how we typically arrived at an event. He wanted to know whether we tended to arrive early, on time, or late to events. Only a few members raised their hands to indicate they usually arrived early. About a quarter of the audience responded that they generally arrived on time, and close to three-fourths indicated they often arrived late. The speaker then explained that for most of his life, he too would consistently arrive five minutes late to events because he never allowed any margin to catch his breath when he arrived, to look for misplaced keys before leaving home, or to deal with unanticipated traffic. This led him to feel rushed, stressed, and even panicked at events as he moved from meeting to meeting.
>
> After making some calculations, with shock he realized that if he arrived fifteen minutes late, three

times a day for fifteen years, it added up to almost six solid months of unnecessary tension—all because he hadn't built any margin into his day. Stunned by this realization, he took a sensible step toward self-care and began adding margins of time into his day. As a result, he found that he felt much more relaxed and at peace. "I am enjoying life more," he told me.

So the old expression "less is more" is true! Part of caring for ourselves means keeping margins of space in our lives—so we should think long and hard before we make commitments. It's so much easier to get into debt than it is to get out of debt. It's easier to get into a relationship than to end one. And it's always easier to get into trouble than to get out of trouble. So, let's devote calendar time to what's truly important and not get distracted my unimportant, unnecessary, or even hurtful commitments.

You can always tell what a person values by looking at his calendar. You can certainly *name* the things you value—the things you *say* are important—but do you put those things on your calendar? Studies show that if it's not on your calendar, it's probably not going to happen. So stop for a few moments to think about your values. Maybe even write them down so you can look at them regularly and remember what you truly see as important! Now, consider how you can fold them into your day. If you named faith as a value, then set aside time every day to practice the First Fifteen method from Chapter 1. If you named valuing your marriage, put that date night onto your calendar right now. If you value your relationships with your family members or friends, decide how to protect dependable time with them. If you named valuing your health, write "going for a walk" every day on your calendar and stick to it like an appointment, or put down going to bed at the same time each day. And what about having fun? That's important for all of us! When was the last time you scheduled in playing a sport, joining a friend for lunch, or reading that book you've been saying for months that you'll read? As the Bible reminds us, our time is limited and precious—we should treat it as such and focus on what's important: "Teach us to number our days and recognize how few they are; help us to spend them as we should" (Ps. 90:12 [The Living Bible]).

Commit to Honoring the Sabbath

Remember, our bodies are vehicles, vessels for our souls. And if we're going to live a high-performance life, we need to schedule pit stops to create margins for our own renewal: to catch our breath and repair ourselves spiritually, emotionally, and physically. Pit stops are keys for allowing our souls to continue performing optimally in accordance with God's dream for our lives. After all, we can't really tune up a vehicle *while* it's racing at two hundred miles per hour or circling a track without stopping, and we all know what happens to a high-performance vehicle that doesn't get regular maintenance.

That's why God commands us to keep a Sabbath rest. In the Book of Hebrews, we hear, "There remains, then, a

Sabbath-rest for the people of God; for anyone who enters God's rest also rests from their works, just as God did from his. Let us, therefore, make every effort to enter that rest" (Heb. 4:9-11 [NIV]). Even God, after creating the world in six days, took the seventh day off to rest, serving as a self-care model for us to follow. This principle of renewal was so important that God even chose to include it in His Ten Commandments: "Remember the Sabbath day by keeping it holy. Six days you shall labor and do all your work, but the seventh day is a sabbath to the LORD your God. On it you shall not do any work" (Ex. 20:8-10 [NIV]). What did God mean? The word *Sabbath* literally means "a time of rest."[11] With the Sabbath, God gave us His plan to keep us renewed in Him by commanding us to hit our own pause button. Father Nick reminds us that even Christ Himself rested from the demands of His ministry in order to be alone with the Father.

> The Bible makes numerous references to times when Christ removed Himself from His work to rest. Even when the crowds gathered to hear Him and have Him heal their sicknesses, He "often withdrew to lonely places and prayed" (Luke 5:16 [NIV]). There are many other accounts of Jesus breaking away from people and tasks in the midst of His work to rest. He even directed His disciples to use rest in preparation for their future ministries: "Because so many people were coming and going that they did not even have a chance to eat, he said to [His disciples], 'Come with

me by yourselves to a quiet place and get some rest.' So they went away by themselves in a boat to a solitary place." (Mark 6:31-32 [NIV])

So, how do we create our Sabbath? We do so by hitting our pause button, and not just on Sunday! We need to put a little bit of Sabbath into every day by creating a daily practice of pausing in the midst of our work. To do this, we create a literal gap in our day—a dedicated time we set aside where everything stops and we disconnect from all work and work-related activities to seek God's solitude without an agenda. Aim for ten to twenty minutes throughout the course of your day, and create a quiet place in your home where you can count on silence. For us, this is our courtyard; for Jesus, this often meant going outside the walls of the city.

Even in the middle of a busy workday, you can find some ways to pause, whether you work from home or at an office. Take a few moments to rest your physical body by sitting back comfortably in your chair. Then, take a deep breath, close your eyes, and drop your shoulders, and allow yourself to rest for five minutes. You'll be surprised at how much, in those few moments, you can create renewal for the next moment. Also, try pausing if you have to wait somewhere, like at a stoplight, the doctor's office, or a grocery line. Force yourself to just wait, instead of grabbing your phone to check your email or make a call. Try saying the Jesus Prayer instead of locking yourself into still more busywork: "Lord Jesus Christ, Son of God, have mercy on me!"

It's great also to pause and *remember the importance of mornings and the conclusions of days.* Try taking a walk early in the morning or after the sun has gone down in the quiet of day. This is when you can set your mind free to wander, to connect to God with transparency and vulnerability, to make insights, and to let God shed light on new perspectives. Or, try sitting outside in nature and pausing to observe and listen to its beauty—this is often the kind of Sabbath pause that invokes a connection to gratitude.

If nothing else, try simply stopping what you're doing at any given moment, and choose to just be. We can even use our commute as a chance to pause: Sometimes, riding in the car on our commute to and from work can bring about stillness, especially if we aren't in a hurry. It's often quiet. We can hear our thoughts, regain perspective, process how we feel about things, and inevitably connect all of it back to God in prayer. Music often begins this process for me (Dr. Roxanne). I have several favorite Christian artists I listen to every morning on my way to work, and their words always have a way of turning down the volume of the world and helping me to refocus into my soul, drawing me into Christ.

As you can see, you can create your Sabbath rest in numerous ways! Let's think about Sundays now. What would our weeks look like if we protected our Sundays as God has commanded us to? For one, imagine how much encouragement and renewal we could carry into our weeks if on Sunday mornings we never missed going to church. Church helps us completely pause, allowing our souls to fully absorb all the prayers said over us and for us and allowing our minds to fully find peace while we worship and connect everything back in prayer. And perhaps when you go to church, you'll hear the very message of renewal you've needed through a sermon that God has inspired just for you. Then, what would our weeks look like if on Sundays *after* church, we dedicated and protected uninterrupted time to do only what truly matters: spend quality time with the people God has blessed us with?

When we honor our Sabbath, we're better able to notice the things that God yearns for us to notice—those things that have perhaps collected during our days and are now operating in the background without our knowledge, affecting the way we feel and the things we do. Our Sabbath rests allow us to notice exhaustion, stress, and maybe even subtle negativity, all of which can fuel our reactions, direct our soul, and affect the way we treat people. Our Sabbath allows God to make us anew every week!

Download Your Thoughts

When we don't rest, we sometimes end up feeling trapped in our stress because our minds start to run in repeated loops. From new demands that arrive to trying to cope with the normal day-to-day demands that already exist, our minds can get overrun. And because we can't cope with, organize, or deal with what we can't see, one key to removing those bouncing thoughts from our head is to get them out onto paper. In my (Dr. Roxanne's) practice, I call this the "brain dump." Seeing our thoughts in writing helps us begin to deal with them, since our minds get so cluttered we sometimes feel overwhelmed or even like we're drowning. Downloading our worries can help us work with them. Whether that means extracting a to-do list, regaining perspective, or realizing where we need help, *removing it helps us work with it.*

The next time you feel your mind racing, simply take out a piece of paper and begin to write down everything that burdens you, removing the clutter. You might think, "Well, that will be overwhelming to see it all," but believe us, you're already *feeling the effects* of it, without the gift of being able to actually *examine it.* On paper, we can see what requires our immediate attention versus what doesn't, or, better yet, what we can control versus what we can't. We begin to see the things we need to fold into our calendars so that they no longer take up valuable headspace. If you don't see yourself as a list-maker, try sitting down with a trusted friend or family member who can help you talk out loud about the things that overwhelm you.

Father Nick and I find ourselves getting stuck in our minds, overthinking everything on our plates, especially during times of trial. For example, the additional responsibilities that came with navigating best treatment options for our dads, being involved during hospital stays and doctor's appointments, and coping with ongoing medical scares could have exhausted us. Plus, we still had to worry about getting to work, packing lunches, getting our kids around, helping with homework, and paying our bills. We coped by adapting our morning coffee routine into a time of talking out loud together about the things that weighed us down. It was incredibly powerful just how much saying things aloud brought perspective, and it helped us solve problems and let some things go. We took tasks off each other's plates, helped one another brainstorm solutions, tag-teamed the child rearing, and, most importantly, we could hear what we both needed most and could help each other see these things with renewed perspective.

When you empty your mind of clutter, you can translate your feelings, thoughts, worries, and burdens into to-do lists. You can find help, solve problems, renew your perspective, and even let go. Collectively, this one aspect of self-care can keep you on track during trials so that you can remain your best self.

Take Care of Your Body

We've talked a lot so far about caring for of our minds and spirits, but we need the cooperation and support of our physical bodies to do these things. Remember, alcohol and drugs and other addictions and bad habits don't give us the clarity of mind we need to navigate through tough moments of growth and struggle, and poor nutrition and lack of physical exercise undercut our ability to cope, too. Here's how Father Nick has learned to approach the care of the body:

> I absolutely love being a priest. In fact, I often wish I'd gotten ordained earlier in life! Still, my calling comes with tremendous stress and struggles. Although now I enjoy running and eating healthy, which helps keep

me mentally, spiritually, and physically well, that wasn't always the case. I used to put my own physical health on the back burner. For example, when you're a priest, people often enjoy feeding you to express their love for you. In fact, if you want to upset someone in your church, say "no, thank you" when they offer you food! In the minds of my parishioners, the more I eat their homemade food, the more it reflects how much I love them.

When you pair people who love to feed you with someone like myself who loves to eat, it makes for a perfect storm. To make matters worse, I love desserts. Well, I don't remember anyone telling me that as you get older, it's not as easy to shed the weight. I just tended to think I could eat whatever I desired. That narrative could not have been further from the truth. In my first year as a priest, I put on close to forty pounds and increased by several pants sizes! At approximately the same time, I also went through some major stressors in the church and, unfortunately, I kept a lot of those stresses pent up inside of me. On the one hand, I was overeating, and on the other hand, I wasn't managing the stress. As a result of the added stress, I even started to develop alopecia, which is an autoimmune disease that attacks your hair growth. Basically, I got larger and started to lose my hair! Not one of the more shining moments of my ministry!

We all know physical exercise and healthy eating habits bring us many benefits—our moods and attitudes improve, our energy levels rise after a workout, and our overall physical health increases. Some studies have shown that regular exercise can even help ease the symptoms of clinical depression.[12] Yet exercise is often the first thing we give up when we feel burdened or overly busy. If you haven't prioritized exercise in your daily routine, it's never too late to start experiencing the benefits. Try something small at first: a walk every night after dinner or a twenty- to thirty-minute midday routine using a YouTube exercise video. And make sure to set a realistic goal so your *anticipation* doesn't outweigh your *participation*.

Why does exercise work so well as a stress reducer? The Bible says we are "fearfully and wonderfully made" (Ps. 139:14 [NIV]), and our bodies respond best when we follow God's design. When we exercise, the increase we experience in body temperature while working up a sweat, followed by a cooling down, sends a signal to the body that it's time for a rest. This allows us to relax and even to sleep more peacefully. Exercise also reduces our body's stress hormones while stimulating the production of certain feel-good neurotransmitters. Interestingly, one of these neurotransmitters, norepinephrine, mediates our brain's response to stress. Simply put, God has designed us to feel better after physical exertion!

Additionally, what we put into our bodies also determines our quality of life. We often use junk food to self-medicate, especially during times of stress. Unfortunately, processed foods high in sugar and salt can stimulate our cravings and undermine our willpower. God never intended us to turn wholesome nutrition grown from the ground into highly processed forms of partial foods that wreak havoc on our blood sugars and our bodies, leaving us with additional cravings and poor energy. You see, God made food perfect in its natural and complete state, but as we do with other forms of nature, we create shortcuts because of our insatiable desire for more abundance, longer shelf life, and more resistance to pests, while wanting to spend less money, time, and energy. And these shortcuts have begun the reformation of what God intended food to be: fuel for the vessel. So try asking yourself this question the next time you reach for food: "Is this choice something that will fuel me to face this day, or will it only feel good in the moment?" When our goal for eating is fuel, sustained energy, sustenance, and clarity of thought, we honor God's perfect design for our body and practice responsible self-care.

Of course, those who under-eat have the opposite problem. If you don't have a good appetite, particularly during stressful times, then aim for four to five small meals a day. Go for nutrient-dense, balanced foods like nuts or legumes that pack in good quality nutrition even when you eat them in small amounts. In times of grief, we can lose our appetites completely, and then we need to consider food as medicine rather than pleasure. We must remember that we need food to survive, so during these times, self-care means learning to eat by the clock rather than trusting your body to signal you that it's time to eat. Like a well-oiled car, food is the energy that keeps our engines going.

Take Care of Your Spiritual Self

All throughout this chapter, we've touched on taking care of your spiritual self, but let's take a moment to really focus on that and remember we can do nothing without the Giver of Life. As Jesus says, "I am the vine, you *are* the branches. He who abides in Me, and I in him, bears much fruit; for without Me you can do nothing" (John 15:5). Nurturing our spiritual lives through our connection with Jesus Christ is how we lay a foundation for all true goodness and peace, as Father Nick reminds us:

> As Psalm 23:1-2 (NIV) beautifully says, "the LORD is [our] shepherd," and because of that, "[we] lack nothing. / He makes [us] lie down in green pastures, / He leads [us] beside quiet waters, / He refreshes [our] soul[s]." What if you spent time with Christ and asked Him, "Lord, what would You say to me?" It's quite possible He would say first, "My child, lie down." Give our Shepherd a chance, and He will restore your soul. Sometimes people say, "I can't hear from God. He doesn't speak to me." Yet we need to realize God doesn't have a speaking problem; we have a hearing problem. Do we quiet our souls long enough to hear Him? In a busy football stadium or at a crowded party, we can't even hear the person next to us. Yet if you go to that restaurant or stadium when it's empty, you'll be able to hear one voice, even if it comes from someone at the opposite end of the room.

We won't hear God's voice if we don't "lie down" in green pastures and quiet our souls.

Remember, a good litmus test for knowing what matters to someone is his or her calendar. If spending time with God isn't on your calendar, it's probably not going to happen. Give calendar time to what you say is important. Come to the Lord first thing in the morning for fifteen minutes and sit quietly. Pray, meditate on some words of Scripture, listen to a worship song, and in your own words say, "Lord, here I am. I'm listening." In time, the habit of putting God first and listening for His voice will bear good fruit in amazing ways, as the Bible says: "But seek first the kingdom of God and His righteousness, and all these things shall be added to you" (Matt. 6:33).

We love Psalmist King David's description: "I remember the days of old; / I meditate on all that you have done; / I ponder the work of Your hands" (Ps. 143:5 [ESV]). King David not only remembered to speak with God, he took time to meditate and reflect on that connection. When we meditate, we focus solely on *one thing in the moment*, turning that one thing over again and again in our minds while simultaneously blocking out everything else. Wouldn't we all be much calmer if we would just take a few moments daily to meditate on the things of God? Here's one way Dr. Roxanne does it:

When I feel stressed, I don't like to hear the TV or any kind of loud music; I crave going outdoors or lying down in a dimly lit room while listening to soft classical music, doing nothing other than breathing slowly and deeply. *Remaining quiet on the outside causes my soul to wake up to prayer on the inside.* As I breathe in—"Lord, be with me!"—then I breathe out, saying, "I know that You are." As we move through life, we must remember that God has designed both our mind and body as a support team for our soul. It's amazing what they can do for us when we care for them in even the smallest of ways.

Care for Each Other

No section on self-care would be complete without reminding ourselves about the incredible importance of relying on other people for support and supporting others who need us, as we talked so much about in the chapter on turning trials into triumphs. Remember, we are to, as Galatians 6:2 puts it, "bear one another's burdens, and so fulfill the law of Christ." The love and assistance God sends to us through other people affirms that His light shines in a dark world. We can say without hesitancy that we remain standing today as a couple and as a family because of the incredible love and support we've received from others. Even Jesus modeled for us the need for support. Remember that in Luke 23, on the road to His Crucifixion, a man named Simon of Cyrene came and helped Jesus carry His Cross? What a picture for us!

So as we end this chapter, we encourage you to open your eyes to the goodness, compassion, and love that surround you. It's not easy navigating through this broken world, but we can find Christ's love everywhere. Maybe today, it's this book you hold in your hands that offers you support. Maybe tomorrow, it will be someone you haven't yet met or the friend you've always been able to lean on. Maybe someday it will be your church family that stands by you in a crisis. When you open your heart to receiving God's love, you'll find that love through the support of others, giving you the strength to carry your cross and to keep yourself healthy through all that you encounter in this life.

PRAYER

✠ ✠ ✠

OH HEAVENLY FATHER, the Prince of Peace, throughout Your Holy Word, You modeled for us the importance of seeking our Sabbath rest. In the Old Testament, You reminded us through the pen of King David to "be still" and know that You are God. In the New Testament, You modeled this by Your frequent withdrawals for prayer. We know that hurry is the enemy of help, both for us and for others, and that we cannot let the busyness of our lives keep us from spending time with You, the Giver of Life. We hear Your warnings through our bodies, as they signal distress. Help us to listen and notice these signals and to care for our bodies as vessels of our souls. We know if we don't make time to care for our bodies and our minds, that in these moments, the devil will make time for us. Therefore, teach us the reward of stillness with You.

✠ ✠ ✠

FOR DISCUSSION:
THE THREE Rs — REST, REFLECT, AND RESPOND

1. As you go to sleep, or in other moments free from distractions, do you think about your worries?

2. In what ways do you currently take care of your mental, spiritual, and physical health?

3. List a few things you could do to improve in each of these areas (for example, read your Bible, start a devotional book, go for a bike ride, take a walk, journal your thoughts and feelings, take the time to eat right).

4. Do you need to learn further skillsets to help you through your stress? (for example, improved stress management, assertiveness skills, time management, or conflict resolution skills).

5. Do you have resources on hand to help you care for your physical and spiritual health, such as a prayer partner, spiritual mentor or priest, a good book on self-care, a therapist, or a doctor for your physical health?

6. What recharges you when you need refueling? To help yourself think about this, try answering these sentence stems:

   - I feel best when . . .
   - I'm happiest when . . .
   - I feel rested when . . .
   - The last best day was when I . . .
   - My day goes best when I start it by . . .
   - The best time of day for me to seek refueling is . . .
   - The time of day I need it most is . . .

SELF-CARE PRACTICES

(Try choosing at least three to fold into your life.)

1. Carve out time this week to shop, meal prep, and prepare healthy, balanced meals and snacks for the week.

2. Try journaling—the "brain dump."

3. Get enough sleep.

4. Meet a friend once a month for lunch, coffee, or a walk.

5. Spend an hour engaging in an interest or hobby you once enjoyed.

6. Protect a regular time for exercise, preferably outside.

7. Ask for help when you need it.

8. Sit outside. Just. Sit.

9. Take a leisurely walk without a goal.

10. Take a twenty-minute nap, go to bed early, or sleep in late.

11. Do something crafty: coloring, knitting, sewing, etc.

12. Organize something.

13. Go to the library or bookstore. Sit in a comfy chair and read.

14. Sit in the grass and watch the clouds float by.

15. Take a walk outside at night and look at the stars.

16. Turn on your favorite music and just dance.

17. Burn a candle or diffuse essential oils (frankincense and myrrh are great) with scents that bring you joy.

18. Sit in a coffee shop and sip coffee at a "European" pace.

19. Walk around a grocery store without a list. Buy some stuff just for fun.

20. Close yourself in a room and listen to the latest episode of your favorite podcast.

21. Have a twenty-minute stretching session.

22. Declutter a spot in your house that's been bugging you.

23. Watch the sun rise or set. Just watch.

24. Research something you've been interested in but haven't had time to dive into.

25. Edit the people you follow on social media; incorporate new positive pages each week so that eventually your feed will fill with positive reminders that reinvigorate your soul.

26. Go to a museum and just appreciate the beauty.

27. Spend time in your garden.

28. Write a list of ten things you're grateful for and why.

29. Write a letter (or an email) to an old friend.

30. Say "no" to someone if you're operating at the edge of your capacity.

31. Be still.

CHAPTER SIX

Make over Your Marriage

I have taken you in my arms, and I love you, and I prefer you to my life itself. For the present life is nothing, and my most ardent dream is to spend it with you in such a way that we may be assured of not being separated in the life reserved for us . . . I place your love above all things, and nothing would be more bitter or painful to me than to be of a different mind than you.[1] —St. John Chrysostom on
WHAT YOUNG HUSBANDS SHOULD SAY TO THEIR WIVES

JUST AS WE need to renew ourselves through self-care before we can effectively share God's renewing power with others, we also need to renew ourselves within our marriages, doing what we can to bring health and healing to one of the most fundamental relationships we have in this life. Unhealthy relationships have a way of depleting our reserves, leaving us spiritually unsettled, cycling in and out of emptiness or loneliness, and filled with anger and negativity. And carrying around this kind of mental and physical anguish affects our soul, making it hard to open ourselves up to our true purpose in Christ. We know that we should "always be humble and gentle. Be patient with each other, making allowances for each other's faults because of [our] love. Make every effort to keep [ourselves] united in the Spirit, binding [ourselves] together with peace" (Eph. 4:2-3 [NLT]), and our spirit desires to live this way, but it's often easier said than done. Marriage, by definition, requires us to merge two completely separate lives in order to become "one flesh," as the Bible tells us, and having the right tools can play an important role in helping us do this successfully. When we remain united in the Spirit and equip ourselves with knowledge about how to better love our spouse in a way that encourages mutual love and support, our relationship becomes another source of renewal and encouragement that can keep us moving toward our purpose.

It seems like we all buy into this notion that "all you need is love," as The Beatles once sang. Indeed, so many movies, TV shows, songs, and books tell us that the secret to a long-lasting relationship is love and being "in love." However, it's a myth that love is all you need for a relationship to prosper! The truth is, while feelings of love or of being "in love" often draw us together in the beginning of a relationship, they're not usually enough to keep the relationship strong in a lasting way. Why? Because our feelings are fleeting. We can feel in love with our partner one day and very angry with them the next. We can go from having fun to tears in a matter of seconds, or to feeling utterly irritated by our spouse's idiosyncratic quirks. And anyone who's been married for a long time knows we can sometimes go for weeks or even months without *feeling* any particular love for the person we once felt constantly thrilled by. What to do?

Once we understand marriage isn't all about *feeling* love but more about *choosing and showing* love, that's when we really start to build a healthy relationship that can last a lifetime. Relationships require a foundation of healthy motivations: behaviors and thoughts driven by a desire for mutual goodness and respect. This requires making a lot of little adjustments along the way and *choosing* to renew our love for our partner every day. When we choose to remain loving, we cultivate patience in the midst of our partner's frustrating qualities. We cultivate a willingness to explore hurt rather than react to it. And we give our partner the benefit of the doubt, rather than taking her behavior personally. We show our love for him even when we're angry, tired, or upset. And we show it despite the hurt feelings and misunderstandings that are bound to appear sooner or later. Does this all sound difficult to do? It is! But the benefits of doing so are beyond compare: a healthy, lifelong, and connected relationship where we learn to grow together in body, mind, and spirit. But we can only do this by constantly resetting and renewing our minds and hearts in Christ, allowing our faith to act as a moral compass we rely on every day to keep us grounded. Without constant renewal in Christ, we can easily drift, allowing division and disconnection to thrive while waiting for the love to return on its own.

For Christians, our relationship with Christ is what allows our choices to transcend our feelings in the midst of hurt, in order to bring about healing. Our intentionality helps us choose well, and in this way, we seek our best selves as we move through conflict and difficulty with patience and self-control. We do what we can to bring about peace through mutual understanding and acceptance of each other, remembering what it says in the Book of Romans: "If possible, as far as it depends on you, live peaceably with all" (12:18 [ESV]).

Living peaceably does not mean, however, tolerating, enabling, or accepting unhealthy behavior in others. In fact, the Book of Proverbs warns us that "a person without self-control / is like a city with broken-down walls" (25:28 [NLT]). A person who acts without boundaries functions as their own spiritual director, without accountability—and when we face this, we are called "not to answer an undiscerning man in relation to his lack of discernment, lest we become like him" (Prov. 26:4 [Orthodox Study Bible]). This means we must practice discernment when our partner falters, knowing that seeking peace doesn't mean taking full ownership of someone else's struggle, but it does mean choosing not to make things worse with blame, condemnation, and judgment. Saint Paul speaks about this when he says, "Brother and sisters, if someone is caught in a sin, you who live by the Spirit should restore that person gently. But watch yourselves, or you also may be tempted" (Gal. 6:1 [NIV]).

So while we must protect ourselves from the temptation of being pulled under the water along with our partner, we cannot kick people when they are down. Rather, God calls us to look for ways to help them lift their heads above the waves again. We do this when we remember their positive traits and why we love them, when we show mercy, and when we seek to understand the struggle causing the behavior, choosing to ask *why*, rather than defining them with *what*. We can also learn how to address—rather than avoid—patterns that lend themselves to destruction. In this way, **loving** *acts as a verb and not simply a noun*, because we express it not only through an active friendship in the joyful times but also in the midst of struggle.

When Christ came into this world, He never stood up and simply said, "I love you." No, He constantly demonstrated His love for us through His actions, showing us that love is sacrificial, unconditional, and without blame or judgment. Through His example we, too, can renew our love for each other on a daily basis by showing compassion, mercy, kindness, affection, and patience. God didn't design love to simply stop at a "feeling" that we experience deep down inside ourselves that our partner can't see or experience. He meant for us to show it in everything we do. It's part of our purpose as human beings and as Christians!

With Christ's example as our guide, here are several important keys for cultivating the spiritual virtues we need in order to have a successful marriage.

Honor individual differences. *The truth is, it's easy to move through life focused on what's wrong with our spouse instead of what's right.* But we must remember that God brought us all into this world with a *different set of gifts, on purpose for a purpose,* and He wants us to love, value, and appreciate one another so we can work together for a greater good. Sometimes He even brings us together with different strengths on purpose so that we can learn from each other and lead in different domains.

Marriage brings particular challenges in this area because it merges two different personalities, two different family backgrounds, experiences, worldviews, and so on. People can easily clash over differences in any one of these areas—it's so much harder when all of them come together in one marriage! While this is the great challenge of marriage, it's also a great strength, because working through differences helps us become better people—and better Christians—in all aspects of our lives. And rather than stifling differences, a good marriage can celebrate them and actually help us each become a better version of our true self, as God intended us to be. So rather than putting ourselves or our spouse on the potter's wheel in an attempt to create a new design, we need to cherish our differences and help one another live even more as our own, unique selves!

If you find yourselves experiencing conflict consistently over the same themes, this may signal that you're not honoring one another's differences: that you haven't yet come to integrate each other's needs and values in effective ways. Self-awareness, again, is key here: Listen to yourself and take stock of the words you use when you talk to your spouse. Do you constantly correct her? Next time, instead of correcting her or arguing about the same old thing, ask yourself, "How can I make allowances for my partner's differences?" "Do I honor those differences, or am I constantly seeking to change them?" "Which of my habits and preferences could I learn to compromise more on?" "How can *I* work on *my part* for both of us to find happiness while co-existing together?" For instance, if you have a passionate and emotionally expressive partner, but you tend to be quiet and reflective, preferring less intense emotional debates, you might have to sustain a little discomfort and practice breathing deeply in order to stay present during moments of conflict. Or, if your partner loves a crowd and you prefer to curl up with a good book at home, you may need to ask your partner to let you know when it really counts for you to go to an event with him and when it matters less, and you can choose to stay home.

In a healthy marriage spouses tend to integrate each other's values and preferences, allowing each person's perspective to influence activities and the culture they build together in the home. They consider and care about what's important to each other, even if they don't always really understand it, and they try to think in terms of "we" instead of "me." They ask themselves, "How would my partner feel about this?" "What makes him comfortable?" "What's important to her, here?" When spouses care for each other's differences in this way, the marriage becomes a space that honors two voices, sees two needs equally, and considers two worlds. You can see how this would create a great deal of harmony!

As you honor and respect each other's differences, it becomes much easier to go one step further and actually give thanks for the unique gifts you each bring to the family and to the world around you. Why? Because making space for each other tends to bring about the best versions of each other. So try to stay focused on the greater good that can exist between you, work together as a team, embrace your differences, and remember to say "thank you." In these ways, your family can become a strong foundation for His will to take place through you both, as you build each other up "according to [each of your] needs, that it may benefit those who listen" (Eph. 4:29 [NIV]).

Pray for your spouse and your marriage. This is one of the greatest gifts you can give your marriage! Pray for God to renew your marriage in Him each day as you work together at finding your purpose in Him. Pray also for God to help you love your spouse in the ways they need most, so they can have every opportunity to be their best self. Pray for Him to help you see your own struggles and to empower you to overcome them, and pray for your spouse when she goes through difficult times. Ask God also to help him in ways you cannot—to perhaps soften his heart, show mercy, or control his temper. Just saying those prayers has the power to soften your own heart and create necessary compassion for your spouse, because your prayers invite empathy into your perspective. Overall, when you invite God into your marriage, you'll find yourself judging less, letting go of more, and giving God the opportunity to heal the hurts that you cannot.

Be generous. It's easy to move through life looking at the people we love without really seeing them, hearing them without really listening to what they have to say. Yet, when we have a generous heart, we choose to notice the people God has placed in our lives to love. As the Bible says, "Do not withhold good from those to whom it is due, / when it is in your power to act" (Prov. 3:27 [NIV]).

Some of the most meaningful gifts people give us aren't extravagant or expensive but are rather small, thoughtful gestures that indicate a generous heart. Love is often in the details! "As I was out running my errands today, I stopped at your favorite coffee shop to bring you that latte you always enjoy!" Or, "I stopped at the hardware store to pick up that tool you need but haven't had time to get." When we interrupt our lives to go out of our way for something our spouse values, we show generosity. We often associate generosity with money, but showing it toward our spouse more often means choosing generosity with our time, our words, and our actions.

Cultivate an attitude of forgiveness. Have you ever felt that your spouse has wronged you? Reacted angrily when you felt you just didn't deserve it? Treated you in a way that felt completely unjust? When these moments happen, most of us get angry—that's natural. But sometimes we allow our minds to attach so much to feeling wronged that we begin to attribute our hurt to more negative and lasting aspects of our partner's character as a whole. This leads us, in turn, toward hypervigilance: before we know it, we're noticing their faults more and more, and forgetting their good qualities, as we silently and secretly disconnect and continue to convince ourselves of the truth of our own narrative.

It's important to stop this cycle in its tracks! Instead, we need to cultivate a willingness to "forgive and forget." "A good marriage," Ruth Graham, Billy Graham's wife, often said, "consists of two good forgivers."[2] This couldn't be more true! When we choose not to forgive our spouse, we become more loyal to our negativity than to our marriage itself. We abide in it, and we follow its supposed truths. Rather, let's seek to follow the instruction of St. Paul, who tells us to "get rid of all bitterness, rage, anger, harsh words, and slander, as well as all types of evil behavior. Instead, be kind to each other, tenderhearted, forgiving one another, just as God through Christ has forgiven you" (Eph. 4:31-32 [NLT]). God calls us to forgive others just as He has forgiven us. "Father Nick and Dr. Roxanne, that's so difficult," you might say. And yes, you're right; it *is* difficult, because forgiving people always is! You might even think, "I'm not someone who forgives easily," to which we would reply, "Join the ranks!" Yet our Lord commanded us to do so, and marriages cannot succeed without it.

Practice kindness and gratitude. Even though we hear in the Book of Proverbs that "gracious words are like a honeycomb, / sweetness to the soul and health to the body" (16:24 [ESV]), when we notice something positive, how often do we share it out loud? Kindness becomes a verb when we see something beautiful in someone *and* we choose to tell them. It may only take a second to share, but those words can last a lifetime within someone's soul.

When was the last time you told your spouse how much you love and appreciate him? Nationally renowned relationship psychologist Dr. John Gottman found, in his over forty years of research on marriage, that successful marriages have at least a 5:1 ratio of positive to negative interactions with each other. He coined this discovery The Magic Ratio. Through his observations, he found that successful couples seem to possess a more positive balance to their interactions. They expressed love, gentleness, and understanding five times more often than harshness, defensiveness, and criticism. They also communicated affirmations and appreciation five times more often than complaints. Gottman's observations specified positive interactions as expressing interest in each other and showing affection, and during conflict, teasing each other to help ease the tension, empathizing with and accepting each other's viewpoints, and remembering the positive about each other.[3] In striving to keep a 5:1 ratio even amidst conflict, we remember the wisdom written over two thousand years prior by King Solomon that "a soft answer turns away wrath, / but a harsh word stirs up anger" (Prov. 15:1 [ESV]).

Practicing kindness and showing appreciation to our partners can make a huge difference in our marriages—so praise your spouse often. Joke with her. Notice him. Listen to and empathize with her struggles. Tell your husband how amazing he is and why he inspires you. Tell your wife how good she makes you feel, how great of a mother she is, and how thankful you feel for all the work she does. And remember to be genuine in your praise: Don't allow your words to say one thing while your face says another, and try to make your praise specific to your partner rather than a generalized statement that would fit any spouse. Your spouse will see through that every time!

Make it a point this week to be intentional in expressing your appreciation to one another by saying two words to the person you love: "Thank you." Pay attention to the small things your spouse does for you every day to love and care for you—and make notice of it aloud—*even if* he doesn't tell you he needs that. You can never go wrong with giving thanks; it's one of life's greatest reinforcers. Those who feel appreciated will often do more than we ever expect of them. Our families are gifts from God, and how we care for them is our gift back to Him.

Show mercy. Remember the Parable of the Prodigal Son (Luke 15:11-32)? Who does the father run toward at the end of the story? The son who had taken his wealth and squandered it in degenerate living! Not only that, but the gospel tells us the father had constantly waited for his son to return, craning his neck to see if he could catch a glimpse of him. Indeed, we could summarize the whole story of the Bible as "God reaching out to us." How, then, could we do less for our spouses? On what grounds could we possibly withhold mercy from them?

God has brought us together for His purposes, and we each possess different strengths and weaknesses. He intends that we form a winning team—a team that glorifies Him. So when someone on the team falters, makes mistakes, or makes us angry, we shouldn't respond with righteous condemnation but rather with mercy and lifting each other up. This is how we help each other in marriage when one of us falls. God has placed you in your marriage to help you both reach *His* purposes, not to judge your spouse along the way.

The recipe for mercy includes empathy as a primary ingredient. Empathy makes mercy easier to practice because it increases our capacity to understand or feel what another person experiences from within their frame of reference. Empathy says, "I care enough about who you are and what you're experiencing to understand better why you might have done what you did or said what you said." It's hard, though, to have empathy when we're upset or when we're the reason someone else is upset, because it's challenging to empathize with or validate someone's feelings when negativity is present. But, oh, how powerfully this can de-escalate our anger toward someone we love and bring about healing. The next time your spouse upsets you, try stepping out of your cause, your agenda, and your defenses, and try instead to understand why he acted the way he did.

Respect your spouse. All of us want our spouses to respect us, but sometimes we fall short of doing for them what we expect them to do for us. Saint Paul, in writing to the people of Rome about the need to show respect and honor, said, "Be devoted to one another in love. Honor one another above yourselves" (Rom. 12:10 [NIV]). God calls us to "outdo" each other and be intentional in the way we show respect to our spouse, not only in the good times, but more importantly when we feel hurt. That means that we avoid disrespectful means of communication like blame, criticism, condescension, and accusation, which work like acid to eventually eat away at the soul of our relationship with our spouse. These forms of disrespect leave lasting hurt that continues to corrupt our friendship even once the hurtful moment has passed. Instead, we need to show respect for our partner through sensitivity in our approach to hurt, being careful not to criticize or overreact but to ask simply for what we need, rather than naming everything we don't. We show respect when we listen actively and attentively enough to understand our spouse's feelings, and we show it when we make room for her needs and preferences—even when they might conflict with our own.

In order to create space for our spouse's needs and preferences, we first need to know what they are! So take some time to consider how your spouse would answer the following questions. And if you don't know—ask!

- What helps your spouse feel loved?
- What's something your spouse most likes to be noticed for?
- How does your spouse like to spend free evenings?
- How does he or she prefer to wind down from a long day?
- How does your spouse like to approach date nights or structure weekends?
- How does your spouse like to be taken care of when stressed?

Keep in mind that getting to know your spouse's needs and preferences is a lifelong process, and that sometimes preferences may change as the marriage evolves. So do this exercise often, and feel free to add your own questions to the list.

Show humility. Sometimes—especially during arguments— we feel tempted to point out all the things we do for the good of the marriage and family because we think this will help us win an argument—or at least demonstrate our goodness and how hard we work, how much we sacrifice, etc. At times, we may even want to show how much *better* we behave than how we feel our spouse is currently behaving. But in reality, only God gives us the strength to do good works, and the Apostle Paul encourages us to act "with all humility and gentleness, with patience, bearing with one another in love" (Eph. 4:2 [ESV]). So, when we don't demonstrate humility, we fall into the trap of having false pride. We can't see the truth of our situations, as we were warned in Proverbs 11:2 (NIV) when King Solomon says, "When pride comes, then comes disgrace, / but with humility comes wisdom."

How does this play out? In arguments, when we lack humility, we may find ourselves digging in, asserting that our perspective is the "right" one—and we're unable to see and make room for opposing viewpoints. This prevents listening openly and genuinely to our partner's perspective with the goal of truly understanding them, recognizing that there are always two valid experiences in any situation. And because our pride keeps us from seeing other valid perspectives, it also means we might struggle to see our own faults and to acknowledge that something we've done might have affected our partner in ways we didn't intend. So without humility, we may fight hard to prove our point and to feel like we've "won" an argument, but it could come at the cost of "losing" our relationship. Having humility means truly listening to our partner's hurts with the goal of understanding, rather than correcting or winning, and then becoming comfortable with saying the words, "I'm sorry," "I regret saying or doing that," or "I understand how you could have felt that way, now that you've explained it." Remember, God often puts people in our lives to help us grow and to enable us to see ourselves better through the lens of the image of Christ. Healthy spouses help each other grow when they allow humility to drive their interactions, because then, their faith becomes more important than whatever argument they face.

Beyond these spiritual virtues, through our practices as priest and psychologist we've found a variety of practical keys that help us renew our marriages and keep our connections with our spouses fresh.

Cultivate a Spirit of Friendship

At times, often because of the busyness of our everyday lives, a marriage can start to feel more like a business partnership than a relationship. Maybe you've experienced this! This tends to happen when we move through our lives so focused on our shared responsibilities of managing finances, the home, our children, and our careers that we forget to take time out to cultivate love and friendship. Though together in the same home physically, moving through life this way can cause us to feel completely alone as our lives run parallel to each other, rarely intersecting long enough for us to even have a real conversation about something other than the things we co-manage. When you can no longer have fun with, be playful with, receive affection from, or have conversations of real depth with your spouse, it's often a sign that your marriage has become a business partnership rather than a real friendship.

The other day, when we went out to dinner as a family, we couldn't help noticing a couple sitting near us. They barely spoke to one another; instead, they alternated between looking off into the distance and checking their cell phones. They sat close to each other yet seemed a world away, and we couldn't help wondering what happened to get them to that place. Surely at one time they were a happy couple, filled with fondness and mutual admiration for each other, with lots to share and hear. While we observed them, we thought about how easy it is for any relationship to fall into this sort of loveless and lonely existence.

During times of distance and disconnection, it's easy for the enemy to get a foothold in our marriage, because we can get preoccupied with everything that's wrong about each other instead of rejoicing in everything that's right. When we haven't spent time prioritizing our relationship with our spouse, we begin to lose sight of what we enjoy most about each other. When was the last time you and your spouse paused to truly immerse yourselves in the moments you share? When did you last contemplate with gratitude *what is good* about each other? Here's a story from Dr. Roxanne that illustrates how this can play out in a marriage:

After returning home from work late one night, one of my clients decided to spend a few minutes sitting with her husband before going to bed. What came out of his mouth next infuriated her. "What, so I guess I have to make my own dinner?" he asked. Filled with anger, she thought, "The audacity!" She told him dinner was on the stove and sarcastically asked, "Do I need to plate it for you?" They both went to bed angry.

The next day, she tried bringing up the issue with him. "What did you really want from me?" she asked. But she got no response. "It felt like a dead end, like it was all just a test," she explained to me. "It's like he just wanted to know that I would do it for him."

When I inquired further, I learned that since having kids, this couple no longer spent much time together, and his new work hours had made this even worse. The husband had been expressing for a long time that he didn't feel like a priority in his wife's life. And this was true, she admitted. When she arranged her day, she didn't include protected time for him, specifically, or for them as a couple. Though not purposefully ignoring him, she instead gave all her time to their kids, the home, her job, and what little remained to her own needs. It became clear that he only wanted her to plate his food because he wanted to see if he was still important to her.

When we continually immerse ourselves in everyday details and don't return to each other to share our lives, or when we find ourselves complaining about our partner and forgetting what it means to be friends—in some cases even thinking the grass might be greener with someone else—then we're headed for trouble. This is often where betrayal is born. When we betray our spouse through our actions, it often means we've already been betraying them in our mind for years by ignoring the friendship and silently simmering about what we don't like about them without ever really communicating any of it.

It's not that healthy couples don't struggle; it's just that despite their struggles, their friendship helps them remember what they love about each other. *Healthy couples know that even in the midst of a fight, they have a reason to repair their relationship! They miss the love because it was there before the fight. They miss the mutual dependence because it was there before the fight. They miss the fun they had, and the laughter, and how much they enjoyed spending time together because, yes, these too were there before the fight.*

So, when we find our friendship with our spouse faltering, how do we rebuild and renew it? One key is to make sure we work together as a team to conquer the responsibilities of life—especially with child-rearing and domestic responsibilities—so that one person doesn't start to resent shouldering a heavier burden. While it's not necessary, or even possible, to come up with a perfectly even, fifty-fifty arrangement, the breakdown of household tasks needs to work for both you and your spouse so that you each feel satisfied with the workload. And the truth is, spouses in healthy relationships don't usually make a decision to do something for their spouse based on what's fair, in a tit-for-tat manner; they make it based on an honest and sincere desire to see that person happy. When you have a good friendship, you don't mind doing things for each other, because you view yourselves as playing for the same team. That sense of connection makes *giving freely* to one another seem natural. Of course, you'll have times when one of you may contribute more, or less, and it may seem unfair, but picking up each other's burdens when the other is down helps to make relationships work.

Chances are, though, if you find yourself getting caught up often in "who did what last" arguments and fights over the dishes, it could signal that the two of you need to give the friendship part of your marriage more attention. Perhaps you haven't had fun together in a while, or maybe you've ignored your personal needs for too long. Try to dig deep the next time you notice yourself keeping track of "who did what," and pay mindful attention to what else you might need (more time to relax, more fun together, more ways to manage your stress, and so on). Then, ask for that in a way that doesn't shovel blame onto your partner but lets her into your world and allows her to know you even better. And don't forget to encourage him to do the same! Check in with each other often and ask questions like, "How can I help?" or "Do you need help with that?" Sometimes just the asking alone is enough to tell your spouse, "I see you. I care about you. I can't wait to spend time with you."

Spend Quality Time Together

Our daily busyness, as well as our human tendency to take for granted the people we've had in our lives for a long time, both lead us to forget the importance of spending quality time together. Let's see how Father Nick has experienced this:

> When you first fall in love, you think of that beloved person all the time! I remember the first time I met Roxanne. I loved how she talked, how she brought such a poised presence into the room, and the graceful way she handled herself. I was just mesmerized!

> One night as we approached the dinner table, I had hoped to sit beside Roxanne, but her dad asked, "Nick, why don't you come and sit next to me?" so I complied. I always enjoyed talking with Roxanne's dad because he was an amazing Renaissance man; he knew a lot about many different topics. But during that dinner, I couldn't stop looking at the other end of the dining room table at Roxanne.

> At one point, her dad posed a question: "So, Nick, tell me about the First Ecumenical Council!" And I replied distractedly, "Well, it began in 325 AD," while still looking over at Roxanne. He tried again, "So, Nick, tell me about the Great Schism." And I answered, "Well, it took place in 1054," and as I spoke, I leaned back to get a better view of Roxanne.

Again he queried, "Nick, so tell me about the fall of the Byzantine Empire," to which I replied, "Well, it took place in 1453," and went back to looking at Roxanne.

Eventually, as I kept staring at Roxanne, she suddenly looked up, and her eyes met mine. Busted! Throughout that dinner, my mind kept saying, "Nick, look down, look away." But no matter how hard I tried, I couldn't. That's how the first blush of love feels!

Fast forward into my ministry as a priest, to a time when we faced some pretty big challenges and struggles in the parish: All I wanted to do was heal the community. I spent all my time visiting people, setting up meetings, and generally trying to solve all the problems. In time our parish did turn a corner, and things became a little easier for me. Through God's grace, our church began to grow.

But one day, in the midst of all my efforts, I looked behind me and it seemed as if my wife and kids stood far away from me, at a great distance. They had supported me and loved me through everything, yet in that moment, I realized *I hadn't been there for them*, and because of my inattention, we were drifting apart. One day my four-year-old son even told me, "Baba, you're a good priest to the people, but you aren't a good priest to us." His innocent comment brought me to my knees. I realized I had been neglecting my first church—my home. That comment changed the course of my life as a parent and a spouse, and today I go on regular date nights with Roxanne and have lunch periodically with the kids at school.

Dr. John Gottman, noted psychologist and marriage researcher, found that two-thirds of couples experience a drop in the quality and satisfaction of their relationship within the first three years following the birth of a child.[4] They now have to plan dates and arrange babysitters, and dinnertime conversations become child-focused. At the other end of the spectrum, numerous studies show happiness actually increases for empty nesters.[5] Why? They experience fewer interruptions and less stress in daily life; couples have more time for conversations and shared activities.

Fortunately, with a few changes, you won't have to wait for your children to leave the house to have a happy marriage again. You can do this by making your time together something you can depend on. In our home, we have many unsaid yet agreed-upon times we spend together. We love to go for walks after dinner or have coffee outside together on Saturday mornings. When our children do come along on walks, they naturally ride ahead on their bikes or dribble with their soccer ball, playful in their own ways, which allows the two of us to truly catch up. It's our time to take deep breaths and connect, free of distraction. We also enjoy spending time together on weeknights after the children head up to bed. Even if we only have an hour, it's still time to ourselves. We may watch our favorite show or do our own work, but we sit on the couch together during this time, allowing for occasional interruptions to share something with each other.

Much of our time together occurs in short spurts sprinkled throughout the week rather than in elaborately planned dates—but these short amounts add up over time. And we try to plan dates too! I (Dr. Roxanne) realized that if I purchase tickets for something, the date becomes a commitment we add to our calendars. So, we love concerts and musicals partly for that very reason. We also try to check in with each other at various points throughout our day with a quick text. And when Father Nick drops off the kids at school, he passes my office on his way to work before I've begun seeing patients. When he approaches my office, he calls on his cell and says, "Look outside!" and begins waving. I return the greeting by moving my office blinds up and down, then we both laugh and hang up. It doesn't take more than thirty seconds, but it's a great start to our day. Small things done frequently provide the backbone to our relationship.

While these small things do add up, also make sure to take time each week to turn off your phones, your computers, your televisions, and your mental to-do lists, and choose instead to focus on protecting time with your spouse with no agenda. And keep in mind, during quality time, we can foster connection with both silence and conversation. Sometimes just existing with each other is enough, while other times we have lots to share. When you have the energy to talk, asking open-ended questions (examples are listed at the end of this chapter) can help you feel more connected. It's amazing what we can learn about the people we love when we ask creative questions! Talk about your hopes, your goals, or what you feel God's purpose is for your life. Talk about how you felt during the day, not just what you did. Talk about the things that made you laugh and the things that made you cry. Share the running tape that has existed in your own head lately, and be mindful of how much you may have forgotten to share with your spouse as your busy week went along. This is your chance to receive love and to invite your partner to know you better as you move through life's journey. Too often we keep these feelings and experiences to ourselves, or we might share only with trusted friends, which can hurt the friendship we have with our spouse.

When your partner shares, try to align with them! This is *not* the time to point out her flaws or what he could be doing better. This is the time to be a friend and to show that you "get it." Show genuine interest and communicate your support, and avoid saying things like "I told you so" or, "Well, you shouldn't have been late turning in that report to your boss." Remember, *he or she is your friend and is sharing in request of support, love, and understanding, not solutions or lessons.*

Consider how to increase your quality time with your spouse. As you come to the end of this section, take a moment right now to think of something simple you can add to your daily routine to help you and your spouse connect. Don't wait for your spouse to make the first move: Take responsibility for your own part in the marriage and think about what *you* can do!

Figure Out Your Conflict Styles

Of course, even when we make our best effort to cultivate our spouse's friendship, we will still have conflict at times. Even those of us in happy marriages can probably rattle off the last time we felt offended by our spouse. No one is perfect, right? It happens to us all! The critical point to remember is that how we handle our grievances will either make—or break—our marriage. Are we holding on to our anger? Are we willing to address areas of unresolved conflict in a way that brings us to solutions? Or has our anger just turned into a dead end, a tunnel of darkness that leaves us disconnected and in despair?

There are two types of anger styles that may trap us and keep us from having a healthy marriage. So when we talk about conflict, it's important to cultivate self-awareness and learn whether we fit into one of these styles.

The angry avoider. We touched on this in Chapter 3, with the "avoiding person" concept—but let's go into more detail here. Some spouses tend toward either "fight" or "flight" reactions during conflict. We call the person prone to flight, the angry avoider. A woman married to such an angry avoider once described her feelings to us:

> "He's jealous when I go out and do things that don't involve him," she said, "and he'll end up giving me the silent treatment if I decide to go out and do them anyway. I try to ignore him, but in my mind, honestly,

I'm thinking, 'How childish.' Sometimes we can go days without talking."

"What if you thought of your spouse as being on your same team?" we asked her. "If he needs something but doesn't know how to articulate it, ask yourself how you could help your team—your relationship—win. What would happen if you gave him the words for what he doesn't know how to express?"

"Try this approach instead," we continued. " 'I know you don't like it when I'm busy' (notice his need without judging him). 'I get that, and I enjoy spending time with you, too' (empathize with him and validate his feelings). 'Let's take a look together at what we can do to protect more time for us while still enabling me to continue those activities that are most important to my well-being.' Remember, your angry-avoider spouse may withdraw simply because he or she doesn't have the tools to communicate strong feelings effectively."

If *you* are the angry avoider, consider your reason for the avoidance. Perhaps you've brought something up previously that didn't go well, and now you choose to avoid any fight at all because you anticipate the conflict will go poorly again. Or perhaps you avoid conflict because one or both of you escalate quickly in hurt and anger. Or maybe you avoid the issue because you aren't exactly sure yet what you're most upset about, or maybe you're trying to decide whether or not you can just let it go. You need to practice discernment here. Sometimes we can let go of things, since it's best to let go of minor, everyday irritations whenever possible. Plenty of small annoyances come up in a marriage! For instance, perhaps your spouse isn't managing her household tasks well due to her increased job responsibilities at work. Or perhaps he snaps at you during a time of extra stress. Not everything requires a conversation!

However, when grievances linger for days on end, it usually indicates a festering issue that God tugs at our hearts to put into words. A lingering grievance can become a distraction to such a point that we're unable to focus on our daily spiritual renewal in Christ—nor even on the rote tasks we need to get done. And buried frustrations will always bubble up to the surface eventually. In fact, because memories are emotionally encoded, when new upsets occur, the floodgates of our minds come crashing open, releasing all the other upsets we've tried to repress that brought on that same feeling. And unfortunately, nothing good comes from overwhelming our spouse with ten years of grievances in one conversation. It's best to stick to one issue in any conflict conversation.

Another thing to consider: *angry avoiders sometimes hope that ignoring a hurt or point of tension will translate into actually letting it go.* Nothing could be further from the truth! Passively avoiding a festering issue while the problem continues will create a slow bleed within the marriage, and as the collection of hurts grows, so does our emotional distance. We end up withdrawing affection and laughter, and playfulness, ease of conversation, and emotional closeness all become distant memories. We struggle to create new positive moments with our spouse, but we're only half-heartedly present because the bad feelings continue to simmer on the back burner. We end up just going through the motions rather than having a real relationship. We also impact our children, because they will intuitively feel the disconnection; they can sense the things we're *not* saying.

So when you just can't let go of a festering feeling, it's time to put words on it. When you do, be patient and kind, as 1 Corinthians 13:4 instructs us, and avoid blame. Try to stick to describing your feelings and preferences rather than defining your spouse's mistakes or intentions. Too often, when we bring up grievances, we not only define what someone did to hurt us, we also assert *why* they did it, too. It's not our job to assign or define someone else's motives, and anytime we do, we're only likely to create defensiveness in the other—which makes the whole conversation counterproductive. Most people respond better to encouragement than criticism! And most spouses want us to give them the tools to help them love us better (as long as we do so kindly and gently), both out of genuine affection for us and also so that we can sing their praises and help them feel more worthwhile as our spouse. It's a win–win situation! And remember, when love tempers our conflicts, we follow what God intends for us as we *speak "the truth in love,"* which allows us to "grow to become in every respect the mature body of him who is the head, that is, Christ" (Eph. 4:15 [NIV]).

The angry reactor. Remember the angry reactor from Chapter 3? Angry reactors unleash anger in ways that can cause lasting hurt in their partners, perhaps even reacting in anger before hearing the whole story. The angry-reactor personality can be highly volatile and not very self-aware, and their reactions cause harm to themselves as well as their partner. As Proverbs 18:13 puts it, "He who answers a matter before he hears *it,* / It *is* folly and shame to him." When upset, this person looks outward for someone to blame, rather than taking ownership for his own moods. During a reactive episode, the angry reactive spouse has difficulty listening to, internalizing, or understanding his spouse's perspective. This type of anger can exist in both the angry reactor and the angry avoider, though it's more common in the reactor. When you're married to an angry reactor, you aren't at ease in your relationship, and keeping your distance may actually seem like the best approach. Yet avoiding a reactive spouse creates a chasm in the marriage that is not easily breached.

Angry reactors tend to base their reactions on a foundation of unhealthy, judgmental, negative, accusatory, or righteous thinking they express in hostile and condemning tones. The common thread here is the angry reactor's disapproval of the other's character, upbringing, or personality. The reactor doesn't usually have a request buried underneath her anger— she simply wants to unleash it and disparage the other person. This type of anger lacks empathy and doesn't allow for individual differences. It doesn't look for a solution or a way out; rather, it seeks an outlet for hostility and judgment.

This type of anger raises our blood pressure and results in a state of agitation in both the giver and the receiver. We should avoid it at all costs! When it comes your way, it's best to respectfully disengage, stating, "I want to understand what you're looking for, but I'm having a very hard time listening right now. I would like to have this conversation again at a later point, when we're both calm enough to honor our needs without inflicting so much hurt."

We need to differentiate the angry reactor from someone who speaks healthfully but struggles with their own emotional intensity, which they may not know how to regulate. How do we know the difference? As a listener you can discern between these two types of anger. Try asking questions such as, "What do you need?" or "What do you hope to see happen?" The angry reactor may only continue their rant, unwilling to work toward solutions. But the healthier person will answer those questions and will usually de-escalate when they feel understood.

If we ourselves are the angry reactor or avoider, we need to learn more productive approaches to our anger. And remember, anger can have productive results when it teaches us about what we value and what we need. For example, if you feel angry when your spouse comes home from work and walks into the house while talking on their cell phone rather than greeting you, this tells you that being greeted is important to you. "Productive anger" like this helps us find—and express—the desire for connection beneath the anger.

So the next time you feel angry, ask yourself "What outcome am I looking for in this situation? Can I ask for something that would solve this problem, or do I just want to vent?" If you're honest with yourself and find your intentions aren't toward growth and a better marriage, take steps to change this pattern! Nursing a spirit of angry criticism will disrupt your own peace and lessen the chances that you and your spouse will ever make a real connection.

Learn How to Fight Well

Someone asked us a great question once: "In a marriage, is it better to never fight or to fight often?" We responded, "Either! What matters is that when we do fight, we must fight well, and if we don't fight, we must be living well."

Marriage requires combining two perspectives, and learning how to face and resolve conflict can be a healthy process that helps us effectively merge our lives. For some couples who happen to share a lot in common—values and perspectives, and sometimes even preferences—not fighting works well, not because they avoid important issues but because they simply have less to argue about!

Most of us encounter conflict in our marriages at some point, though, and when this happens, we encourage you to channel any anger you feel toward your spouse into trying to understand the "why" so you can better seek the "what"— doing what you can to bring healing to your relationship. Fighting well means accepting each other well, making room for each other by keeping our focus on bringing unity and collective good to the bond we share. It's doing what honors the relationship instead of what honors only our own agenda.

Through all conflict, it's helpful to keep this scripture in mind: "May God, who gives this patience and encouragement, help you live in complete harmony with each other, as is fitting for followers of Christ Jesus. Then all of you can join together with one voice, giving praise and glory to God. . . . Therefore, accept each other just as Christ has accepted you so that God will be given glory" (Rom. 15:5-7 [NLT]). God doesn't call us to judge or criticize our spouses for who they are or what they need, but to accept them—just as Christ has accepted us.

To do this, we must operate on the premise that *it's not our job to convince our partner that the way we see things is the "right way" or the "only way"—or that the way they see things is "completely wrong."* Fighting well isn't about determining who's right and who's wrong, because there's usually no firm answer to that; it's solely determined by the perspective of the person. Our goal in a conflict, then, is to explain our view with transparency and vulnerability and to seek to understand our spouse well enough to try to reach some common ground. When this happens, the relationship grows based on newfound understandings of one another, and it makes room for two valid realities, two sets of emotions about those realities, and two different experiences and perspectives.

So the next time you feel defensive in response to your spouse's anger, try thinking, "Just because my spouse feels upset doesn't mean I've done something wrong. This is her perspective on something she needs. My job is to understand it, try to make room for it, and definitely not judge it." Remembering this may help you listen more intently for the raw and vulnerable feelings and desires that underly your spouse's words.

In fighting well, we must also remember God has equipped us for survival in life, and so we often react quickly, without thinking it through first, to situations we see as threatening. Approaching a fight with accusations, strong tones, and personal attacks will cause our spouse to feel threatened and only evoke the fight-or-flight response in him. *Once a conversation triggers this, the goal often shifts to self-preservation rather than marital preservation.* The attack—whether real or perceived—causes our brain to switch from its typical slow-paced, thoughtful, problem-solving, empathetic, and reasonable regulation in our prefrontal cortex (the most sophisticated part of our brains) to the more reflexive and rapid emotional response dictated by the amygdala (a more primitive region of our brain).

When this switch occurs, we go from responding to reacting, and our bodies channel all our resources toward self-protection. We can no longer listen calmly to see other perspectives or take in new information to seek understanding; instead, we now fight, freeze, or flee for protection. We've left the conversation physically, or emotionally, or both. This happens because our heart rate increases, our lungs expand to take in more oxygen, our vision narrows, our blood pressure increases, our digestion slows, and blood flows away from the prefrontal cortex—the region necessary for rational thought—and toward our extremities. Said simply, when we feel threatened, our prefrontal cortex no longer guides our reasoning, self-control, inhibition, problem-solving abilities, and decision-making. Yet we need that part of our brain to stay active during conflict!

So, how can we stay calm in the midst of conflict? Psychologist and marriage therapist Dr. John Gottman found in his forty years of marriage research that 96 percent of the time, the way a conversation ends has everything to do with *how it began within the first three minutes.*[6] So it's important to practice gentleness in the face of anger from the very beginning of an argument. As King Solomon wrote in Proverbs (ESV), "A soft answer turns away wrath, / but a harsh word stirs up anger" (15:1) and, "A gentle tongue is a tree of life, / but perverseness in it breaks the spirit" (15:4).

Dr. Gottman further helps us fight well when he describes four bad habits in marriage that he calls the Four Horsemen of the Apocalypse.[7] These actions destroy relationships, so we need to do our best to avoid them! The first is **criticism,** in which we globally attack our spouse's character or personality with statements about what he did wrong or what's wrong with her as a person. It often begins with statements such as "you always" or "you never." Criticism often indicates judgment, not a truth, and will invariably create defensiveness in those on the receiving end. Instead, try to make a specific request for what you'd like your spouse to do differently in the future, rather than throwing out an accusation about what's wrong with her because of what she did. For example, instead of saying, "You never make any plans for us; everything you do is all about you," try, "I sometimes feel left out of all you do outside of us. How about if we start protecting more time to spend together?"

Defensiveness often happens in response to criticism, because we want to protect ourselves. We correct our partner's accusations in an attempt to clear our name of the crime. It doesn't work, because critical attacks are judgments, not simply facts that we can clear up with reasonable evidence. Defensiveness can sometimes be disguised by a victim stance, when people say things like, "Oh sure, right, it's always me. I never do anything to help." Here, mutual understanding disappears, and only entrenched positions remain. To help avoid defensiveness, we need to hear each other out without preparing our defense while the other person is still talking, and we need to make sure the listener doesn't feel attacked! When we receive polite requests rather than global attacks about who we are, we're much more likely to try to accommodate our spouse and understand his or her perspective.

Gottman's third Horseman of the Apocalypse is **contempt,** which means treating your spouse as undeserving of respect by calling him names or engaging in other toxic behaviors. (Gottman's research has shown this as the number-one predictor of failed relationships.) And the fourth is **stonewalling,** which happens when one spouse communicates nonverbally that he or she has "checked out" of the interaction. With stonewalling, you might notice behaviors like looking away with crossed arms, appearing uninterested, or one-word answers with a facial expression that says, "I'm not hearing anything you're saying." Stonewalling, left unattended, can morph into the silent treatment. We must recognize that stonewalling often comes about when someone feels overwhelmed with emotion and doesn't know how to calm down, which can happen in fight-or-flight mode. When this happens, we need to take time off to self-soothe and come back when we feel more able to engage and less threatened.

One way to keep the Four Horsemen from invading your marriage is to create pre-fight plans that help you fight well. In our marriage, Father Nick and I have a set of pre-fight plans guided by I Corinthians 13:4-7 (NIV): "Love is patient, love is kind. It does not envy, it does not boast, it is not proud. It does not dishonor others, it is not self-seeking, it is not easily angered, it keeps no record of wrongs. Love does not delight in evil but rejoices with the truth. It always protects, always trusts, always hopes, always perseveres." With God's grace, we try to abide by these principles as best as possible. Our pre-fight plan includes not swearing or using bad language in our arguments. It says that we don't keep score, so a statement such as, "Roxanne, you did this five years ago on that one Tuesday, don't you remember?" isn't allowed. We also try to keep current, handling each offense as it comes up so resentment doesn't build up. We don't criticize or name-call or make generalizations about each other. We try to avoid words like *always* and *never*, and we attempt to stick to just the argument of the moment. We don't carry these plans out with perfection, but they guide us so that we can realize when we've strayed, and they help us know how to reset. They've saved the day for us many times, since in many ways, we have completely opposite personalities and temperaments!

We've found that having some simple scripts on hand as part of our pre-fight plan can help so much.

For example, try using this one for your next conflict: "When _____ happened, I noticed feeling _____, and I thought _____. I now realize that I would prefer if, moving forward, we _____, because I've realized that I _____." So, rather than saying, "You don't do anything in this house to help me; you leave it all for me," try instead, "When I came home the other night, I felt overwhelmed by all that needed to be done and I thought, I just don't have the energy for this. I realize now that I need your help in keeping up with certain things at home because I can't do as much as I thought I could, and when I try, I just feel run down and too tired to do anything that actually makes me happy. How about if, moving forward, you spend more time with the kids during dinner prep so I can take on dinner without so much distraction?"

Here's another example. Rather than saying, "All you ever do is work, and you don't even look my way or make me a priority," try, "I've been feeling really alone lately; I think sometimes I'm not sure anymore of how you feel about me. I realize now that it's probably just that I'd like to make spending more time with each other a priority, because I don't like to feel so distant from you. Can we take a look at our calendars and map out some time to spend together?"

And another. Rather than, "You never back me up with the kids," try, "I notice you often stay quiet when I discipline the kids, and sometimes it feels like you don't agree with what I'm doing. I need your support with the children so we can be a more unified front. Can we talk about how you could support me in those moments? Is there something

I do that makes that hard for you? If you don't always agree with the value I am teaching, can we agree to talk about that in private?"

These approaches require a bit of thinking and preparation before you begin. However, you'll find the payoff greater than the effort it took to approach it intentionally. The next time you find yourself wanting to accuse, blame, or criticize your spouse, decide how you can turn it into a request instead. If you can't do that, you may not be ready to talk about it.

Here's a great, real-life example of how using requests can work better than accusing, blaming, and so on. In our marriage seminars, a common area of stress people mention is relationships with in-laws. A young woman complained to us recently about her husband's unpleasant and rather negative feelings toward her mother. "Every time my parents visit, he points out everything he dislikes about my mother," she said. "In the beginning it wasn't such a big deal, but now, I'm tired of it. She isn't that bad!" Over time, this woman had become increasingly more closed off from her husband and more defensive about—and protective of—her mother. This caused her husband to feel distant from his wife and completely alone.

Her husband could have turned the situation around if he'd taken the time to formulate intentional comments rather than just speaking critically. In taking ownership of his feelings, he could have figured out how to ask for what he hoped for. Perhaps he could have thought more about what was really bothering him and why before beginning to complain, and whether those changes were even possible or in his wife's control to make! And instead of criticizing the woman who raised his wife, he could have suggested a few changes in the way they handled her visits. Even though his wife might have felt similar frustrations toward her mother, she was too busy defending her mother to him to even connect to her own emotions on the issue, making it very hard for her to validate any level of his frustrations.

Before we leave this topic, we also want to encourage you to pray before speaking to your spouse about something that has deeply upset you or that the two of you strongly disagree about. Perhaps there might even be a prayer you need to say right now as you read this very section and think about a request you have been needing to make but have been avoiding. Resist the temptation to depend solely on your own will to move through your anger, as we can become quickly derailed even when we have the best of intentions. We need God's help to move through these moments with the grace and love that only His Spirit can provide. Before you begin, ask God to give you a gentle spirit and the words that will bring healing to your marriage in the most fruitful way. Ask Him to give you an open heart and a loving perspective so that together you can find solutions rather than score individual victories. Ask God to give you a soft tone, and pray for your partner's heart to be open to seeing the goodness in yours. Our Lord's words guide us on this: "I am the vine, you *are* the branches. He who abides in Me, and I in him, bears much fruit; for without Me you can do nothing" (John 15:5).

Be a Good Listener

In our marriage, we often joke that God gave us two ears and only one mouth because He intended for us to listen twice as much as we speak! Two headstrong leaders live under our roof; listening well doesn't always come naturally to us, since we both like to talk and have strong emotions and convictions. Yet, since we work in ministry and psychology, we've learned over time what works and what doesn't when it comes to building healthy marriages. This we know: we must learn both how to express ourselves *and* how to listen. Father Nick says:

> As a society, we used to believe that women talked more than men. Although studies now show that's actually a myth,[8] often, I seem to spend all of my words while I'm at work, but Dr. Roxanne saves many of hers for when I get home! But really, she needs to talk to me, and honestly, it doesn't require much from me beyond sitting down and looking her in the eye to make sure we've connected. Husbands, do you want to know the four most romantic words in the world? They are: "And then what happened?"

> We especially focus on three areas in our daily conversations. First, we talk about how our individual lives are going outside of each other—this includes how we feel about current events in the world or the things that happen to us in our day-to-day lives. We also discuss our children—the things they bring to our attention, our hopes for them, our worries and

our joys—*and* lastly, we discuss our schedules so that in our busy lives, we don't fail to plan time for each other, our children, and the other things that are important to us both. We didn't always do this, but since we started sharing our calendars and two major parts of our separate experiences, it's made a big difference in our relationship. And we don't let much time go by before we catch up on what's going on in our lives, which helps us feel consistently connected to one another.

When you sit down to talk and listen to one another, we suggest listening in several specific ways, to make the most of your communication:

Listen to know. Do you ever wonder what your spouse really thinks about? Do you wonder who he really is and what he truly feels? Or what has been keeping her up at night? It's amazing what you can learn about someone when you stop to ask just a few open-ended questions *and* really listen to the response. The truth is, every successful relationship needs a foundation of meaningful conversation, and in our busy world, we rarely find out much from the "How was your day?" question. Rather, take some time every now and then to ask your spouse more specific questions to get to know her better. Trust me, much has changed since the time you first met. At the end of this chapter, you'll find some questions to get you started—but don't feel you need to limit yourself to just those. Try making up some of your own as well!

Listen to support. To show support, let the people you love vent about their lives. And when your partner opens up, you always want to send the message, "It's okay to talk to me, and I'm glad you did." This builds the type of trust your spouse needs in order to feel relief when he's in a tough spot, and the person he loves and feels closest to is the best person to provide that relief. Your supportive and validating response says to your spouse, "You aren't crazy for feeling this way." And when you listen, don't give instructions or advice for how to fix problems or tell your spouse things really aren't that bad. Don't tell her how she could have responded to the situation better or that she shouldn't feel the way she does. All of that only makes people feel more alone in their feelings. What people need most when they share their troubles is comfort, connection, and a safe place to explore their feelings and their interpretations about what they're experiencing. In the end, feeling loved and heard calms the waters of their soul enough so they can eventually solve their own problems.

Listen attentively. Even though we're both trained listeners and we practice the art of listening every day in our jobs, it's still hard for us to do it at home sometimes! Listening well takes practice and patience. Additionally, it's hard to listen when *we* are the reason someone else is upset: it's hard to empathize with or validate someone's feelings when they feel negatively about something *we* have done. Yet, through attentive listening we have the power to change our marriages for the good and to help our spouse, if we can just decide to put aside our egos and "set a guard over [our] mouth[s]"

(Ps. 141:3 [NIV]) while our spouse speaks. Try these techniques the next time you sit down to listen to your spouse:

- Listen without preparing your own reactions or defense.
- Listen to understand something you may not have already known.
- Listen to hear what your partner values underneath the frustration.
- Respond with, "I can see where you're coming from."
- Or respond with, "I understand how you would have felt that way."

Listening well and responding with these sorts of validations can de-escalate a situation with someone who feels hurt and increase his or her ability to now hear you! And keep in mind that you don't need to defend yourself, because in the end, it doesn't matter, since convictions are emotionally encoded and not changed by facts listed in a debate. And people won't usually change their minds until they've first felt completely heard and understood. You'll help this process along if you own up to your own behaviors that may have caused offense or admit regret for any unkind words you've spoken. If you were in the wrong, try to find a way to acknowledge that. When healing the relationship after a conflict, hear out each other's feelings and then acknowledge if, in fact, there's something you regret or wish you hadn't done or said. This step goes a long way toward creating healing that lasts.

Know When to Give It a Rest

Have you ever shared strong feelings but felt like your partner just wouldn't listen? Did you feel like you spoke with conviction, appropriateness, reason, and heartfelt love, but your spouse just attached even more strongly to his own entrenched position and inappropriately displayed anger? Did you feel defeated? Or hopeless? Did you find it hard to maintain your best self? It's hard to remain at our best when someone else isn't acting like his best self. But remember this: "A hot-tempered person stirs up conflict, / but the one who is patient calms a quarrel" (Prov. 15:18 [NIV]). Sometimes it's up to us to give it a rest and calm the quarrel.

We must remember that we can't force someone to listen, and attempting to follow, coerce, convince, or otherwise make someone listen will only end poorly for you both. So how do we treat a non-listener gently? We give her space by taking a break and waiting patiently. And why do we need that space? The Bible is clear, because "starting a quarrel is like opening a floodgate, / so stop before a dispute breaks out" (Prov. 17:14 [NLT]). When our emotions are acute and elevated, we can't have a healthy conversation, because our heart rate shoots up and blood moves from the problem-solving section of our brain into the part of the brain that controls the muscles for fight or flight. When anger is triggered, it takes less than a quarter of a second for our amygdala to respond. What happens then? Adrenaline surges, and our attention narrows as we home in on the target of the anger. Body temperature rises, skin perspires, and blood floods into our extremities to aid us if we need to fight (our hands) or to run (our feet). If we're forced to remain in an argument after this is triggered, this is when we end up saying things we later regret. So, in order to regain control over our anger, it means taking steps to undo the threat response, which will give us more conscious control over how we react to angry feelings. We do this by taking space and using relaxation techniques while trying to reel our thoughts back into healthy and productive territory.

Several things indicate that it's time to take a break from an argument. If you or your spouse find it difficult to listen without becoming defensive, if one of you begins to disengage from the conversation or think about other things, or if you or your spouse talk over each other or have begun chastising each other (*either* in your mind or out loud), then it's time for a break. Continuing the conversation will likely lead to escalation.

So, whether you're stewing in bed or facing off in the kitchen, take a break to think about something else. Listen to soothing music. Breathe deeply to settle your emotions and your pulse. If you can, go for a walk: Physical activity is a powerful mediator of emotional angst. Pray while you walk, and ask God for His guidance. Ask Him to keep your thoughts helpful, to heal you, and to help you keep an open heart. Also, try not to think about the argument from the perspective of what you dislike about your partner, since, as the Bible asks us, "Why do you look at the speck that is in your brother's eye, but do not notice the log that is in your own eye?" (Matt. 7:3 [New American Standard Bible]).

Doing so will only make things worse, so instead, try to think about it from the perspective of what you originally needed and how to come back and ask for that with sensitivity. During your break, bring your mind back to God's love for you and your spouse. Remind yourself that no one is perfect and that your problems have solutions. And then keep your thoughts on those solutions rather than marinating in the problem, and continue to pray that God will help your words bring healing.

As you navigate the landscape of your marriage overall, remember that prayer and your relationship to God are at the root of all! Good communication techniques, building up your friendship, etc., all help—but ultimately, without God we can do nothing.

PRAYER

✠ ✠ ✠

LORD JESUS CHRIST, Your first miracle took place
at a wedding in Cana of Galilee. By Your presence

there, You showed how essential You are in marriage.

You showed us through Your life what a marriage is,

through the wedding band of Christianity when You

gave us the ring of the Holy Cross. We thank You

that You blessed our marriages there, by bringing us

together in love and trust. The day You brought us

together in marriage was a day filled with LOVE.

However, like every relationship, we have times when

we get off course, when we need to be reminded of

what true love is, and more importantly, of Your daily

presence in our lives. Lord, we ask You to enrich

our relationship with love for each other. Remind us that You have blessed us to support each other by forgiving each other's wrongs like You have forgiven us. Empower us in our words and actions to lift each other up and not tear each other down. Equip us to daily look for opportunities to engage each other, constantly learning and growing with each other. Challenge us to not try and make each other who we want each other to be but who You have created us to be. Arm us with Your power to not give the enemy, who desires to destroy this marriage, a foothold. As we journey through this *renewal* in our lives, help us to work toward a renewed marriage, with You at the center of it, so that we may truly live "happily ever after." We praise and glorify the Father, Son, and Holy Spirit. Amen.

✠ ✠ ✠

FOR DISCUSSION:
THE THREE Rs—REST, REFLECT,
AND RESPOND

1. Which of the marriage virtues do you feel your marriage possesses? Which would you like to build up? What are some steps you could take to build those virtues into your marriage?

2. What could you regularly commit to doing with your spouse every day/week/month?

3. What do you love most about your spouse? Have you shared it with him or her recently? If not, please do!

4. Do you have protected time on your calendar for your spouse? If not, think about a good time to connect and ask for it.

5. How do you feel about the division of labor in your household? Is there anything you need that you haven't asked for that may give you more time to spend with your partner?

6. Are there any lingering feelings you haven't addressed but know you probably need to? If so, use the sentence template under the "Fighting Well" section to help you bring this up with your spouse.

7. What changes do you notice in your body when you're angry? Does conflict with your spouse bring you closer or divide you further? Why?

8. What tools can you use from this chapter to help you confront your anger? Listen better?

9. What three steps could you take next time to respond better when a conflict has gone poorly?

10. Give an example of a time when you could have gotten angry, but you showed empathy instead. What was the result?

DR. ROXANNE'S TEN
OPEN-ENDED QUESTIONS

1. If you could wave a magic wand and everything in your life would become exactly as you wished it would be, what three things might be different?

2. Who do you admire most in this world? Why? What three traits do you admire most about that person?

3. What's the best compliment you've ever received?

4. If you could be anyone else in the world for twenty-four hours, who would you choose to be? Why?

5. What's the best thing that's ever happened to you?

6. What's the worst thing that's ever happened to you?

7. What's the one criticism you received that you never could forget?

8. If you could change one characteristic about yourself, what would it be, and why?

9. What do you feel are your greatest gifts?

10. If someone wrote your biography, what would you want them to say about you? What would you want to be known for?

FATHER NICK'S TWELVE MARRIAGE TIPS

1. Keep God first.

2. Show your love for your partner every day in different ways.

3. Make space for your partner's preferences in your day.

4. Spend intentional time with each other, scheduled every week.

5. Express affection unexpectedly.

6. Be humble—apologize sincerely and state your regrets.

7. Compliment freely and often.

8. Be merciful—don't let your mind attach to judgment.

9. Start and end each day with a hug or a kiss.

10. Have fun together—laugh at each other's silliness.

11. Have humor about the qualities of your spouse that would otherwise annoy you.

12. Ask questions and show interest any time your partner shares.

CHAPTER SEVEN

Equip Your Children

*Teach children how they should live, and they will remember
it all their life.* —PROVERBS 22:6 (GNT)

*Parents, do not treat your children in such a way as to make
them angry. Instead, raise them with Christian discipline
and instruction.* —EPHESIANS 6:4 (GNT)

JUST LIKE WE need to renew our marriages in order to
have the strength, energy, and inner peace to go out into
the world and do the work God has given us to do, we also
need to seek renewal in our relationships with our children.
Our home is our base of operations, and if things aren't
working well at home, we'll find ourselves too distracted and
weary to do much good out in the world. Do you know that
this especially holds true for women?[1] While men tend to
feel better when things in the workplace go well, the health
of relationships is key for women. So husbands, even if you
don't feel as distracted by the tensions in your household
as your wife may, take it upon yourself to contribute to the
well-being of your household as well—for the good of all!

In any case, whatever our gender, we all feel more content when we have a peaceful household to return to after a busy day of doing God's work in the world. After all, as parents we all know that blissful feeling of inner peace we get when we've spent real time connecting with our children—the type that's free from distraction, relaxed, and fulfilling to our core. When we've kept our emotions in check, responding rather than reacting, even when our children push our every button. When we've provided spiritual discernment on those blessed occasions when our children come to us for guidance with problems at school—and we don't solve things for them but ask just the right questions to help them solve things themselves. On those days, we go to bed with a full heart, at peace about our children, feeling like we've finally figured out what good parenting looks and feels like.

And then, tomorrow happens.

It's the inevitable pendulum swing. Frustration sets in with your tired children, who stayed up later than they should have and are now melting down during homework hours. You find an uneaten lunch in its entirety in a backpack, or receive an email from a teacher that your child forgot to study for an important test and didn't do well. You overhear siblings bickering over the rules of how to play a game, and then you get pushback on basic responsibilities. "I'll do it later," you hear, but "later" never actually arrives. What felt like parental bliss only twelve hours earlier has morphed into complete chaos, and you feel you're coming unglued. "How did I lose control so quickly?" you wonder. And now you're reacting like you're in a war zone, trying to put out all the fires while keeping your head just above the water—not even thinking about how to best deal with it all. It's just enough to deal. Yet, the stress begins to take its toll, and rather than desiring that sweet closeness with your children you felt only the day before, you prefer space from their exhausting choices and sour moods. "How did we get from yesterday to today? What happened to my parental bliss?" you think. "How do I get back there?"

This cycle should sound familiar to anyone who's raised children. And while there's no perfect approach to parenting, many books promise that their tried and true methods can help us avoid these inevitable cyclical patterns and easily renew our relationships with our children. But moments like these land in the lap of every parent—well read, equipped with all the latest trendy tools, or not. It's just life. And childhood is a series of opportunities for children (and parents!) to learn a whole lot of new things in a whole lot of ways. Much of that learning taking place on difficult days, just like these. We can get through the hard days better when we remember that these pendulum swings are completely normal and serve only to prune our children in ways that will better equip them to fulfill God's calling as they grow into His purpose.

From our experience, parenting is a process, so we shouldn't define it by a single moment, a single interaction, or a single day. It's one of the hardest yet most fulfilling jobs in the world. And as parents, we must love ourselves through these moments, just as we choose to love our children through theirs. Life as a parent equals struggle, realization, growth, and reset: a continual process of renewal, just as our marriages, emotional health, and spiritual lives also require! And in order to focus on this renewal and parent well through the ups and downs, we must practice self-awareness—as well as an awareness of the world in which we raise our children.

Push Back against the World's Influence

One key to renewing our families is acknowledging the world that surrounds our children. We don't parent in a Bubble-Wrapped home, after all! Like most adults, children face enormous amounts of pressure in a world that changes so quickly it feels impossible for any of us to keep up. We find ourselves constantly imprisoned by doubt as parents, trying to guess what's best for them along the way as we struggle to make constant adjustments and find success in a world that seems to spin ever faster every day.

A parent who watches their children grow up in today's world will notice several things: Children must grow up far too fast, the world encourages a "too much, too soon" mentality, children are expected to develop much faster than their brain's *actual* rate of development, and an ever-increasing, changing set of pressures from the outside world ups the ante with every passing year, changing the criteria for success. Our children are over-busy and overscheduled as societal norms encourage them to pack their days with extra-curricular activities—yet so many of the activities they participate in are laced with additional competition, angst, and pressure or are driven purely by the desire to live up to yet another factor that determines their success. A high level of competition now exists in everything our children participate in, from sports to music to academics, so that these things can no longer function as simple sources of enjoyment and renewal. To top it all off, because of all the pressure our society places on children to be the best, many parents feel parenting has become the latest competitive adult sport in which we compete for the "best parent" prize. And whether children express it or not, they feel pressure to live up to all the busyness and competition; when they don't, many feel bad about themselves.

Also, most parents today didn't have a constant source of distraction right at our fingertips when we were young, which meant our souls could exist more simply, and we had the time and space to hear ourselves think. We had enough time, space, and quiet to figure out who we were and what we wanted out of life, to ponder our hopes and dreams, to have fun, to create, and also just to rest our souls. Most of our children today don't have this type of quiet space for renewal that is free of distraction, where their minds can rest. When we pair the high intensity of pressures from the outside world with little to no recovery or renewal on the inside of their souls, it shows in the struggles we now see within our children's physical and emotional well-being.

Even as pressure continues to mount, causing stressful conditions and issues with physical and mental health, children have additional pressure at home to cope well with it, to not raise their voices, not push back, not melt down, and to continue to welcome the demands of performing well without a means of relief from the mounting pressure. And even as they have less time for sleep, the expectations remain—yet even most adults struggle to perform well with less than eight hours of sleep per night, and chronic sleep deprivation in adults has been shown to mimic signs of clinical depression.[2] Additionally, even though children have less down time and opportunities to renew, society continues to expect them to figure out how to solve problems independently in new and creative ways. Yet research tells us that only a "mind at rest" will truly allow effectual problem-solving and "aha" moments to occur.[3]

As parents, how should we respond to all these pressures the world puts on our children? We encourage you to push back against them in order to help you keep your kids healthier. While we and our children have to participate in our world to some degree, we suggest trying to find more of a middle ground than what society pulls for. Just as we have to keep our own spiritual and emotional well-being in mind, and to keep renewing ourselves daily to stay strong against the world's influence, we have to help our children with these things too. Our bodies and minds weren't meant to sustain such consistently high levels of stress and anxiety over long periods of time, and as a result we see reactive coping behaviors at an all-time high in our children today. What's happening beneath the surface? Stress and dysregulation. What's happening on the surface? Meltdowns, withdrawal, disrespectful attitudes, apathy. Remember that stress happens when we operate at the edge of capacity. And how do our children cope? Not well! We're seeing sky-rocketing rates of self-injury,[4] increasing rates of depression[5] and anxiety,[6] and a nation-wide struggle with alcohol and drugs.[7] Is this what God intended for our children? How should we respond?

Sometimes we find ourselves responding by *overparenting* in an attempt to fill the gap between unrealistic demands and our children's natural capabilities to keep up, which are still developing. And in many ways, this reaction makes sense, that as insurmountable pressures in today's world increase, parents will want to jump in more than they once did! Yet parenting experts often tell us to step back, to let children figure things out for themselves, and to let the consequences teach them. Recent trends now seem to assert that watching over the emotional and physical well-being of our children has become reprehensible! Buzzwords like "grit" and "resilience" show up in parenting books that promise amazing outcomes if parents would just step back from being overinvolved. Yet, the realities of what it takes to actually "make it" in today's world send conflicting messages. The demands *are* higher. The pressures *are* higher, and the criteria for success *are* higher. So backing off only leaves our children floundering with more than they can cope with. Even many adults still struggle with how to effectively manage stress, regulate tough emotions, and be disciplined enough to follow through with what it takes to create and maintain success—so why should we presume that our children, whose brains are still developing, would be able to manage these pressures better than we can?

In fact, in a meta-analysis of more than two hundred coping and emotion regulation studies that included more than eighty thousand young people, Bruce Compas, professor of psychology and human development at Vanderbilt University, found that "stress can disrupt the still-developing white matter in the brain, causing long-term problems with complex thinking and memory skills, attention, learning and behavior." He also found that the methods children use to cope, if left on their own, do not often lead to improving the adverse effects of stress. Children need parents to help them learn more adaptive strategies, such as how to look at their problems in other ways and from other perspectives, how to engage in problem-solving, and how to pursue constructive communication in whatever situation faces them. Compas maintains that stress is the "single most potent risk factor for mental health problems in children and adolescents, including depression, anxiety, post-traumatic stress syndrome, eating disorders, and substance use."[8] We can help our children mediate these effects if we are present, accessible, and ready to step in to teach them the skills they need to flourish.

Yet, it's so easy to unconsciously internalize societal trends about parenting and begin backing off in all the *wrong* places because we doubt ourselves. When we do this, we leave our children overwhelmed and unsure of how to get back to level ground, and unfortunately, they may reach out to all the wrong sources of renewal, as the Compas study found. Family support is incredibly beneficial to children at every stage, but this especially holds true during the teenage years. In a recent study by Melissa Milkie at the University of Toronto, she found that the amount of "parent time"—the time mothers and fathers spent engaged in the life and activities of their adolescents (age twelve through eighteen)—was linked to fewer behavioral problems, higher math scores, less substance abuse, and fewer delinquent behaviors like skipping school, staying out at night without permission, or getting into trouble at school.[9]

Now, please don't see this as an excuse to "rescue" your child from every struggle. Many times, natural consequences do work as great teachers—like when your child forgets a school book at home but you don't go get it for them; or when they ask to bake, and they make a gigantic mess and have to clean it all up themselves; or when they stay up too late but still have to wake up for their responsibilities. These types of lessons teach kids very natural, developmentally appropriate, and organic things so that they will alter their choices in the future. Notice the key words here: natural, developmentally appropriate, and organic. These expectations and lessons *are* within the reach of our children. But when children feel stressed and unsure of how to manage all the feelings that come with the fast-paced, overachieving world, "natural consequences" simply don't work. In those times, we need to teach them how to effectively grow into their brains, bodies, and souls.

Let's not forget that children's brains don't fully develop until their mid-to-late twenties (up until then, the emotional center of their brain is more well-developed than their reasoning, impulse control, and problem-solving areas). Before that time, their brains *are* led chiefly by the more primitive limbic system, and their executive functioning (problem-solving, reasoning, decision making—essentially the capacities that help them manage stress effectively) lags behind. So, while our children's brains are still developing, parents will need to play an active role in supporting them physically, emotionally, and spiritually.

As parents, we have a hard enough time keeping our own heads above water amidst the craziness of the world, so we all too easily forget that the home should be a source of spiritual renewal—a place where we can rest our physical bodies and recharge emotionally, restoring what we've lost through the stress of the day. For the sake of our children, we need to make sure our home doesn't end up just reminding them of added expectations, demands, and pressure to perform. How many times have you found yourself barking out constant demands at your children? "Come on, you need to get started on things." "Stop playing around." "What homework do you have?" "Can you feed the dog?" "When are you going to take the trash out?" "How many times have I asked you to pick up your room? It's a complete disaster." "Watch your tone." "Get off your phone." It's so easy to continually provide directions, corrections, and expectations, all the while not realizing our children are in a constant state of stress. We need to make sure that we see our children, rather than seeing only what needs to get done.

And no, it's not wrong to have high standards or hold your children accountable! Of course we want them to have a clean room and keep a respectful tone when they talk. In fact, it's our job as parents to instill good values in our children. *However, when we don't teach children how to manage their stress, the expectation that they will continue to perform well in this high-pressure world without an "attitude" is unlikely*. After all, irritability, agitation, and withdrawal all signal dysregulation from stress that's not being managed well. Our children still need our help because they haven't yet figured out how to do it all, and they need *more teaching and less preaching*. Remember, if adults are *still* learning how to effectively manage stress and balance expectations, and how to do so with grace, we shouldn't expect our children to have it all figured out already.

So if we want to parent effectively, to guide our children and help them find their own purpose in Christ without falling into the traps of either overparenting or underparenting, what should we do? A middle ground does exist—and the rest of this chapter provides keys to help you teach your kids how to navigate the challenges of this complex world in a healthy and godly way. Try putting one or more of these into practice today!

Practice Mindfulness

Practicing mindfulness as parents means paying attention to our children's emotional experiences as they unfold and trying to see things from their point of view. We can do this simply by choosing to make a connection with our children before giving them yet another command. "What was your day like today?" we can ask. "You look upset—do you need a hug?" "Are you stressed about anything in particular?" "What's your biggest worry right now?" "Is there anything I can do to help?" "What do you need before you get started?" It means pursuing our children in real time to ask about their experiences—and then truly listening, empathizing with understanding, and giving them the words to express what they may not even be aware they are feeling. *Learning to identify feelings is the first step to managing them,* and it's important to teach our children how to manage their feelings before their feelings start to manage them. We can help our children learn this skill when we notice and articulate what they feel; this helps them learn to practice mindfulness themselves, through increased self-awareness. Mindfulness helps equip our children to make values-based decisions that are in line with who God calls them to be, rather than simply reacting to the moments of their everyday lives without awareness, discernment, or direction.

Mindfulness also involves parenting in a way that helps your children pay attention to when their basic needs aren't being met. Even as adults, when we aren't tired, hungry, etc., we make better choices, follow our values more closely, manage stress in a healthier manner, and better renew ourselves spiritually with God's grace! So we need to teach our children to read these signals too: Fatigue signals a need for sleep, hunger indicates a meal is in order, and so on. When we help children recognize signs of their own stress, fatigue, hunger, or worry, they eventually begin to recognize these need-states within themselves. Then they can take steps to resolve their needs in a way that gives their souls more room to take the lead, choose well, and remain more on the path of making intentional, values-based decisions.

Allow for Free Time

We tend to have very little free time in our lives, which makes us so weary! And who can feel renewed in themselves or with each other when weariness prevails? When we give our children free time to just sit and do nothing much—the space to "just be" and rest versus rushing them to "hurry up" and get to everything the world says is important—we model the priority of stillness and renewal. We can give them the space to just relax and listen to music, read a book for fun, take a long shower, etc. Even letting our children play mindless games on their phone for a short period of time can help them relax and is a form of seeking stillness. Children need downtime to allow their souls some freedom from the demands of the world around them. Additionally, in order to learn to respond to their inner world, they need the space to feel it, hear it, and respond to it.

Encourage Your Children to Express Their Feelings

Making room for every emotion is evident in Scripture, when Ecclesiastes 3:3-4 (ESV) says there's a time for every-thing: "A time to break down, and a time to build up; / a time to weep, and a time to laugh; / a time to mourn, and a time to dance." When we permit children to have feelings and to express their feelings freely to us aloud, they learn how to explore their emotional experiences enough to under-stand them and to figure out what their emotions are trying to tell them. And when we listen without reacting, we lay a

foundation for encouraging this process, by modeling understanding through reflection and compassion—tools they'll
need later in order to respond to their own emotions with
care and discernment.

How do you most often respond to your children's feelings? Do your own reactions ever get in the way of helping your child to fully empty out her own perspectives
and feelings? Sometimes, as parents we may notice ourselves becoming impatient with our children's perspectives
or wanting to jump in and tell them why they shouldn't
feel what they feel, or that things really aren't that big of a
deal. But it's important to be patient, because we know that
getting comfortable with and understanding feelings will
help our children take control of their emotions so that the
emotions don't take control of them. We must also remain
patient and listen well because we don't want our children
to learn to avoid, invalidate, or judge their feelings, since
that usually make things worse. Dr. Roxanne saw this in
action recently:

> The other day a child told me, "My whole life is a
> mess. Everything is just messed up." (Yes, you can
> hear the thinking error—all-or-nothing thinking—
> when one thing goes wrong and we think our whole
> world is falling apart). Knowing how powerfully
> emotions can impact our interpretations, I knew the
> child needed to explore this. "What happened? Let's
> start from the beginning," I said.

"Well, I forgot to study for a test, did horrible, then I said something that upset my dad, and now everything is just a mess. It's stupid that I'm even this upset," he said. "I should be able to handle this. I don't know what's wrong with me. Everything feels wrong with me." Once he began emptying out his feelings, we realized that rather than dealing with the original upsetting events one by one—and focusing on finding solutions—he was beating himself up for being upset and for not handling life better. Perhaps he was right, but getting mad at himself at this point wouldn't help the original problem!

By emptying everything out aloud, this young man learned it was okay to be upset about a grade—it just meant that school was important to him! He also learned that it was okay to feel bad about upsetting his dad—it just meant he cared about their relationship and wanted to repair it! And he began to hear all the blame and self-judgment and could realize it was only making him feel worse and had little to do with the original problem. It's our role as parents to teach our children to make room for their emotions so that their emotions can inform them, rather than derail them.

Don't Lose Your Temper

Instead, express vulnerability. Losing your temper may stop an unpleasant exchange with your child, but it doesn't teach them good emotional skills. And our goal in these moments is to impart values, not just stop the behavior. So instead, if your child says or does something that hurts you, rather than jumping in with retaliation, tell them how their words or actions made you feel. This is the key to teaching compassion without preaching it, and we allow our children to experience the natural consequence their words and behaviors have on others. We hold up a mirror of love that allows them to see themselves. When we attack back, we muddy the waters of their reflection with our own charged emotional reactions, robbing them of the valuable gift of seeing themselves and instead giving them the chance to point their finger back at us as the reason for their behavior.

Also, *don't get angry and overreact to talking back*. The next time your children talk back to you, remember, they're not usually trying to hurt you, they're in the process of learning how to channel their own emotions into positive outlets. That's where we can help, as parents! We want to be a mirror for our children, giving them the opportunity to see themselves, and to reset and describe what's really going on. "Let's try that again" often works as a simple prompt to give them the opportunity to catch their own disrespectful tone. It's possible to set firm limits that encourage compliance while *also* fostering emotional growth.

Let's say you asked your child to clean his room and he complies, but with a sour attitude. Perhaps he doesn't have the tools to communicate effectively what he feels. If you react with anger to his bad attitude, you risk escalating an already problematic situation or encouraging your child to repress his feelings in the pattern of the "avoider." Not understanding the true cause of his emotions, your child may also blame you for his anger, completely missing his own signals! By the time the episode ends, you'll both be fuming, and the room will still be a mess. Sound familiar? What our children need most in this type of moment are two things: they need to learn to take ownership of their own feelings and how to manage them, and yes, they also need to comply with your request. But to do any of this, they have to catch what affects their compliance. Try giving your child the words they might be struggling to find: "Looks like you're overwhelmed. Do you need help breaking this mess up into sections?" Or, "Do you need to eat first, so that you have the energy?" "What do you think you need in order to get this done?" Then calmly remind your child of the consequences: "Remember, you won't be going out this evening until this task is done."

A recent experience Dr. Roxanne had in her practice demonstrates what a change expressing vulnerability instead of reacting in anger can make, and how it can help us renew our relationships with our children through a better understanding of one another:

> An adolescent girl in one of my counseling sessions looked over at her mother with utter disdain and said, "I just can't stand you sometimes. You're so annoying and overbearing." Her mom, hurt, and probably a little embarrassed, angrily retorted, "I wouldn't be so overbearing if you did what you were supposed to do. You're just so frustrating to deal with sometimes!" With this

exchange, the girl expressed her frustration with her mother, and her mom retaliated by describing her contempt for her daughter. This brought the conversation to a complete standstill while they both stewed in silence. Then they each glanced over in my direction as if to say, "See—I told you she was like this!"

It's so easy to let anger and misunderstandings disrupt the peace and tranquility in our homes, robbing us of joy and connection. Even the most docile parent can react with hostility when wounded by a child's words, and vice versa. And parents usually don't share these types of episodes with other parents, so they feel alone in their tremendous guilt over having lost their cool with their kids. "A good parent/child would never react this way," they think.

But we must learn to navigate through these choppy emotional waters if we are to be victorious with our children. It's our responsibility to offer good examples of how to handle strong emotions while not losing sight of the values we want to cultivate in our children. So when this girl snapped at her mom, in an attempt to help her develop compassion and the ability to take another's perspective, I asked the mother, "Did that hurt your feelings?"

"Of course it did," the mother replied, tears welling up in her eyes. "Tell her that," I said. "Let her know what you felt when she spoke to you that way." She turned to her daughter and said, "Your words just now, they hurt me. It always hurts me when you speak to me like that, and it happens often." The daughter sat quietly, but you could see the tears in her own eyes as she witnessed her mother's vulnerability (self-reflection rather than finger-pointing).

"What do you feel as you hear your mother's vulnerability when she expresses her feelings?" I asked the daughter. "Bad, I guess," she said. "What makes you feel bad? Was it not your intention to hurt your mom?" I asked the girl. "No," she said, "I just don't like when she asks me to do a hundred things right when I get home from school."

"What would happen if you just shared that with her—shared what you're actually feeling and needing?" I said. With tears in her eyes she said, "When I first get home from school, Mom, you don't realize that I need a little bit of down time before I start doing more stuff. I'm tired and have so much on my plate and am just coming home from doing stuff all day."

When she heard that, her mom replied with kindness, "All you had to do was tell me that. I get that! I just need your chores to get done. I don't care when you do them. How about I commit to not nagging you when you first come home, and you commit to getting things done at your own pace, but by 8:00 p.m."

It was a win! When each person expressed her real emotions with vulnerability, this enabled them to come to an understanding and a resolution that worked for them both. In making room to express the "why," it's always easier to reach a compromise on the "what." And when the mother controlled her temper, stopped overreacting, and gave her daughter the chance to honestly share her feelings, these things helped the daughter identify her own emotions and learn valuable emotional skills.

Set Limits

As parents, we sometimes feel sheer defeat at the inappropriate choices our children make; we feel powerless and lose our cool, relying on threats and strong emotion to intimidate our children into listening. We've all been there, but we've learned from the examples above—as well as from our own experiences—that reacting harshly damages our own peace and our relationships with our children if we do so as our default mode of parenting. Also, there will come a time when our children no longer fear us, so this tactic is ineffective in the long run. Instead, we can use our own escalating emotions as a signal of where we need to set a limit *and* enforce that limit.

Of course, if your children don't make responsible choices on their own, it makes sense to limit their independence until they prove they can act responsibly. And whenever possible, where it makes sense, we need to allow for developmentally appropriate, natural consequences to their actions and choices. Any consequences we give our kids should connect as closely as possible to the crime. For instance, if they fail to do their chores on any given day, it makes sense they would then have double the next. If they fail to self-regulate the amount of time they spend on their phones, it makes sense to impose a limit for them. Also, remember that consequences work best when children know about them in advance and when you consistently follow through with them. So make sure you don't name a consequence you're unwilling to stand behind! Remember too, that just because you impose a consequence doesn't always mean kids will comply; ultimately, we don't truly have control over our children's choices, and consequences only provide a bit of added motivation for them to choose well.

If your child has misbehaved in some way and you can't think of a consequence right away, we encourage you to use the *delay technique*. As parents, we don't have to offer a response immediately; we only have to let our children know that there will be one. When this happens, we can say something like, "We need some time to think about how we're going to handle this; we'll let you know in the morning." Give yourself time away from the situation to figure out what makes sense and what seems logical, and then come back when your mind is fresh and you know the value you wish to teach. Then you can let them know what their behavior has earned them, as well as addressing the value that was compromised. Don't be afraid to use this tactic—it's very effective!

Show Respect

Sometimes, even when we've set clear limits, children will push up against them by showing disrespect for us and our rules. But have you ever heard parents complain that their children are disrespectful, but then those very same parents turn around and show disrespect toward each other or their children? Children are imitators, and respect is a two-way street. We don't always *feel* respect toward our children when they do things that upset us, yet we expect our children to treat us with respect unconditionally—even when *we* do something to upset *them*. So the key to gaining our children's respect is that we must think of respect as something we, too, must strive to show unconditionally to them.

When we're upset about something our child has said or done, it can be so hard to approach the issue with care, love, compassion, and respect. However, approaching our child with the right attitude helps create an atmosphere of trust and respect in the relationship rather than a culture of resentment. And this sort of atmosphere helps us renew our relationships with one another and leads to far better outcomes than alternative environments. In a seven-year longitudinal study, researchers examined the influence of supportive parenting (which included warmth, proactive teaching, discipline that involved explanation and reasoning, and positive parental involvement) versus a less supportive, more harsh parenting style that lacked respect for children. The study found that supportive parenting was associated with more positive school adjustment and fewer behavior problems, and it even mitigated the negative impact of socioeconomic stress, family stress, and single parenthood on children's behavioral problems.[10]

So, as you consider how best to create a culture of support and respect in your family, remember that your children are always watching. They see how you speak to your spouse, your friends, and the bank teller. Be mindful of your tone of voice, your facial expressions, and your words, because all three parts of our communication convey respect or a lack of it. Ultimately, being respectful means that we show our children we care about their well-being and the way they feel, even when they upset us. We give respect when we truly see our children, when we listen to them, when we tend to them with care, and when we speak to them with kindness and understanding. So strive to lead your family in a kind and compassionate way, and avoid shaming, criticizing, and belittling family members or others.

Also, ask God for guidance! Every night in our own prayers with our children, we say aloud, "Lord, please continue to help our family have patience, love, kindness, and wisdom in all that we do. Help us to have kindness in our hearts and values in our minds, and help us to honor You in our choices." Also keep in mind what St. Paul wrote in his letter to the people of Rome, "Be devoted to one another in love. Honor one another above yourselves" (Rom. 12:10

[NIV]). What a beautiful passage! God calls us to "outdo" each other and go on the offensive to show respect to our families. Put simply, how we respect our children teaches them something very important about the love and kindness they will eventually learn to show themselves and the world around them. And in those difficult moments where we find it hard to show respect to our children, it can help us to remember that Christ lives inside of them, and He has entrusted them to us in order that we may "train up a child in the way he should go: and when he is old, he will not depart from it" (Prov. 22:6 [King James Version]).

Remember the Power of Words

We've seen that the language we use contributes to how we show respect to one another, and generally, what we say can affect another human being in powerful ways. It's true for both the joy we bring to others when we recognize something positive within them, as well as for the sadness we can bring through negativity or the complete absence of uplifting words. Our words can inspire, encourage, and motivate our family members to do the extraordinary things God intends them to do, but it's easy to move through life looking at the people we love without really noticing them. Hearing them without really listening to what they have to say. Yet, our children need us to notice them. They need us to speak life-giving words over them. If we don't notice our children, the world will.

The world sends out messages every day, telling our children who they are and who they should strive to become. As parents, we need to counter these messages by reminding our children who God designed them to be—and also by noticing their unique qualities. Most children learn to identify themselves early in life through what the important people in their lives notice about them. *So we need to be the people who notice!* We need to help our children value themselves beyond physical appearance, material possessions, and outward success—those things the world sees and encourages them for. When the world speaks loudly, children's identities and self-worth become tied to things like the clothes they wear, the kind of car they drive, or how many followers they have on Twitter. And whether we know it or not, sometimes we encourage and perpetuate these societal norms.

Instead, we must strive to notice and point out the gifts God has uniquely woven into our child's character. Perhaps you might complement your child for her fun personality, contagious smile, the joy she brings others, her warmth, her witty humor; his creativity and curiosity, his tendency to persevere through any challenge, or his kind and compassionate nature. When you see it, notice it out loud! And try to notice the thousands of things your family members do *right* instead of the one thing they do wrong. Remember the Gottman study that found the perfect ratio of positive to negative comments was 5:1? So, praise often! Let your children know how grateful you feel that God gave them to you. Thank them for their ability to make you laugh and for helping you out when they do, and make sure to encourage them daily. The word *encourage* means "to inspire [someone] with courage, spirit, or hope."[II] Our words should give our children the confidence to pursue their dreams and practice their God-given gifts. This is one of the best ways to renew our relationships with them—by creating a positive environment!

In much the same way, resist angry, hurtful, critical, or negative words, no matter how tired or frustrated you feel. It's better to say nothing at all then to say words you might regret. When you find yourself being hypercritical, stop talking, take a deep breath, take a break from the conversation, and come back when you feel constructive and know the value you wish to teach. Remember, as St. Paul wrote in Ephesians, "Let no corrupting talk come out of your mouths, but only such as is good for building up, as fits the occasion, that it may give grace to those who hear" (4:29 [ESV]). And as King Solomon said, "Pleasant words are *as* a honeycomb, / Sweet to the soul, and health to the bones" (Prov. 16:24 [American Standard Version]). Our words carry long-lasting weight; what we say to our children can impact them for a lifetime.

Listen to Each Other

Our words play such an important role in renewing our relationships with our children, and listening well is even more important! Indeed, like we discussed in the marriage chapter, communicating well requires that we listen more than we speak. This is hard to do! In our own family, we're always working on becoming better listeners. We often talk about our values of "listening to each other" and "acknowledging each other," and we ask this question a lot: "What do you hear me saying?" We also encourage asking questions of the person talking to demonstrate our interest in listening, before we move on to another topic. We discourage interruption as well. One study concluded that the average person listens for only seventeen seconds before they interrupt the person talking![12] It's so important to work consciously on being patient and *truly listening* to what our children say prior to interjecting our own thoughts, needs, and assumptions.

One key to good listening is to practice *reflective listening*, which requires accurately repeating back the speaker's thoughts, perspectives, associated feelings, and needs. The next time one of your children is upset, listen intently, and then before responding with your own thoughts, repeat back what you think you heard. You could begin like this, "What I think you're trying to say is . . . have I heard you correctly?" "Is that it?" "Is there more?" Then ask whether you've captured what they've said correctly. This tool doesn't typically come naturally to us during conversation, as our brains process quickly and move on to our own thoughts and ideas about what the speaker has shared before they have even finished talking. But when we slow down and take the time to hear our children correctly, they are more likely to feel heard and valued by us, and as we do so, we also model to them good listening behavior.

Show Humility

Renewing our relationships also involves showing humility to one another. The dictionary defines a *humble* person as someone who is "not proud or haughty; not arrogant or assertive."[13] Practicing humility makes for a healthier family, as family members put aside selfishness to adopt a "we" philosophy instead of a "me" philosophy. How does this play out? Remember that if you have a disagreement with your child and dig in because you are "right," then you might ultimately "win" the argument, but just like in marriage, you may have lost the relationship (the "we") in the process.

So instead of focusing on being right and "winning" arguments, practice humility by becoming comfortable with saying the words "I'm sorry," or "I understand how you feel," or "I regret that." We're not perfect, and we can all strive to be better tomorrow than we are today. It's okay to let your children see that you're only human, continually learning from today's mistakes so you can do better tomorrow. Apologize to your children if you regret how you've reacted in any way—they won't forget it! And they will learn to practice humility themselves from your example. Another beautiful way to integrate this value is in your prayers. Bring your regrets and hard lessons into your prayers in the evening with your children. Evening prayers with your children allow for open hearts and listening ears to review the day, and during this time, we can acknowledge our faults when our emotions are less active and our hearts are connected through prayer.

Set Priorities

How often do you find yourself spending so much time on daily tasks that you look up and realize you've barely interacted with your children all week? How can we practice humility, make room for emotions, listen well, and so on, if we become so busy with our to-do lists that we don't even stop to notice the people we live with? After our spouses, our most important relationships are with our children, and we need a strong, healthy home base before we can cooperate with God's purposes and minister to the greater world. It's important to remind ourselves daily that our tasks will always be here, but our children will grow up. We often hear people say, "Well, when things slow down, I'm going to make it a point to . . ." Yet life never does slow down; as our children get older, we merely shift into new and different areas of oversight. Father Nick remembers an illustration from one of his professors that really drove home to him the necessity of making family a priority:

> One day in my doctoral program, my professor walked into the classroom with a lunchbox in his hands, and we wondered what he was going to do next. He sat the lunchbox down and then put a large glass jar on the desk. While we watched with curiosity, he pulled out about a dozen golf balls and placed them inside the jar. He then asked us, "Is this jar full?"
>
> When we said "yes," he then poured a cup of rock pebbles into the jar and asked, "How about now? Is the jar full?" We said, "Yes, it's really full now." Then he added a cup of sand into the jar. The sand

filled in nicely all around the golf balls and pebbles. Then he asked us, "Okay, now is the jar full?" And we responded, "Yes, it's now completely full."

In reply to our quizzical expressions, he looked at us and said, "This jar represents your life. The golf balls are the things that are most important in life— your relationship with God, your family, and your health. If you lost everything but these three things, your life would still be full. The pebbles are everything we must do to function in life but that are less important—going to work, paying bills, and fulfilling deadlines. The sand is everything else—the little things we stress about, like keeping up with the house, mowing the lawn, cruising on social media, or cleaning up our email."

Our professor continued, "If I changed the order of filling up the jar, suddenly everything would no longer fit. If I put the pebbles in first, and then the sand, then the golf balls would no longer fit. Life is like this. What are you putting in the jar first? What things do you devote your hours and days to?" he asked.

This question has always stayed with me, and as my life has become busier, I find there are days when the "sand" in my life fills the entire jar, leaving little to no room for God's greatest gift—my family.

How can we re-shift our priorities to place our family at the top? Try taking a moment each day to truly *see and listen* to your children. Ask a question or acknowledge out loud what they want to talk to you about. Spend time connecting with them by watching their favorite show with them or playing their favorite game with them on the Xbox. Or put the devices away and talk to each other over an after-school snack.

Also, pay attention when your own body signals that you need rest, so that you don't take your fatigue out on family members. As parents, paying attention to our own happiness is also an integral part of creating a culture of happiness for our children. Remember, children often live in what we feel, rather than what we tell them. If we don't feel at peace, chances are they won't either. So, attempt to carve out more stress-free time for yourself and for your family. Laugh together, play together, find ways to be silly.

Get on the Same Page

Have you ever found yourself trying to set a limit for your child by saying "no," but your spouse jumps in and tells you, "It's no big deal"? None of our advice for renewing your family relationships will work if you and your spouse continually sabotage each other's attempts at parenting! You and your spouse might not be on the same page when it comes to priorities or values; even so, it's important to present a united front to your children. Children are smart, and they know where limits exist and where they don't. They know when a limit you've set isn't firm because both parents don't support it. These situations set children up to push limits, which then sets parents up for exhaustion, frustration, and escalating anger. And when children don't see clear and consistent limits, they find this confusing, since they'll never know which behaviors will meet with consequences and which will not. So, when it feels like your children "just won't listen," and they seem to constantly act out, consider whether you and your spouse unintentionally undermine your own parenting efforts because of a lack of consistency.

You see, children don't just come out responsible, respectful, and patient beings. In fact, our brains still mature, change, and develop well into our mid-twenties. So, children need lots of guidance that's consistent across situations and people. It's important to know the limits and values you want to encourage with your children. To begin, decide what behaviors bother you both most and what values you wish to instill. Then, most importantly, talk to your spouse to get on the same page about these. Try to listen to and respect each other's viewpoints about what makes for effective parenting in your home; this will lead to a mutually agreed-upon set of values you *both* commit to enforcing—otherwise, your efforts will be lost, along with your energy and sense of peace and well-being as a parent. We suggest even writing these down so you both remember what you've agreed on together and can reference it often.

Model Godly Values

Godly values lie at the heart of all the ways we equip our children and renew our relationships with them. But because many families today work more and sleep less—and are involved in more than that they can effectively handle—stress is often at the forefront of our family relationships and may motivate many of our parenting decisions. As a result, we sometimes look for ways to escape the pressure: We work long hours or exit the dinner table with the excuse of cleaning up the kitchen, or we overreact, sending our kids to their rooms in a state of fury. Yet we lose great parenting opportunities when we choose to escape or react rather than engage, *because our children are always watching us. Through observing us they learn how to be a grown-up and how to manage stress, and they learn what's important—what values they should hold dear.*

Albert Bandura, a renowned psychologist, studied the phenomenon of learned behavior and is most well known for something he called Social Learning Theory. Bandura's theory holds that children observe the behavior of others and then model that same behavior in other settings, when given the opportunity. This was illustrated during his famous Bobo doll experiment in 1961. He and his team placed children aged three to six together in a room with a blow-up doll and another adult. In one test, the adult behaved aggressively and unkindly toward the blow-up doll and at times even knocked it over. In another test, the adult did not behave aggressively toward the doll and rather played in a quiet and subdued manner, and in a third test there was no adult model at all. Unsurprisingly, the study concluded that children imitate exactly what they see. Those in the aggressive observation group exhibited significantly more imitation of the model's physical and verbal aggression than did those in the other two conditions. Interestingly, Bandura also found that children are more influenced by same-sex models. So, boys exhibited far more aggression when exposed to an aggressive male model than an aggressive female model. Results for the girls showed similar findings. Overall, the children in the non-aggressive observation condition and the control group exhibited few aggressive behaviors, indicating that children can learn social behavior simply through the process of observing adults around them. Bandura concluded that *children will always act out the behavior they have observed over the instructions they have been given.*[14]

Our children "live in our unconscious," and they know what we feel and think, and sense our deepest commitments and values, without us ever saying a word. Because they live in what they see and feel, if we want them to see our spouse in a positive light, we must *truly hold* our spouse in a positive light. So often we see children who act out and don't have respect for one of their parents; interestingly, in talking to the favored parent, we often discover they have negative thoughts about their spouse. In the mysterious synergy that exists in family life, your children will mirror the things you feel and think, even if you don't verbalize those feelings and thoughts.

Do we want our children to have self-control? Then we must exercise self-control. Do we want them to tell the truth? Then we must do likewise. Do we want them to love God with all their heart, soul, and mind? Then we must prioritize our relationship with God over everything else. As parents, we have an obligation to raise children who are compassionate, respectful, gentle, loving, patient, merciful, and kind, but they don't come out of the womb knowing how to do this. They only come equipped with the *potential* to learn, and then they are imprinted by what they observe, experience, and feel in the homes we make for them. *In truth, what our children will most remember about their childhood is how we made them feel.*

To help yourself consider what you may be unconsciously teaching your children, think about these questions: What do your children observe when they watch you handle a difficult project or a challenge? Do they see you frustrated and wanting to give up, or do they see someone who pushes through with calm perseverance? When someone feels angry in your home, do you snap back with a reactive comment, or do you take a step back and listen for understanding? When your children aren't getting along, do you attempt to fix it for them, or do you teach them how to talk to each other with respect and honesty, putting into action those values you want to instill? Try adding your own questions to this list to further increase your awareness of what you do or do not model in terms of godly values for your children—then consider how you might change your behavior to do better.

Take Care of Yourself

Sometimes, loving our children drives us to express love for them *at the cost of our own limits*—and we may even fail to realize that our own fuel tanks are empty. We may think we model godly values when we totally sacrifice our own good for the good of our family, but one of the keys to parenting well is actually taking time to renew our own body, mind, and spirit. As parents, we often make sure to provide our children with proper nutrition, adequate sleep, social interaction, mental stimulation, and physical play, and we generally help them to have fun and be successful—but sometimes we forget the importance of giving these same things to ourselves! *The truth is, most parents feel happier when they make these same needs a priority in their own lives.* Most parents also feel happier when they have interests that *go beyond* their children's interests: for example, when they take a weekly exercise class, join a book club or volunteer ministry, play a game of golf with friends, or take a class to learn a new skill like cake decorating. And don't forget to build in some daily time to renew yourself in Christ by practicing the First Fifteen or some other daily spiritual practice. Remember, you're more than just a parent. God has designed you with a multi-faceted identity, and to truly feel fulfilled, we have to devote time to each area of our lives that makes us who we are. Aim for at least thirty minutes a day to do something for yourself. Then, take note of how taking care of you allows you to better take care of others!

Not only do parents feel happier when their needs are met, but there's another fabulous hidden benefit! Watching us feed our soul and take care of our own nutrition, physical body, and interests teaches children, among many things, *to be more patient, less self-indulgent, and more empathetic.* They realize, "I'm not the only person in the world" and "I have to make room for other people." They also learn through our example that they too must nurture their own mental, emotional, spiritual, and physical needs if they want to live life as their best selves.

Teach Your Values

Research consistently shows that children are much more likely to internalize values when parents are involved and present in their lives *and* when they see their children as autonomous beings who must choose to take on their values, rather than believing they can externally control and regulate that process.[15] That means that children need to understand the rationale behind our parenting moments if they are to take on our values. In other words, in any teachable moment, try to *give your children the "why" for the "what."* "What's important here? And why is it important?" "How does this tie back into a value God has called us to live by?" Try asking yourself, "What do I want my child to learn from this, and why?" "What do I want my child to learn to say to himself in these moments, to use as a framework for his own thinking?"

Godly values lie at the core of all the parenting advice in this chapter. We can't renew our relationships and parent well if we don't first know our values and then strive to live them out and instill them in our children in every possible way. We can't be a family that preaches we "love the Lord" on Sunday unless we do our best to live out our faith in our homes on Monday!

One way you can help your children learn your values is to reward them every time you catch them embodying one of them. Children and adults alike enjoy getting rewarded for good behavior (think of the way you feel when you get a raise at work for doing a good job), and it's been proven that we can shape positive behavior by reinforcing it. Positive experiences get hardwired into our brains so that we want to repeat the behavior that brought it on: in this case, the reward. So, when a good behavior is happening, if we notice and reward it, we're likely to then see more of it. For instance, we can say, "Great job! I love the way you patiently and calmly spoke to your brother about what just upset you."

Some parents worry that by praising or rewarding a behavior, they set themselves up to always have to reward it. But that's not the case, because we tend to get good at anything we do frequently enough. Remember, neurons that fire together, wire together. Behaviors we do often enough become hardwired and thus, down the road, no longer require reinforcement. So, once those behaviors are shaped, the wiring is there, and the behavior continues even in the absence of reward.

One way we rewarded our children when they were young was through a mason-jar system. You might want to try this! With this system, each of our children had a jar, and we added "gems" (small rocks we collected from a mining trip we took to North Carolina) to their jars each time we caught them in a voluntary action that aligned with our values. These "gems" appeared in their jars when they did things like used their manners, took initiative with their responsibilities, chose to help someone without being asked (we call this the "unseen hero"), used good communication skills, and when they chose kindness, patience, or problem-solving over bickering. We gave them gems when they chose to honor

God with their actions, even when it would have been easier not to. When the jars were full, they could redeem their gems for extra privileges like outings with friends, staying up late, or small extras we wouldn't normally indulge. Now that they are older, the concept remains—only they no longer need to see the gems; we simply connect their extra privileges to their behaviors and choices throughout the week.

Practically speaking, the values you decide on will also guide your decisions about how to best intervene in the midst of frustrations. Here's an example from our home: When one of our children would complain about his or her sibling, because we value communication and effective problem-solving, first we would ask them to address each other, not us—but they had to do so using our values. Not easy! They used to get gems if they could look at each other and talk about what happened; if they could share what they were feeling appropriately without blame; if they could tell their sibling what they needed; and if the listener could acknowledge it. Even adults find this difficult! Because we value problem-solving, we would then ask them to brain-storm solutions that would make them both happy. The solution that won was the one that best captured both of their needs.

This process also takes the pressure off of us as parents to figure things out for them. Yes, we do need to guide them, especially when they're young, but we don't do our kids a favor when we attempt to solve their conflicts for them. This also helps us avoid scolding them for feelings they simply don't know how to manage and allows them to learn skills they'll need for the rest of their lives. When we teach our kids these conflict-resolution skills, and reinforce other behaviors and values early on through rewards, we help them build habits that will serve them well in adulthood.

Sometimes it can be hard to figure out which values we want to focus on for our families, so here's a list of possible values to consider as foundational for your home. Also, try having a brainstorming session with your spouse to come up with some of your own!

- mutual respect
- encouragement
- kindness
- generosity
- integrity and honesty
- helping each other without being asked
- gratitude
- problem-solving
- compromise
- patience
- persistence
- good listening
- emotion regulation
- showing mercy and forgiveness
- owning feelings
- admitting wrongs
- accountability
- noticing and making room for other people's needs

Something to watch out for: If you don't see your family members living out the values you cherish, first *look to yourself* to see whether your own behavior reflects that value. Remember, more will always be caught than taught. Also, after you *reinforce a value*, make it a point to *verbalize that value.* (For example, "We value respect in our home, so let's try what you just said again, but this time, please be respectful. When you do this, you'll get your toy/phone/privileges back. Otherwise, we'll keep it until you can.") Or *model the value* in your response to your child—"I need some time before I can talk about this since I don't want to say something hurtful. I'll be back." Try also to *demonstrate and put words on the value even in the midst of a struggle*: "You seem upset! Can you tell your brother what you need, rather than rolling your eyes?"

Remember, all of our actions begin in our thoughts, so we must guard our thoughts if we expect to successfully express our values through our actions. We can't expect to show kindness toward one of our children if we've been thinking negative and judgmental thoughts about him all day. We can't expect to show patience with our child if we've already decided, "she's just the difficult one who keeps making poor choices."

One mom noticed her daughter often acted grouchy after coming home from school. After closely observing her daughter, the mother concluded that—like many of us—her daughter felt overwhelmed by her life and didn't have an effective approach for managing her feelings. The mother decided to model two of her deeply held values in her response: she chose to be a vessel of God's mercy and self-control by acknowledging her daughter's feelings and then suggesting an appropriate next step. "You're clearly upset. Do you need to talk about it, or do you need some time alone first?" This simple approach helped her daughter realize that when she felt angry, she needed space to sort it out so that she didn't take it out on others.

Likewise, we can teach values to our children even in the ways we model them with each other as parents. One man at a marriage retreat recently shared with us that he was struggling with his wife's moodiness when she came home from work. She'd feel so run down that she would just sit silently at the dinner table. His former response was to tiptoe around her, but inevitably, they would end up fighting. One of his stated core values was *unconditional love*, so he decided he'd make more progress changing his own behavior rather than trying to change his wife. He began to show this value by giving her a hug every now and then when she came home from work and sending kind text messages to her throughout the day. *He stopped allowing her actions to determine his reactions.* "It felt good," he said. "It was a relief." His wife began to soften in her responses to him, and peace in the home was restored—all from his decision to comply, himself, with a value he wished to see in others.

Every day we have opportunities like this to communicate our values to our children through our actions—and most people would prefer to *see* a sermon through our actions than to just *hear* a sermon through our words. So whenever you can, choose to offer forgiveness rather than holding a grudge;

to show respect rather than disdain; to honor integrity and honesty over lies, secrets, and deception; to show understanding of your child's needs rather than being judgmental. And, "above all, keep loving one another earnestly, since love covers a multitude of sins" (I Pet. 4:8 [ESV]).

PRAYER

✠ ✠ ✠

OH HEAVENLY FATHER, one of the greatest gifts
You gave humanity was the opportunity to be a parent.
You blessed me with the ability to shape and guide my
children toward Your purpose. There have been times
when I felt that I was working toward this, while many
other times, I've struggled. I've had times when I've lost
my cool, didn't say the right words, handled a situation
the wrong way, and wasn't the parent You want me to
be. Lord, as I read *Renewing You,* I ask You to help me
renew my relationship with my child. Help me to be
a better parent by listening, loving, and learning from
them. Daily remind me that my children are simply on
loan to me, and that my ministry is to plant seeds that
allow them to grow in their faith, in their education,

in society, and in Your purpose for them. When I struggle with how to guide them, let me not lean on my own understanding but go to You first in prayer. When I make a mistake, keep me humble enough to seek both Your and their forgiveness. Awaken me in times when I'm not living the way You wish, and help me to remember that my children learn more from what I do than from what I say. Strengthen me so that as I close out this prayer, I am a renewed parent, ready and willing to lead my child in my words and actions toward the dream You have for them. Heavenly Father, I want to act in ways that will make You proud of me. I thank You again for the opportunity you blessed me with to be a parent, and I honor the Father, Son, and Holy Spirit. Amen.

FOR DISCUSSION:
THE THREE Rs——REST, REFLECT, AND RESPOND

1. How well can your children identify, articulate, and understand their emotions to solve problems? What are a few steps you could take to help them improve this ability?

2. What behavior have you noticed in your children that may require more firm limits because of how much it affects you? What limit will you put in place? What value does it relate to?

3. Provide an example of how you turned your anger into a constructive request for your child.

4. Could you have done anything differently this past week to communicate more respectfully with your spouse or children? If so, what might have helped?

5. Identify a disrespectful behavior you've noticed in your children. Have you ever acted that way yourself toward others?

6. When was the last time you apologized to your child? In what ways do you model the virtue of humility?

7. Under what circumstances are you most likely to use hurtful words, and how could you be more mindful during these times?

8. Practice reflective listening this week. How did the situation go when you focused your attention on listening instead of offering your own thoughts?

9. What are your values? What does your family see you protecting? Tolerating? Acting flippantly about? What would your children say are your values? Do they match with what *you* think your values are?

10. What do your children most often observe about you when you feel upset or stressed?

11. What do you think when you think about each of your children? You should know, because they will know. How about your spouse? You should know, because your children will ultimately think the same thing.

12. Spend quality time this week with each family member, without an agenda.

13. Do you take daily time for healthy pauses to connect with your family and God?

14. How often do you pause to check into your own body's signals? Your own needs? Your own happiness? What will you do for yourself this week?

CHAPTER EIGHT

Share Your Light

In the same way your light must shine before people, so that they will see the good things you do and praise your Father in heaven. —MATTHEW 5:16 (GNT)

THROUGHOUT THIS BOOK, we've talked about seeking God's renewal in so many parts of our lives. And perhaps you've noticed this renewal focuses mostly on our private activities and our homes: our own spiritual and thought lives, our family relationships, how we care for our bodies, and so on. Yet, we know God has called us out into the world to shine our light before all people: it's part of His purpose for our lives! So where does our role as Christians in the world come in? The thing is, your light is only as strong as your mind, spirit, and body. And if you don't care for those things first, you'll find your light won't shine as brightly as it could. That's why this chapter on sharing your light comes last. And of course, none of us ever reach peak renewal—we're all works in progress, and renewal, by its very definition, involves a lot of "doing again." That means, even as we go out into the world to shine our light, our internal renewing work, and our work at home, in our relationships, never stops.

So, yes, we believe that God has a plan and a purpose *out in the world* for each of our lives—that when we've experienced His renewal in our lives, we can then go out and help others renew their lives. We believe that God has made every one of us *on* purpose, for *His* purpose, and He yearns for us to share His light with the world. We are "fearfully and wonderfully made" (Ps. 139:14 [NIV]), with specific gifts, talents, and abilities we can share, and the Bible says that "we are God's masterpiece. He has created us anew in Christ Jesus, so we can do the good things He planned for us long ago" (Eph. 2:10 [NLT]). Our good works flow out of the intersection of our authentic faith, our God-given gifts, and the renewing, inner work we continue to do. And when we follow God's purpose for us, we don't hold on to our gifts, but we unwrap them and share them with others. The Bible mentions giving to others *so* often, especially in the New Testament—which indicates that we should place a lot of importance on it in our lives. You've probably even experienced the importance of giving for yourself, since much of who we are today stems from others who chose to unwrap their gifts and share them with us. Think for a moment about all the people who have helped you get where you are today: parents, a family friend, a mentor, a teacher, or maybe even a perfect stranger!

We meet so many people during our lifetime, it would be impossible to count them all! Some simply *walk into our day.* We see them, and we might even speak to them—but they don't really leave an impression on our life. Other people not only walk into our day, they *walk into our life* and leave a lasting impression on our heart. They live their light, and their gifts ultimately help us cultivate our gifts. They inspire us to want to be better than we were before we met them. A young man we will just call "Samson" was one such person for Father Nick:

> Samson not only walked into my day, he walked into my life. Samson was an eight-year-old boy who lived in one of the poorest regions of Kenya, Africa. His family, along with other members of their tribe, often went days without anything to eat or drink. Seeing their gaunt faces broke my heart. Every day, Samson walked beside me as I went from village to village during a mission trip. He didn't say much, but he always wanted to help, whether it was unloading and setting up tents or gathering wood for a campfire.

> On the night before we left his village, I took Samson for a walk. I had one last granola bar in my backpack, and I wanted to give him this small treat to thank him for his help. I said, "Samson, I want you to eat this granola bar. It's a small gift to thank you for all of your help." I thought for sure he would scarf down the whole granola bar without skipping a beat, especially since he hadn't eaten in more than three days.

> What happened in the next twenty minutes left a lasting impression on my heart: I'll never forget it,

and I'll feel forever inspired by it. Samson proceeded to break almost every little individual oat off that granola bar. He then lifted his shirt up, creating a pocket, and put every little piece in his shirt. I figured he wanted to save it for later, but I couldn't believe what he did next. He gave me a hug, took all those small pieces of granola bar, and distributed them to every child in the village. He was starving, and he needed to eat—but he chose instead to think of others.

I said to Samson, "I know you're hungry. I know you wanted this bar. Why didn't you just eat it all by yourself?" He looked at me and said, "These people are *all* hungry, and they are *all* my family." I was touched. Not only did most of the people in this village not belong to his family, but many were not even a part of his tribe. Here I was, standing before a young boy I had come to inspire and teach, and yet he was the one who inspired me.

We live in a world that desperately needs our light. On any given day, according to the World Health Organization, 821 million people, or one in nine, go to bed hungry,[1] and 2.1 billion people globally lack access to safe drinking water.[2] According to UNICEF, approximately 3.1 million children die every year from malnutrition,[3] and 385 million children live in extreme poverty.[4] And how about disease? According to the National Cancer Institute, this year alone roughly 1.8

million people will be diagnosed with cancer in the United States, and an estimated 606,520 people will die from the disease.[5] And as of this writing, nearly 600,000 people have died globally from the COVID-19 pandemic.[6]

How does God call us to respond to these alarming statistics? The Bible says, "Cast off the works of darkness, and . . . put on the armour of light" (Rom. 13:12 [KJV]). Whether we see darkness in the form of poverty, hunger, and disease, or whether we see it in the form of hate, selfish desire, or condemnation, Christ commands us to live a different example—to "let [our] light shine before others" (Matt. 5:16 [NIV]). We do this by putting on the character of Christ, the "true light" who lives within us. Like Samson, God calls us to mend the hurts of those in the greater world around us because we are all one family in Christ. Ultimately, as one family, the value of our lives does not lie in what we accumulate but in what we give away. And comparatively speaking, most of us have great wealth, according to these numbers.

What might it look like to come into contact with a modern-day light in *this* world? Think of the person who lights up a room with her mere presence because of the joy she radiates—not from vainglory but from pureness of heart. Think of the person who makes you feel at ease because he knows how to comfort you, no matter what wound you expose. Or the person whose encouraging words bring growth and healing, without blame, judgment, or criticism. Think of the person whose mere presence feels like a warm hug and whose support always leaves you feeling blessed, lifted, and inspired. Think of the person who doesn't think only about him or herself but also thinks of others and sees the hurt in the world around them. Or the person who is quick to forgive; who makes you feel important in a roomful of people. Think of the person who never has a negative thing to say and who finds the silver lining in every circumstance. These traits exist on a continuum inside all of us. Our light shines brightest when we seek to cultivate these gifts within ourselves so that we can bless and bring light to others. And remember, light shines brightest in darkness, so it doesn't take much to cast off the darkness when we do what we can to exude even a little bit of light.

Psychologist Scott Barry Kaufman has actually investigated what it means to be a "light" in this world. Essentially, he studied what personality traits "everyday saints" have. He did his research as a contrast to what was originally coined the Dark Triad by Delroy Paulhus and Kevin Williams. The Dark Triad is a paradigm used to explain why some people don't think twice before they do something malevolent. The researchers found a certain set of personality traits to be a common thread in clinical populations such as criminals: entitled self-importance, exploitation and deceit, callousness, and cynicism. In contrast, everyday saints who seem to live in the light possess very different traits! The Light Triad, Kaufman says, is composed of three personality traits: 1. valuing the inherent dignity and worth of each individual human being; 2. treating people as ends unto themselves, not just as a means to another end; 3. believing that other human beings are fundamentally good and not out to get us.[7]

Are we not all deeply touched when we encounter these kinds of everyday saints who share their light with us? When they reach out to us in a big-hearted way to bring us comfort, compassion, words of encouragement, or their own time when we need it most? Yet, how often do we evaluate our *own* lives according to these principles, to see if these God-honoring qualities live in our own actions toward those around us?

Think of it like this: Each day, we get 86,400 gifts of grace. Why 86,400? That's the number of seconds we have in one day. This precious time passes us by so quickly, and once those seconds are over, we will never have them back. The world needs us to be intentional with how we use our seconds, and in this final chapter, we offer some ways you can share God's light with the people He places in your path.

Bring the Light of Compassion

One day, when our daughter was about seven, we woke up after a long and trying week to find a remote-control kitty sitting at our bedroom door. Our daughter had neatly dressed the cat in a skirt and button-down shirt, and it wore the glasses from our daughter's look-alike doll. The kitty carried a note that read, "Dear Mom and Dad, I love you with all my heart and am so thankful you are my parents. I know this week has been hard for you, so I wanted to write you a card to tell you how much I love you." Now, not much can make us smile first thing in the morning before we've each had our first cup of coffee, but that sure did. Being on the receiving end of compassion just felt good.

In our household, we commonly talk about the word *love*. We like to say that although it's both a noun and a verb, it's best used as a verb. Yes, it's nice to hear the words, "I love you," but if we're honest, we feel most loved when someone takes the time to truly notice us and care for us in specific ways, or when they unexpectedly go out of their way to help when we're struggling, or when they choose to do the right thing even when it's the harder option. And when we have compassion for the people in this world who God places in our lives, we express godly love so beautifully.

Think about Christ: He never stood up and *just* simply said the words, "I love you." No, He actively expressed His love as a verb, showing His love for us in everything He did. His actions showed us that love is sacrificial, compassionate, unconditional, generous, and without judgment or expectation. We can follow Christ's example by showing this same kind of renewing love to the world! His example inspires us to demonstrate our love for people in a real way through our own compassion. God never designed love to simply stop at a "feeling" we experience deep down inside, which other people can't see. No, He calls us to let our love be seen, as the epigraph of this chapter says: "Let your light so shine before men, that they may see your good works and glorify your Father in heaven" (Matt. 5:16). You see, it's through our good works that we show the goodness of God to others.

The greatest sermon we can preach is the one that we live, and the actions we take in our everyday life are a testament to our beliefs. Samson showed us that. And yes, even our daughter, in her own little way, showed us that. Now, we don't get a kitty with a note every day, but the simplicity of what she did reminded us that we don't have to wait for a special occasion to share our light with those in need: Every day presents a renewed opportunity for us to notice family, friends, or people in our greater community who might need our light of compassion. Maybe the elderly neighbor down the street needs help getting her groceries, or the newcomer at church could use a friend, or the server in your local restaurant could use an extra tip in recognition of how hard she works. Whatever the situation, showing compassion doesn't have to involve a grandiose act; it doesn't need to be complicated or overly orchestrated. Showing compassion to others comes from our heart, and it happens in all the small things we do. It happens when we choose to notice others whose struggles we may not have even known about.

Recently, we heard a pastor friend share a moving story about a father and his three children riding a New York City subway. The father sat at the back of the car, holding his head in his hands while his children ran around, laughing and playing. Three couples sat just a few seats away, all well dressed, apparently on their way to a Broadway play. It didn't take long for them to notice these three young children who were carrying on and having fun. The women repeatedly glanced over at the children with exasperated expressions and then glanced at the father as if to say, "Don't you see your children causing such a ruckus?" Eventually, one of the women very loudly remarked, "This generation of parents has clearly forgotten how to raise their children." A few minutes later, one of them stood up and approached the father and said, "Your children are making so much noise and running around. Could you please control them?" The man looked up at her and said, "I'm so sorry; I guess I didn't realize how loud they were. I can't bring myself to take their joy away by telling them I've come from the hospital where their mother has just died." The woman was noticeably taken aback, uttering in embarrassment, "Sir, I'm so sorry. I had no idea."

The truth is, we never truly know what people are going through. It's easier to show compassion once we know someone's story, because we can then see their life through the lens of their hurt. But if we don't have that lens, we must use God's lens. If we judge someone else's actions too quickly, we never reach the ability to love them and be a light in the midst of their darkness. Christ tells us not to judge (Matt. 7:1) but rather to love others without qualifiers.

When we open our eyes, ears, and hearts without qualifiers, we begin to see people standing right in front of us who might need a smile, a check-in, a listening ear, a "hello," an uplifting card, or a warm embrace. We just need to notice and be willing to stop and offer support. Sometimes we get so focused on our own needs and our own day-to-day agenda that we simply forget to look up and notice the people God has placed directly in our path. A woman who was a widow shared with me (Dr. Roxanne) the other day that she lives in a condominium complex full of neighbors, yet no one ever checks in on her to see if she needs anything—even though she, herself, has surprised many of them with baked goods on random occasions, just because. What a difference it could make if her neighbors returned the favor in some small way of their own, seeing that perhaps her gifts to them could have even been a subtle indication of what she, herself, might need: the gift of connection!

The story of the Good Samaritan in Luke 10:25-37 (NIV) reminds us of how to be this sort of "good neighbor." In this parable, a leader in the Jewish law asked Jesus what he must do to get into the Kingdom of heaven. Jesus asked him, "What is written in the Law? How do you read it?" The man answered that he needed to love God with all his heart, strength, mind, and soul and to "love [his] neighbor as [himself]." And Jesus responded, "You have answered correctly." When the man asked, "And who is my neighbor?" Jesus answered by sharing a story of a Jewish man on his way to Jericho who was robbed, beaten, and left for dead on the side of a road, and the three people who came across this man. First, a priest on his way to the temple passed by without stopping; then, another high-ranking Jewish man also walked right by the injured man, on the other side of the street. But a Samaritan, who wasn't even supposed to associate with a Jewish person, decided to stop. He took care of the man: He bandaged his wounds, then put him on his own donkey and took him to a nearby inn. He asked the innkeeper to take care of him and, with what little money he had, promised to return to reimburse the innkeeper for any additional costs. Jesus said, "Which of these three do you think was a neighbor to the man who fell into the hands of robbers?" The man answered correctly, saying, "The one who had mercy on him." Then Jesus said, "Go and do likewise." Sometimes we, too, can get so wrapped up in our own world that we forget to "go and do likewise."

Social psychologists have studied helping behavior for a long time, and although it's generally accepted that we are hardwired to help others,[8] certain circumstances get in the way of us doing so. For one, when we feel rushed, like the first two people who didn't stop to help the injured man, studies show we're less likely to look up, take notice, and help others. Even well-intentioned people striving consciously to do good in this world can walk right by someone who needs their love and compassion. Drs. John Darley and Daniel Batson conducted a study related to this topic, composed of students at Princeton Theological Seminary. They gathered sixty-seven students and placed them into two groups. They gave one of the groups the Parable of the Good Samaritan to read and then asked them to give a sermon on that parable within a few minutes of reading it. The researchers asked the other group to develop a presentation on employment opportunities for seminarians. They told all of the students to go to an adjacent building to complete their presentations, and they asked some to "rush" and told others they could take their time getting there. The seminarians didn't know that Darley and Batson had placed an actor, dressed as a poor homeless man, in a doorway right outside the building. He looked like someone in obvious need of help.

Out of these sixty-seven seminary students—devout people of faith—only 40 percent, or twenty-seven of them, actually stopped to help. Interestingly, fewer of the students who were asked to "rush" *and* who had not just read the parable on helping actually stopped to help. Conversely, more of those who didn't feel hurried and had just read the Parable of the Good Samaritan did help the man.[9] This study reminds us of the importance of slowing down and also of making sure to renew ourselves daily in God's Word. Otherwise, we can easily overlook opportunities to share God's compassion.

God depends on *all of us* to leave *His* mark in this world. And we can find people who need compassion all around us—within our families, when we shop at the grocery store, at our workplaces, when we wait in line at the bank, in our churches, in restaurants, and even when we walk out to get our mail. Just take the time to notice them! And to take it a step further, we can also try to get to know the people we encounter in our daily life. Try taking a few minutes to chat with the dry cleaner, the lawn service workers, the quiet coworker, and the cashier or bagger at the grocery store. Even just taking a moment to look up from our smart phones and ask people how their days are going can make a difference to someone. We once heard it said that the problem with our world is that we draw the circle of family too small. Like Samson, we need to see everyone in our surrounding community as part of our family, both inside and outside our inner circle. Many of us look only to our own friends and family to offer our light—and these are wonderful places to start, of course. But our circle can expand to encompass everyone we come across.

Practice Generosity

Oftentimes, we view giving to others and generosity as the amount we write on a check; however, Scripture teaches us multiple ways to show generosity. The Apostle Paul exhorted the people of Corinth: "But since you excel in everything— in faith, in speech, in knowledge, in complete earnestness and in the love we have kindled in you—see that you also excel in this grace of giving" (2 Cor. 8:7 [NIV]). And he continues in the next chapter: "You will be enriched *in every way* so that you can be generous on every occasion, and . . . your generosity will result in thanksgiving to God" (2 Cor. 9:11 [NIV]). What does it mean to be rich in every way? If we feel rich in happiness, perhaps God has gifted us with a joyful spirit, and we can lift others up. Or we can be rich in friendship, in strength, good health, or in virtues like patience and kindness. All these allow us to sow seeds of God's love in the lives of others, which can result in people knowing God, being renewed by Him, and thanking Him.

Here are some specific ways we can show generosity to others:

We can be generous with our time. People we help often see our time as more valuable than our money, as it demands more of us and takes a greater commitment than simply writing out a check. And since we live in a culture that is over-busy and values this over-busyness, giving of our time can make a huge difference to someone and also demonstrate how we, as Christians, value God's work over the values of our culture. What a wonderful witness to others! We can offer up this precious commodity to people in our community in many ways: When you go outside to get your mail or walk your dog, try looking up and saying "hello" to the people you see. Smile, and ask how they are doing! Or visit a nursing home, meet an elderly person for coffee, serve food to the homeless, volunteer in local youth ministries or community service organizations, or serve on ministries that reach out to those who are sick or in need of visitation—to name just a few possibilities.

When we do these things, we follow the outline Jesus gave us in the Gospel of Matthew when He described the actions that define a true disciple of Christ: "I was hungry and you gave me something to eat, I was thirsty and you gave me something to drink, I was a stranger and you invited me in, I needed clothes and you clothed me, I was sick and you looked after me, I was in prison and you came to visit me" (Matt. 25:35-36 [NIV]). When the disciples asked when it was that they saw Jesus in need and did not help, He responded, "Whatever you did for one of the least of these brothers and sisters of mine, you did for me" (Matt. 25:40 [NIV]). So when we give of our time to help others, we give to Christ, Himself, as well.

We can be generous with our talent. People often say to us, "I'm not that talented!" Yet in Ephesians 4:7 (NIV), the Apostle Paul wrote that "to each one of us grace has been given as Christ apportioned it." The word *grace*, in this instance, means "spiritual gift." Each of you has a divine enablement from God that you can use generously for the benefit of others. You *are* good at something, and when you do that something, you know it because it feels good and right! When you use the spiritual gift God has given you, you will change the lives of people around you for the better.

We feel "divinely enabled" to listen and communicate; you might feel "divinely enabled" to connect to others, to bring joy, to help physically, to serve, to cook or bake for others, to write cards, or to make others laugh. Whatever your gift, you have a place!

We can be generous with our touch. An old telephone company slogan once encouraged people to "reach out and touch someone." Never have we needed this more than in a world that relies so much on social media—a world of virtual connecting where great detachment often occurs between people in their homes and communities. With the isolation our society brings, it's more important than ever to reach out in more personal ways. How do we do this? Try some of these things. Right now, you could grab your phone and text someone just to say, "I'm thinking about you and praying for you. I just wanted you to know I'm in your corner this week!" Or, drop a handwritten note in the mail to someone, just to say "hello." (Even though we don't use the post office much anymore, we all still love to get mail!) Try taking it a step further, even, and call that friend you haven't seen in a while and ask them how they've been. And when you ask people how they're doing, stop to actually listen with your eyes and your ears. Try asking a question to get them to further elaborate. Show interest, and take the time to really hear the sorrow in someone's voice when they're dealing with loss or stress. You'll be surprised how often people come back later and tell you that your generous gesture was exactly what they needed that day: that it was just what they needed in order to feel renewed. Small acts of kindness make a real difference in this world!

Be a Light of Encouragement

One night we were reading a book about animals to our kids. We turned to the section on geese, kind of as a laugh, since we have so many geese walking around our neighborhood. In fact, we sometimes have to come to a complete stop while driving because a family of geese appears to be a having a conversation in the middle of the road! The book said that if we watch geese fly, we'll notice they fly in a V-shaped pattern. The goose at the tip of the V works the hardest, pumping his wings in a specific way to make it easier for all the other geese to coast off his momentum and use less of their energy. After some time, that lead goose falls to the back of the V and another goose moves forward to lead the pack. They operate like a family, constantly helping one another to get to their destination. Plus, while they fly, they make very loud squawking sounds, and animal scientists say these are actually cheers of encouragement for each other, which helps them keep flying. How profound, we thought, coming from animals we find to be such a nuisance! But hasn't God created all of us to fly through life like that? Carrying one another to new destinations while encouraging each other along the way?

The truth is, though we are all different, each of us has a contribution to make in this world—but we need each other's support to get there. We need people in our pack to encourage us and help us feel renewed along the way. Remember how the word *encourage* means "to inspire [someone] with courage, spirit, or hope"? We need courage to believe in ourselves when we must face circumstances we don't think we can handle. We need courage to use our gifts to do great things in this world. We need reminders that we have what it takes and that someone believes in us and our gifts, and a few words of encouragement can often be the key that unlocks the door to our potential.

We need to remember that other people need encouragement too, though it's hard to offer encouragement if we focus on what we find discouraging about others. It helps us to remember that God tells us not to work toward shaping others but rather to remember that *He* is the potter. A story in Jeremiah 18 reminds us so well of this:

In the Old Testament, God often sent prophets to the Jewish people because they would follow God for a little while before they would inevitably go off course. One such prophet was Jeremiah, who lived around 627 BC, during the time of the Jewish exile into Babylon. Jeremiah uses a beautiful analogy about how God molds us: he tells us that God is the "potter" and we are the clay, and that He has us on a "potter's wheel," molding and shaping us into who *He* wishes us to be. Jeremiah says, "So I went down to the potter's house, and I saw him working at the wheel. But the pot he was shaping from the clay was marred in his hands; so the potter formed it into another pot, shaping it as seemed best to him" (18:3-4 [NIV]).

So often in life, we try to play the role of the "potter," and we put our friends, spouses, and children on this wheel, telling them how they should act, who they should be, how they should think, or what they should feel, in an attempt to shape their lives to our liking. But we must remember that it's not our job to fix people and that pointing out their faults actually keeps them from feeling renewed in Christ; it's our job to love them and encourage them. God is the potter and is always at work within those we love, creating something beautiful even in broken vessels. Our job is to remain loving and encouraging in order to help cultivate the unique strengths God has woven into others, letting our words of encouragement water His seeds of goodness.

Let's consider also the Book of Romans, where St. Paul tells the people of Rome about the new salvation that comes to us through Christ. In speaking about how we should treat others, he says, "Accept one another, then, just as Christ accepted you, in order to bring praise to God" (Rom. 15:7 [NIV]). The key word here is *accept,* which means to "receive willingly" and "to give approval to."[10] People don't need us to mold them; they need us to accept them. They don't need us to make them into who *we* want them to be; they need us to dig around and help them find the seeds of who *God* wants them to be. Then, we can water those seeds with our encouragement, because what we say and how we say it can influence the people around us for years to come.

The TV show *Mister Roger's Neighborhood* spoke encouragement to people, and especially to children. It's a great example of how encouragement can stick with people for a lifetime! The show first aired in 1968 and was the longest-running children's program ever to air on PBS—and it continues to influence the lives of children and adults around the world today. Mr. Rogers was a minister who wanted to change children's lives. He ended up receiving some forty honorary degrees and the presidential Medal of Freedom, and he was inducted into the Television Hall of Fame. In his acceptance speech, he said these unforgettable words about encouragement:

> Those of us in television are chosen to be servants . . . to help meet the deeper needs of those who watch and listen . . . to show and tell what the good in life is all about. But how do we make goodness attractive? By doing whatever we can do to bring *courage* to those whose lives move near our own—by treating our "neighbor" at least as well as we treat ourselves and allowing that to inform everything that we produce.[11]

He then asked the audience to think for a moment about a person in their own lives who encouraged them and helped them to become who they are today.

Try taking a few moments now to think about who has encouraged you on your journey. Dr. Roxanne would say her parents taught her the value of encouragement:

> They never doubted me: I could always feel their belief in me, in my abilities and in my potential. It was a constant backdrop that created a foundation for what my life would become. We joke to this day that I was the "talker" in our family, but they

encouraged my personality, even though I stood out as the highly sociable one in a family full of mathematicians. They watered the seeds that God placed within me, always seeing my strengths and helping me nurture them no matter what stage of life I was in. And their unwavering belief in me and unconditional support gave me the courage to look past my own insecurities and remember my worth as I journeyed on the road to becoming all I have become. In short, their belief in me gave me strength. Even to this very day, if I get nervous about something, my mom always says, "Why would you ever feel nervous? You've always done great, and today will be no different."

As for Father Nick, his parents taught him his value by showing that they valued him:

> They saw my gifts and encouraged me even when I decided to go to seminary, which they had reservations about: they worried about how challenging a pastor's life can be. Yet they encouraged me because they looked beyond their own reservations and believed in the greater plan God had for me. They encouraged my extroverted nature, and they valued my sense of humor, which I believe God gave to me as a way to help me cope with being short when I was younger. Today, Roxanne says that two of my greatest gifts are my ability to relate to people and how

much I make her laugh. My parents were always there to praise me when I did well, but they were also there to give me honest feedback when I didn't.

I also remember a particular teacher whose encouragement changed my life. Prior to the sixth grade, I didn't always take school seriously. I struggled to grasp the material, and I wasn't always a great student—I often wondered how I was going to get through school successfully. But my sixth-grade teacher, Mr. Larson, changed everything for me. He said, "Nick, you have so much potential. You can do great things if you just apply yourself. I see it in you." Those might seem like simple words, but here I am, remembering them some thirty years later. He didn't just speak *at* me, he spoke *to* me. He built me up and made me feel like I could, indeed, do anything I wanted to do.

So, you see, the way we encourage other people can change their lives in profound ways! We challenge you to go out and leave an impression on someone else by encouraging them today.

Enjoy the Blessings of Giving

When we give to others by being encouraging, kind, compassionate, and generous, we bring them great blessings. But did you know that when we bring light to others, we also bring blessings upon ourselves? A popular Chinese proverb says,

"If you want happiness for an hour, take a nap. If you want happiness for a day, go fishing. If you want happiness for a year, inherit a fortune. If you want happiness for a lifetime, help somebody."[12] Turns out there's immense wisdom in this Chinese proverb, as happiness researcher Sonja Lyubomirsky and two of her colleagues found that only 10 percent of our happiness is determined by our life circumstance, whereas 40 percent is determined by the way we choose to live our lives and the things we do. (Our genes dictate the other 50 percent.) Lyubomirsky concluded that when we participate in daily activities that involve helping others and various other deliberate acts of kindness, it directly causes an increase in our own happiness.[13] So the good feeling we get when we help others can, in and of itself, renew us daily, helping us feel refreshed and renewed in Christ! I (Dr. Roxanne) spoke to a young woman recently who reminded me of this:

> This young woman told me she had gone to buy her grandmother some fudge at a local shop. The store sat on a touristy street filled with lots of people, restaurants, and specialty shops. After purchasing the fudge, she came outside and saw an elderly man who appeared to be homeless, sitting in an electric wheelchair. He asked the woman and her two friends if they wouldn't mind helping him. A little taken aback, they asked, "What do you need?" He quietly said, "Food. Please."
>
> The friends checked their funds and decided they had enough money to buy this man some pizza. They

told the man, "If you can meet us at the pizza parlor, we can get you a slice of pizza." The man said, "Thank you, but my wheelchair has run out of batteries, and it needs to be charged before it can move again." The women, undeterred, said, "Well, okay, then we can push you."

And they did. When they arrived at the pizza shop, they asked for a table near an electrical outlet so the man could charge his wheelchair. They plugged his chair in, and before ordering, asked him what his favorite type of pizza was. He said, "Supreme." They got him two slices and a refillable drink cup, and then they sat with him while he ate, and they talked with him for a while.

As she pondered this experience, the young woman told me, "I'm sure it felt good to be cared for, but truthfully, I was the one who felt good." That's what giving does! When we choose to leave our mark on someone else, it ends up leaving a greater mark upon us.

Caring for others feels good because God's plan for interconnection and communion is woven into our DNA! When we freely express generosity or even have the very intent to engage in a generous act, it can trigger changes in the brain associated with increased happiness. Did you know that the moment we go out and make a difference—when we lift the fallen, when we bring light to someone else's darkness—we experience what's called the Happiness Trifecta? Basically, dopamine, serotonin, and oxytocin all release to give us a happy sensation. The neurochemicals associated with the Happiness Trifecta even counter the effects of cortisol (our stress hormone). The effect is so powerful that therapists use giving to others as a tool in certain counseling methods to help individuals better tolerate their own strong, negative emotions during times of acute emotional crisis. Reaching outside of ourselves even in the midst of dealing with our own burdens genuinely helps us feel better. And it doesn't take a grand display of giving in order to experience these benefits, either. Even small acts of generosity, altruism, and service can reduce stress, support our immune system, forge social connections, and enhance our sense of purpose.[14] It continues to amaze us just how much God has equipped our bodies to respond favorably to His teachings. The Bible speaks of this concept as well, as I Timothy 6:17-19 (NIV) states:

> Command those who are rich in this present world not to be arrogant nor to put their hope in wealth, which is so uncertain, but to put their hope in God, who richly provides us with everything for our enjoyment. Command them to do good, to be rich in good deeds, and to be generous and willing to share. In this way they will lay up treasure for themselves as a firm foundation for the coming age, so that they may take hold of the life that is truly life.

Simply said, not only do our works of service help those around us and strengthen and renew the community, they also allow us to "lay up treasure" for ourselves so that we can live a full and rich life.

Even when we don't directly experience blessings from our giving (or maybe we don't see those blessing until much later), St. Peter emphasizes that giving to one another is so important, we must keep doing it even during difficult times—those times when our first instinct is often to withdraw into ourselves or our families. Writing to the churches of Asia Minor during a time of persecution, he said, "Above everything, love one another earnestly, because love covers over many sins. Open your homes to each other without complaining. Each one, as a good manager of God's different gifts, must use for the good of others the special gift he has received from God" (I Pet. 4:8-10 [GNT]). It's hard for us to imagine the persecution the early Christians suffered—if these Christians could continue to give to one another during their times of trial, so can we! So let's strive to follow their example.

Be the Solution

During times of persecution or other community or global types of stress, the human reaction is often to feel sorry and think, "That's sad; I wish things were different." Yet, we do nothing. Or we feel that we have enough problems in our own life, so we can't possibly worry about the world's troubles. Or perhaps we believe someone else will take care of the problem. It's easy to look the other way when problems don't directly affect our children, our family, or our country, but God calls us to care. He calls us to serve. He calls us today to do whatever we can to make a difference in our world—whether in our community, our country, or the world at large.

Jesus, Himself, is our example, for He didn't come into this world to be served, nor did He retreat into his own problems and ignore the suffering of others. He came to serve, and He calls us to follow His example. "Now that I, your Lord and Teacher, have washed your feet, you also should wash one another's feet. I have set you an example that you should do as I have done for you" (John 13:14-15 [NIV]). You can see here that He also calls us to serve one another with humility. If the last person we would expect to wash the feet of others chose to do so for His disciples on the night before His Crucifixion, then nothing should be beneath us. Peter even said to Jesus before Jesus washed his feet, "No, You shall never wash my feet," to which Jesus answered, "Unless I wash you, you have no part with me" (John 13:8 [NIV]). In other words, Jesus is saying, "This is who I am and what I'm all about. If you want to follow me, we must serve one another willingly and in genuine deference and humility."

Unfortunately, throughout history, instead of fulfilling God's dreams for us to serve one another willingly and with humility, as a society we often fall short. Today, when we turn on the news, we don't see a world where people serve one another. We see a very messy world. We watch the international scene as innocent people die every day. People are being persecuted simply for their faith, their beliefs, or their culture. We watch humans suffer from economic hardship in multiple regions around the globe and as wars devastate countries and whole societies. We watch as world leaders allow money, power, and greed to corrupt how they lead their countries, taking without giving to their people. We watch in sadness as senseless killings, robberies, and abductions take place in our own country. We look around and see poverty: people without food, water, and shelter.

Some people look at the mess and say to God, "There's so much sadness in the world, so much conflict. Why don't You do something? What are You waiting for?" But God says to us, "I did do something; I created you." And then we remember, light can best be seen in the darkness. So, as we look at a dark world, God says, "You have the greatest opportunity to let your light shine." We are the solution that God created to help solve the problems of this world. We are called the "salt of the earth" (Matt. 5:13), a city on the hill, "the light of the world" (Matt. 5:14), and we can't change this world by standing still or hiding our light. God calls us to restore— not ignore—the people in our world.

Yet, even sometimes when we see people in need, studies show we generally leave it to someone else if we believe someone else is available to help. Social psychologists Bibb Latané and John Darley studied something they referred to as the Bystander Effect. They found that the more people there were present witnessing a situation where someone needed help, the less likely any of them were to actually help.[15] Researchers studied this phenomenon because of a senseless murder that took place in 1964. Onlookers watched as twenty-eight-year-old Kitty Genovese was murdered. At least thirty-eight neighbors heard the repeated screams during her brutal attack, which lasted over half an hour, but none of them called the police. The attacker was later asked how he dared to attack a woman in front of so many witnesses, and he calmly replied, "I knew they wouldn't do anything; people never do." Many were probably convinced that someone else would do something. Darley and Latané concluded from their own research that this phenomenon occurs because each witness feels less responsible for helping, a process they referred to as "diffusion of responsibility."

We must remember that God calls *us* to be that someone. We aren't advising that you put your life in danger, but we believe we shouldn't count on the hundreds of other bystanders to be that "someone" when they pass by a homeless man or a mother with three kids trying to get her stroller through a heavy door. In our role as bringers of God's light, we don't want to leave these opportunities for someone else to deal with. As Galatians 6:10 (NIV) says, "As we have opportunity, let us do good to all people."

And, as we have opportunity, let us also show a willingness to be interrupted—because opportunities to make a difference often come in the form of an interruption in our day. We might receive a call from a friend who needs our support with a tough matter, or our help getting home from the hospital, or a meal once she's home. Or maybe someone needs our help for something even as small as lending a book from our bookshelf when they are going through a tough time. What about when the wait at a doctor's office feels like an eternity? Instead of letting our stress and impatience boil over, we could take the opportunity to show kindness to the elderly woman sitting next to us. Perhaps she lives alone, and if we talk to her, it might be the only conversation she will have all day. Or, we could choose to say "hello" or kindly offer a smile to anyone we meet as we go about our day! Just look around you: there are so many opportunities to allow for interruptions in order to serve your world with your time, talents, and treasure. We find that it's easiest not to overthink how to help others or to try to achieve grandiose plans, but to simply start small, with the person nearest you, remembering that God often puts people directly in our path that are in need of His light.

And look at Jesus' life. People constantly interrupted Him! When His friend John the Baptist was beheaded, Jesus tried to go to a lonely place to mourn, but the crowds beat Him there, and though struggling Himself, He showed compassion by serving them. He chose to heal their sick, and then He served them all dinner. Only then, in the evening, did He get a chance to be alone. And even then, He was interrupted (Matt. 14:10-25). Another time when Jesus had sought solitude to pray, Peter found Him to let Him know everyone was looking for Him (Mark 1:35-39). Jesus didn't respond irritably; instead, He decided to go out and reach more people through preaching some more. Even in the Book of Matthew when the Pharisees conspired against Him, Jesus tried to withdraw, yet many followed Him. Again, He didn't say, "I don't have time for this." No, He allowed for the interruption and healed them all (Matt. 12:14-15). Jesus turned His interruptions into opportunities to let God's light shine before people—and He calls us to do the same. Several weeks ago, Father Nick visited a friend and heard her story of how a stranger interrupted his day to share God's light with her:

> This friend had recently lost her husband. During our visit, she told me what had happened to her at the grocery store the other day. She was shopping near the floral department, and a young man approached her and said, "Ma'am, I need some help. I need to get some flowers for a friend, and I know nothing about flowers. Can you recommend something?"
>
> She was a little startled at first, but then she said, "Sure. Well, lilies are nice, but then, they don't last long. And this flower has already bloomed, so it won't be bright for long. I don't know your friend, but when my husband was alive, he would plant the most beautiful hydrangeas, and they always made me smile with their large, colorful blooms. Why don't you try a hydrangea?" The man said, "Perfect. I wouldn't have thought of that." Then, they went their separate ways, and she finished buying her groceries.
>
> Well, as she walked out of the store, she heard a voice saying, "Ma'am, ma'am, excuse me!" She turned around and saw the same young man again. He came up to her and said, "Here, thought you might like one of these," and he handed her the same hydrangeas he had just bought for his friend. She teared up, and

as he walked away, she felt such warmth. "People do care," she said. This man didn't know her—he had no idea what her story was. But that moment of interruption opened his heart to hers. His thoughtful gesture brought God's light into the world for someone right there in front of him!

When we talk about bringing God's renewing light to others, we sometimes hear, "But I don't know how to get involved. I don't know where to begin." We encourage you to look within your own community. Perhaps you feel passionate about a certain cause or a group you want to support. Give those organizations a call and see what opportunities they offer for getting involved. Nonprofit organizations always need more help. If you enjoy being around people, you could offer to volunteer in a hospital setting, forging social connections and bringing joy to those who need it. Maybe you enjoy meal preparation; you could serve meals at your local homeless shelter or offer to prepare meals at your local hospital-based housing facility for families of those receiving care at the hospital who don't live locally. Whatever the cause, look for how you can give back, based on *your* gifts. It could be as simple as going through your own home and making piles of things you no longer need. Have your children decide which toys they no longer use, and go as a family to make a donation to a shelter. Whatever motivates your giving, we encourage you to find a way to serve.

During the holidays, we often make visits to nursing homes, and this past holiday, we went with several young people from our church. All the children were asked to write as many cards or make as many drawings as they could to hand out to the seniors upon our visit. As we were handing out cards, we watched as smiles began forming all around the room, like a wave of light. I (Dr. Roxanne) will never forget the response from one woman who received a card. As we were about to leave, she stopped us, and with tears in her eyes, she said, "I want you to know that this is the only card I, and many others here, have received all year. Please know how much these children being here has changed my life today." I was speechless. Something so simple, that took so little time, was powerful enough to change someone's life. Her words felt like God reminding us just how important it is to share His light.

One thing we enjoy doing with our church community is preparing what we call "homeless kits": bags filled with supplies like toiletries, food, and water. We always keep one on hand in our car so that when the opportunity presents itself, we have something to give. I will never forget reaching into our car one day to hand out one of those bags, and the woman who received it suddenly teared up and said, "You don't know how much we love receiving bags like these. My kids have benefited from the supplies for weeks. God bless you and what you do."

If you find yourself thinking "someone else will do it," remember the story of Noah and the ark. This is one of the most well-known stories in Scripture. Only six chapters into the first book of the Old Testament, we hear God's disappointment with His people. He feels frustrated because He sees a people that are divided. They undermine each other and don't care for one another. He sees the people—the faithful—not acting as difference-makers in this world, and the Bible says that filled God's heart with pain. He was frustrated by how far from His teachings the people had strayed, "but Noah found favor in the eyes of the LORD" (Gen. 6:5-8 [NIV]). In the midst of God's frustration, He found someone who could help Him transform the world. God found a solution, and it was Noah. Could it be that as you read this book, God feels pained by all the sadness He sees and is looking for someone to help Him transform the world? Could He be looking at you and seeing a Noah?

When we accept God's call to act as Noah and bring His light to the world, our altruism can spread by up to three degrees. Studies have shown this![16] This happens because when we offer even something as simple as a smile, we engage our mirror neurons. Mirror neurons make us smile when others smile, cry when others cry, and laugh when others laugh. God has built into our brains the tendency to mirror each other, so when we smile, we literally impact other people's brains in a positive way. This is why, when we do something kind for one person, they're motivated to show kindness toward someone else, and that person's gratitude inspires yet another act of kindness toward someone else. So, if you go out today choosing to serve, know that in your serving you generate a ripple effect of light that could lead to dozens or even hundreds of people choosing to serve someone else—simply from something you chose to do for one person.

So commit to a cause, and call to find out how you can volunteer or get involved. Allow for interruptions in your day when you see someone in need. Give to those less fortunate. Think about the talents you have been given and commit to serving a particular ministry, outreach opportunity, or charitable organization with your gifts. You are the someone God is waiting on to transform His world.

We once heard this saying that we absolutely love, that describes so well how God wants us to shine our light in the world: "I'm a little pencil in the hand of a writing God, who is sending a love letter to the world." We are the tools God uses to write His love letter to the world. So, let's ask ourselves today, what kind of letter are *we* writing to the world? What kind of light do *we* share? We must recognize that there's so much sadness and heartache in the world and that people all around us are starving for God's light. So we must go out today and share God's light by being a light of compassion, encouragement, forgiveness, peace, and service. Don't just walk into someone's day. Recognize that God wants you to be like Samson and walk into their life. Leave a lasting impression. Today, God is giving you His pencil. Let's go out and write His love letter to the world. Write the first word now!

PRAYER

✠ ✠ ✠

FATHER, YOU TELL us that our life is like mist,

that we are here for only a small amount of time

on this earth. And I want to be a shining light to

the people You put across my path. I want to be a

shining light for You. But I know that when I make

that step toward You, the devil will give me every

excuse to step away. He will tell me that I have too

much baggage in my past to make a difference. He

will whisper in my ear that I don't have time. He

will want me to be like him, a judger and accuser of

men. I ask You to help me not to listen to his voice

but instead to Your promise. Let me remember that

You need me to be an answer to the problems in

the world. You need my voice to be Your voice of comfort in the world. You want my arms to be Your arms, loving those who suffer. You yearn for my feet to be Your feet, to spread compassion to those in need. You hope that my ears can be Your ears to listen to the needs of those around me. Lord, help me to be Your vessel and Your pencil, so I can make a difference and help make Your dreams come true for this earth. Amen.

✠ ✠ ✠

FOR DISCUSSION:
THE THREE Rs—REST, REFLECT, AND RESPOND

Compassion and Generosity

1. What kind of lens do you generally see people through? Do you look through a godly lens or a judging lens?

2. Try assessing the positive and negative statements you make inside your own head when you look at others; are they judgmental, or are they merciful overall?

3. Think of the last time you judged someone else. How could you have shown compassion instead? How does it feel to practice compassion?

4. How could you go out of your way to show compassion this week? Name three different people you think could use your compassion.

Encouragement

1. Do you think you have inspired others? What kind of mark do you generally leave on people?

2. What are some ways you can reflect God's light of encouragement during your workday? At home? In your neighborhood? In your community?

3. Take inventory of all the inspiring words you shared today.

4. Who could use your encouragement? What could you say or do to encourage that person?

Be the Solution

1. What are some of the gifts, talents, and abilities God has given you, and how can you share these gifts with others? Be specific! (Examples: volunteering, helping to tutor children, being a mentor, knitting for a ministry or charity organization, feeding the hungry, collecting donations for the needy.)

2. Do you love people the way Jesus would love them?

3. Do you set conditions on loving others by only loving those who think like you, dress like you, or believe what you believe?

4. What are some ways you can learn to show your love toward those who are in need?

CONCLUSION

As we close this book and take its principles out into our lives, it's important to remember that God is never done renewing us! Our renewal continues on a daily basis as we work on getting closer to Him, on loving our spouses and children better, on taking care of ourselves more carefully, on turning our trials into testimonies—and also on shining our renewed selves into the world as God's light. New aspirations, new goals, new accomplishments, and new dreams all wait for us to grab hold of them, and God has a wonderful purpose for us as we grow closer and closer to a life lived in His image. To a life of freedom and love, rather than a life locked inside the prison of our own flesh.

But remember, real growth is never linear. You will have ups and downs, peaks and valleys. And as you try to integrate these principles into your daily life, picture in your mind the persistence you will show along this journey. No matter which way the pendulum swings, whether you breeze through some strategies or struggle to implement others, learning and growing always take place in our lives. Every day is a new opportunity to use your tools for renewal, to seek a better version of yourself than you were the day before. Everything we experience benefits us in some way. So never give up!

Remember, too, that the difference between renewing and staying stagnant in all areas of our life lies in how we view our setbacks. *Persistence* is a state of constantly pursuing something, and most of you reading this book are doing so, because you have chosen to pursue a better you by learning more about how to renew yourself in Christ. You aren't done seeking God's potential for your life. You're still looking for ways to grow and improve. So if you stumble, get right back up, let God strengthen you, and try again. And remember the words of Nelson Mandela: "It always seems impossible until it's done."[1]

The beauty of setting goals is not only the joy you feel when you reach the end result but also how much you learn as you embrace the journey. What brings us a full life in our faith, a renewed spirit, and an ability to reflect the image of God has more to do with how we persevere through challenges than it does with our innate ability. And when we hold on to our inner peace and happiness, and increase our own self-awareness as we intentionally pursue our goals, we experience even greater success.

Know that your birth was not an accident or some random act in history. We all have a mark God meant for us to leave on this world: in our families, our workplaces, our communities, and the larger world. And God equips us with all the gifts to do so, only asking that we continue to cultivate that which He has already given us and woven into our beings. *When we seek constant renewal, we empower our spirit to overcome the obstacles of our flesh that threaten to stand in the way of shining our light in this world.*

We hope this book has left you feeling more equipped and inspired to take the plunge into the next chapter of your life. If you're thinking about or have already begun using any of the tools presented in this book, you're already one step closer to bringing God's ultimate plan into fruition in your life. Keep your head up and remember that life is like a mountain—we keep climbing until we reach the top! Thank you for allowing us to join you on this journey. And now, let's all go out and start living a life of renewal!

ENDNOTES

Introduction

1. *Merriam-Webster*, s.v. "renew (v.)," accessed June 15, 2020, https://www.merriam-webster.com/dictionary/renew.
2. *Merriam-Webster*, s.v. "*ne plus ultra* (n.)," accessed June 15, 2020, https://www.merriam-webster.com/dictionary/ne plus ultra.
3. Viktor Frankl, *Man's Search for Meaning* (Cutchogue, NY: Buccaneer Books, Inc., 1992), 112.

Chapter I: Make Faith Your Foundation

1. Peter Winebrenner Stoner, *Science Speaks: Scientific Proof of the Accuracy of Prophecy and the Bible* (Chicago: Moody Press, 1976).

Chapter 2: Remodel Your Mind

1. Ana Smiljanic, trans., *Our Thoughts Determine our Lives: The Life and Teachings of Elder Thadius of Vitovnica* (Platina, CA: St. Herman of Alaska Brotherhood, 2012).
2. Steve Bradt, "Wandering mind not a happy mind," *The Harvard Gazette*, November 11, 2010, https://news.harvard.edu/gazette/story/2010/11/wandering-mind-not-a-happy-mind/.
3. G.E.H. Palmer, Philip Sherrard, and Kallistos Ware, trans., *The Philokalia: The Complete Text (Vol. 2): Compiled by St. Nikodimos of Holy Mountain and St. Markarios of Corinth* (London: Faber & Faber, 1982).
4. Robin Amis, *A Different Christianity: Early Christian Esotericism and Modern Thought* (Hermitage, TN: Praxis Institute Press, 2003), 308-309.
5. Dorothy Bass, et al., *Christian Practical Wisdom: What It Is, Why It Matters* (Grand Rapids, MI: Eerdmans, 2016), 299.
6. Amis, 77.
7. Archimandrite Lazarus Moore, trans., *The Ladder of Divine Ascent: St. John Climacus* (London: SPCK, 1982).

8. G.E.H. Palmer, et al.

9. Michael Craig Miller, "Commentary: Dr. Aaron T. Beck's enduring impact on mental health," *Harvard Mental Health Letter,* October, 2011, https://www.health.harvard.edu/newsletter _article/dr-aaron-t-becks-enduring-impact-on-mental-health.

10. John Gottman and Julie Gottman, "The Natural Principles of Love," *Journal of Family Theory and Review* 9, no. 1 (March 2017): 7-26, https://onlinelibrary.wiley.com/doi/abs/10.1111 /jftr.12182.

Chapter 3: Find Victory over Your Vices

1. William Shephard Walsh, *The International Encyclopedia of Prose and Poetical Quotations from the Literature of the World* (Marrickville, NSW, Australia: Wentworth Press, 2016), 133.

2. Phillippa Lally, et al., "How are habits formed: modeling habit formation in the real world," *European Journal of Social Psychology* 40, no. 6 (October 2010).

3. Jessica A. Chen, Eliot Fearey, and Ronald E. Smith, "'That Which Is Measured Improves': A Theoretical and Empirical Review of Self-Monitoring in Self-Management and Adaptive Behavior Change," *Journal of Behavior Therapy and Mental Health* 1, no. 4 (May 24, 2017): 19-38, https://openaccesspub.org/jbtm /article/386.

4. Saint Nicholas the Wonderworker, "Introduction and Beginning Prayers," *Great Vespers of Saint Nicholas,* https://www.stnicholas center.org/how-to-celebrate/resources/music/hymns/hymns -orthodox-byzantine/great-vespers-chant.

5. Janice K. Kiecolt-Glaser, et al., "Negative Behavior During Marital Conflict Is Associated with Immunological Down-Regulation," *Psychosomatic Medicine* 55, no. 5 (Sept.-Oct. 1993): 395-409, http:// pni.osumc.edu/KG%20Publications%20(pdf)/076.pdf.

6. Jeremy J. Day and Regina M. Carelli, "The Nucleus Accumbens and Pavlovian Reward Learning," *Neuroscientist* 13, no. 2 (April

2007): 148-159, https://www.ncbi.nlm.nih.gov/pmc/articles/PMC3130622/.

7. C.S. Lewis, *The Weight of Glory* (San Francisco: HarperOne, 2001), 136.

8. Loren Toussaint, Alyssa C.D. Cheadle, and Amy D. Owen, "Forgive to Live: Forgiveness, Health, and Longevity," *Journal of Behavioral Medicine* 35, no. 4 (June 2011): 375-86, https://wwwresearchgate.net/publication/51250786_Forgive_to_Live_Forgiveness_Health_and_Longevity.

9. Robert D. Enright and Richard P. Fitzgibbons, *Forgiveness Therapy: An Empirical Guide for Resolving Anger and Restoring Hope* (Washington, DC: American Psychological Association, 2014).

10. Loren Toussaint, et al., "The effects of brief prayer on the experience of forgiveness: an American and Indian comparison," *International Journal of Psychology* 51, no. 4 (January 16, 2015).

11. Vani A. Mathur, et al., "Neural basis of extraordinary empathy and altruistic motivation," *NeuroImage* 51, no. 4 (July 15, 2010): 1468-1475, https://www.sciencedirect.com/science/article/abs/pii/S1053811910003125?via%3Dihub.

12. Dalai Lama, Desmond Tutu, and Douglas Carlton Abrams, *The Book of Joy: Lasting Happiness in a Changing World* (New York: Penguin Random House, 2016).

13. *The Oxford English Dictionary*, 7ᵗʰ ed. (2001), s.v. "bless."

14. Jennifer Thompson-Cannino, Ronald Cotton, and Erin Torneo, *Picking Cotton: Our Memoir of Injustice and Redemption* (New York: St. Martin's, Griffin, 2010).

15. "O Heavenly King and Psalm 51 (Psalm of Repentance)," Orthodox Church in America, https://www.oca.org/orthodoxy/prayers/trisagion.

Chapter 4: Turn Your Trials into Triumphs

1. Mark Hart, *The "R" Father: 14 Ways to Respond to the Lord's Prayer* (Frederick, MD: Word Among Us Press, 2010).

2. "Hematidrosis: Can people sweat blood?" *Medical News Today,* last medically review on August 26, 2017.

3. *Merriam-Webster,* s.v. "surrender (v.)," accessed July 13, 2020, https://www.merriam-webster.com/dictionary/surrender.

4. *Dictionary.com,* s.v. "anxious (adj.)," accessed July 13, 2020, https://www.dictionary.com/browse/anxious.

5. Benedict Carey, "Expert on Mental Illness Reveals Her Own Struggle," *The New York Times,* June 23, 2011, https://www.ny times.com/2011/06/23/health/23lives.html.

6. *Wikipedia,* s.v. "paraclete," last modified May 31, 2020, 00:44, https://en.wikipedia.org/wiki/Paraclete.

7. "80% of Thoughts Are Negative . . . 95% are repetitive," *The Miracle Zone* (blog), March 2, 2012, https://faithhopeand psychology.wordpress.com/2012/03/02/80-of-thoughts-are -negative-95-are-repetitive/.

8. "Language Studies: Greek Thoughts," Studylight.org, https:// www.studylight.org/language-studies/greek-thoughts.html ?article=35.

9. *Wikipedia,* s.v. "confirmation bias," last modified July 12, 2020, 21:13, https://en.wikipedia.org/wiki/Confirmation_bias.

10. Serge Brand, et al., "Acute Bouts of Exercising Improved Mood, Rumination and Social Interaction in Inpatients with Mental Disorders," *Frontiers in Psychology* 13 (March 2018), https://www .frontiersin.org/articles/10.3389/fpsyg.2018.00249/full.

Chapter 5: Tend to Yourself

1. "New study shows people sleep even less than they think: Whites, women and wealthy sleep longer, better," UChicagoMedicine, July 2, 2006, https://www.uchicagomedicine.org/forefront /news/new-study-shows-people-sleep-even-less-than-they-think -whites-women-and-wealthy-sleep-longer-better.

2. Derek Thompson, "Workism Is Making Americans Miserable," *The Atlantic,* February 24, 2019, https://www.theatlantic.com

/ideas/archive/2019/02/religion-workism-making-americans
-miserable/583441/.

3. Liz Stevens, "What Percentage of Americans Spend More Than They Earn?" *Best Money Moves*, October 3, 2018, https://bestmoneymoves.com/blog/2018/10/03/what-percentage-of-americans-spend-more-than-they-earn/.

4. Lisa Damour, "Why Stress and Anxiety Aren't Always Bad," American Psychological Association, August 10, 2019, https://www.apa.org/news/press/releases/2019/08/stress-anxiety.

5. "National Sleep Foundation 2009 Sleep in America Poll," Sleep Foundation.org, https://www.sleepfoundation.org/professionals/sleep-americar-polls/2009-health-and-safety.

6. Lilian Wiegner, et al., "Prevalence of perceived stress and associations to symptoms of exhaustion, depression and anxiety in a working age population seeking primary care—an observational study," *BMC Family Practice* 16, no. 38 (March 19, 2015): https://bmcfampract.biomedcentral.com/articles/10.1186/s12875-015-0252-7.

7. Adam Gazzaley and Larry D. Rosen, *The Distracted Mind: Ancient Brains in a High-Tech World* (Cambridge, MA: The MIT Press, 2017).

8. John Pencavel, "The Productivity of Working Hours," *The Economic Journal* 125, no. 589 (December 2015): 2052-2076, https://onlinelibrary.wiley.com/doi/abs/10.1111/ecoj.12166.

9. Carlos Eduardo Macedo, et al., "Prefrontal dopamine release and sensory-specific satiety altered in rats with neonatal ventral hippocampal lesions," *Behavioural Brain Research* 231, no. 1 (May 16, 2012): 97-104, https://www.sciencedirect.com/science/article/pii/S0166432812001702?via%3Dihub.

10. Neel Burton, "Our Hierarchy of Needs," *Psychology Today*, May 23, 2012, https://www.psychologytoday.com/us/blog/hide-and-seek/201205/our-hierarchy-needs.

11. *Merriam-Webster*, s.v. "Sabbath (n.)," accessed July 11, 2020, https://www.merriam-webster.com/dictionary/Sabbath.

12. Lynette L. Craft and Frank M. Perna, "The Benefits of Exercise for the Clinically Depressed," *The Primary Care Companion to the Journal of Clinical Psychiatry* 6, no. 3 (2004): 104-111, https://www.ncbi.nlm.nih.gov/pmc/articles/PMC474733/.

Chapter 6: Make over Your Marriage

1. Saint John Chrysostom, *Sentences by St. John Chrysostom: Quotes and Translations—Part 1*, trans. Vladimir Djambov (Independently published, 2019), 7.

2. "Billy Graham Trivia: What Was Crucial to Billy and Ruth's Happy Marriage?" Billy Graham Evangelical Association, February 8, 2017, https://billygraham.org/story/billy-graham-trivia-what-was-crucial-to-billy-and-ruths-happy-marriage/.

3. John M. Gottman and Robert W. Levenson, "What Predicts Change in Marital Interaction Over Time? A Study of Alternative Models," *Family Process* 38, no. 2 (June 1999): 143-158, https://onlinelibrary.wiley.com/doi/abs/10.1111/j.1545-5300.1999.00143.x?sid=nlm%3Apubmed.

4. Alyson F. Shapiro and John M. Gottman, "Effects on Marriage of a Psycho-Communicative-Educational Intervention with Couples Undergoing the Transition to Parenthood, Evaluation at 1-Year Post Intervention," *The Journal of Family Communication* 5, no. 1 (2005): 1-24, http://citeseerx.ist.psu.edu/viewdoc/download?doi=10.1.1.527.7354&rep=rep1&type=pdf.

5. Robert W. Levenson, Laura L. Carstensen, and John M. Gottman, "Long-term marriage: Age, gender, and satisfaction," *Psychology and Aging* 8, no. 2 (1993): 301-313, https://psycnet.apa.org/record/1993-41063-001.

6. John M. Gottman, "The 6 Things That Predict Divorce," The Gottman Institute, October 10, 2014, https://www.gottman.com/blog/the-6-things-that-predict-divorce/.

7. Ellie Lisitsa, "The Four Horsemen: Criticism, Contempt, Defensiveness, and Stonewalling," *Gottman Relationship Blog*, The Gottman Institute, April 23, 2013, https://www.gottman.com

/blog/the-four-horsemen-recognizing-criticism-contempt
-defensiveness-and-stonewalling/.

8. Deborah James and Janice Drakich, "Understanding gender differences in amount of talk: A critical review of research," in *Oxford Studies in Sociolinguistics: Gender and Conversational Interaction*, ed. Deborah Tannen (Oxford: Oxford University Press, 1993), 281-312.

Chapter 7: Equip Your Children

1. D. Bilsker, D. Schiedel, and J. Marcia, "Sex differences in identity status," *Sex Roles: A Journal of Research* 18, no. 3-4 (1988): 231-236, https://psycnet.apa.org/record/1989-08074-001.

2. Arianna Novati, et al., "Chronically Restricted Sleep Leads to Depression-Like Changes in Neurotransmitter Receptor Sensitivity and Neuroendocrine Stress Reactivity in Rats," *Sleep* 31, no. 11 (November 2008): 1579-1585, https://academic .oup.com/sleep/article/31/11/1579/2454130.

3. John Kounios, et al., "The origins of insight in resting-state brain activity," *Neuropsychologia* 46, no. 1 (Jan. 15, 2008): 281-291, https://pubmed.ncbi.nlm.nih.gov/17765273/.

4. Sarah A. Ting, et al., "Trends in US emergency department visits for attempted suicide and self-inflicted injury," *General Hospital Psychiatry* 34, no. 5 (September-October 2012): 557-565, https://www.sciencedirect.com/science/article/abs/pii /S016383431200103X?via%3Dihub.

5. Jean M. Twenge, et al., "Age, Period, and Cohort Trends in Mood Disorder Indicators and Suicide-Related Outcomes in a Nationally Representative Dataset, 2005-2017," *Journal of Abnormal Psychology* 128, no. 3 (2019): 185-199, https://www.apa .org/pubs/journals/releases/abn-abn0000410.pdf.

6. Ayelet Meron Ruscio, et al., "Cross-sectional Comparison of the Epidemiology of DSM-5 Generalized Anxiety Disorder Across the Globe," *JAMA Psychiatry* 74, no. 5 (May 1, 2017): 465-475, https://pubmed.ncbi.nlm.nih.gov/28297020/.

7. "Monitoring the Future Survey: High School and Youth Trends DrugFacts," National Institute on Drug Abuse, July 6, 2020, https://www.drugabuse.gov/publications/drugfacts/monitoring-future-survey-high-school-youth-trends.

8. Bruce E. Compas, et al., "Coping, emotion regulation, and psychopathology in childhood and adolescence: A meta-analysis and narrative review," *Psychological Bulletin* 143, no. 9 (2017): 939-991, https://psycnet.apa.org/record/2017-26062-001.

9. Melissa A. Milkie, Kei M. Nomaguchi, and Kathleen E. Denny, "Does the Amount of Time Mothers Spend with Children or Adolescents Matter?" *Journal of Marriage and Family* 77, no. 2 (April 2015): 355-372, https://onlinelibrary.wiley.com/doi/abs/10.1111/jomf.12170.

10. Gregory S. Pettit, John E. Bates, and Kenneth A. Dodge, "Supportive Parenting, Ecological Context, and Children's Adjustment: A Seven-Year Longitudinal Study," *Child Development* 68, no. 5 (October 1997): 908-923, https://www.jstor.org/stable/1132041?seq=1.

11. *Merriam-Webster*, s.v. "encourage (v.)," accessed July 11, 2020, https://www.merriam-webster.com/dictionary/encourage.

12. Gary Chapman, *The Five Love Languages: The Secret to Love that Lasts* (Chicago: Moody Publishers, 2015).

13. *Merriam-Webster*, s.v. "humble (adj.)," accessed July 11, 2020, https://www.merriam-webster.com/dictionary/humble.

14. Albert Bandura, Dorothea Ross, and Sheila A. Ross, "Transmission of aggression through imitation of aggressive models," *The Journal of Abnormal and Social Psychology* 63, no. 3 (1961): 575-582, https://psycnet.apa.org/doiLanding?doi=10.1037%2Fh0045925.

15. S.A. Hardy, L.M. Padilla-Walker, and G. Carlo, "Parenting Dimensions and Adolescents' Internalization of Moral Values," *Journal of Moral Education* 37 (2008): 205-223, http://selfdeterminationtheory.org/SDT/documents/08_Hardy_etal_JME.pdf.

Chapter 8: Share Your Light

1. "Global hunger continues to rise, new UN report says," World Health Organization, September 11, 2018, https://www.who.int/news-room/detail/11-09-2018-global-hunger-continues-to-rise---new-un-report-says.

2. "2.1 billion people lack safe drinking water at home, more than twice as many lack safe sanitation," World Health Organization, July 12, 2017, https://www.who.int/news-room/detail/12-07-2017-2-1-billion-people-lack-safe-drinking-water-at-home-more-than-twice-as-many-lack-safe-sanitation.

3. "UNICEF: Too Many Children Dying of Malnutrition," UNICEF USA, June 6, 2013, https://www.unicefusa.org/press/releases/unicef-too-many-children-dying-malnutrition/8259.

4. "Nearly 385 million children living in extreme poverty, says joint World Bank Group-UNICEF study," UNICEF, October 3, 2016, https://www.unicef.org/press-releases/nearly-385-million-children-living-extreme-poverty-says-joint-world-bank-group.

5. "Cancer Stat Facts: Common Cancer Sites," National Cancer Institute, https://seer.cancer.gov/statfacts/html/common.html.

6. "Coronavirus Death Toll," *Worldometer,* July, 13, 2020, https://www.worldometers.info/coronavirus/coronavirus-death-toll/.

7. Scott Barry Kaufman, et al., "The Light vs. Dark Triad of Personality: Contrasting Two Very Different Profiles of Human Nature," *Personality and Social Psychology* 10, no. 467 (March 12, 2019), https://www.frontiersin.org/articles/10.3389/fpsyg.2019.00467/full.

8. Jamil Zaki and Jason P. Mitchell, "Equitable decision making is associated with neural markers of intrinsic value," *Proceedings of the National Academy of Sciences of the United States of America* 108, no. 49 (Dec. 6, 2011): 19761-19766, https://www.ncbi.nlm.nih.gov/pmc/articles/PMC3241792/.

9. J.M. Darley and C.D. Batson, "From Jerusalem to Jericho: A Study of Situational and Dispositional Variables in Helping

Behavior," *Journal of Personality and Social Psychology* 27, no. 1 (1973): 100-108, https://psycnet.apa.org/record/1973-31215-001.

10. *Merriam-Webster*, s.v. "accept (v.)," accessed July 13, 2020, https://www.merriam-webster.com/dictionary/accept.

11. Fred Rogers, *The World According to Mister Rogers: Important Things to Remember* (Lebanon, IN: Hachette Books, 2019).

12. Jenny Santi, "The Secret of Happiness Is Helping Others," *Time* magazine, https://time.com/collection/guide-to-happiness /4070299/secret-to-happiness/.

13. Sonja Lyubomirsky, Kennon M. Sheldon, and David Schkade, "Pursuing Happiness: The Architecture of Sustainable Change," *Review of General Psychology* 9, no. 2 (2005): 111-131, http://sonjalyubomirsky.com/wp-content/themes/sonjalyubomirsky /papers/LSS2005.pdf.

14. Tristen K. Inagaki, et al., "The Neurobiology of Giving Versus Receiving Support: The Role of Stress-Related and Social Reward-Related Neural Activity," *Psychosomatic Medicine* 78, no. 4 (May 2016): 443-453, https://journals .lww.com/psychosomaticmedicine/Abstract/2016/05000 /The_Neurobiology_of_Giving_Versus_Receiving.7.aspx.

15. John M. Darley and Bibb Latané, "Bystander Intervention in Emergencies: Diffusion of Responsibility," *Journal of Personality and Social Psychology* 8, no. 4 (1968): 377-383, https://pdfs.semantic scholar.org/432a/51ae6e67a9c7fdb7b97c4917da96bb3140cf.pdf.

16. James H. Fowler and Nicholas A. Christakis, "Cooperative behavior cascades in human social networks," *Proceedings of the National Academy of Sciences of the United States of America* 107, no. 12 (March 23, 2010): 5334-5338, https://www.pnas.org/content /107/12/5334.

Conclusion

1. Jessica Durando, "15 of Nelson Mandela's best quotes," *USA Today*, Dec. 6, 2013, https://www.usatoday.com/story/news /nation-now/2013/12/05/nelson-mandela-quotes/3775255/.

(continued)

Ancient Faith Publishing hopes you have enjoyed
and benefited from this book. The proceeds from the
sales of our books only partially cover the costs of operating
our nonprofit ministry—which includes both the work
of Ancient Faith Publishing and the work of
Ancient Faith Radio. Your financial support makes
it possible to continue this ministry both in print and
online. Donations are tax deductible and can be
made at www.ancientfaith.com.

To view our other publications,
please visit our website:

store.ancientfaith.com

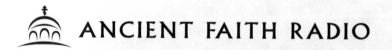

ANCIENT FAITH RADIO

Bringing you Orthodox Christian music, readings,
prayers, teaching, and podcasts 24 hours a day since 2004 at

www.ancientfaith.com